First published in January 2012

British Library Cataloguing in Publication Data
A catalogue record for this book is available from the British Library.

ISBN 978 0 85733 078 9

Library of Congress catalog card no. 2011935257

Published by Haynes Publishing,
Sparkford, Yeovil, Somerset BA22 7JJ, UK
Tel: 01963 442030 Fax: 01963 440001
Int. tel: +44 1963 442030 Int. fax: +44 1963 440001
E-mail: sales@haynes.co.uk
Website: www.haynes.co.uk

Haynes North America Inc.
861 Lawrence Drive, Newbury Park,
California 91320, USA

Printed and bound in the USA

While every effort is taken to ensure the accuracy
of the information given in this book, no liability
can be accepted by the author or publishers for
any loss, damage or injury caused by errors in,
or omissions from the information given.

Author:	Sean Lerwill
Project Manager:	Louise McIntyre
Copy editor:	Ian Heath
Design:	Richard Parsons
Photography:	Bill Gidda
	Kevin Winebold
	Jonathan Josephs
Library photography:	Alamy (pages 6, 7, 165)
	Getty Images (page 12)

Author Acknowledgments

A big thank you to ASICS, Nike, UnderArmour, Adidas, Maximuscle, Maxitone, WaterBobble, HydraCoach, KTBPR and High Definition Fitness for supplying kit and equipment for the book. Without your generosity the images wouldn't be as colourful!

Special thanks to Bill Gidda, Jon Josephs and Kevin Winebold for such an amazing selection of images.

A huge thank you to Louise McIntrye, Ian Heath, Richard Parsons and the whole team at Haynes. Thanks also go to Judith McGough; your kindness and hospitality aided me no end during this project, and to The Royal Marines, without who I would not be writing at all.

As always a big thank you to Gill Lerwill for the opportunities to run competitively from a young age and for your general support and encouragement.

Above all a massive thank you to Kate Braithwaite for supporting in every possible way: sports modelling, proof reading, location finding, photographer finding and everything else you did to make this book possible. Without you, it wouldn't be what it is.

Haynes

Running
Manual

Contents

RUNNING MANUAL
INTRODUCTION

Running has been one of the most popular pastimes and methods of getting fit across the UK, and the world, for some time. A simple look around our parks and gyms in the mornings, at lunchtimes or in the evenings illustrates this. Running is simply accessible to everyone – all that's necessary is a decent pair of trainers, a pair of shorts and a T-shirt. Gyms these days seem to have at least as many treadmills as bikes and cross-trainers, again indicating the fact that running is as popular as ever.

Furthermore, the hero status obtained by runners such as Usain Bolt, Paula Radcliffe or Haile Gebrselassie has propelled the sport into the realms of football status. Interest in marathons and other distance runs like 'The Grizzly' as something to aim for, either as a fitness goal or a way of generating money for charity, has likewise increased the popularity of running hugely.

Personally, I always appreciate it if, at the beginning of a manual or textbook, the author explains to me who the book is for; it saves me having to read a few paragraphs, pages or chapters before I find out that it's not quite right for me. So, who is this book for? In simple terms, I've aimed it at all types of runners of almost any standard. It contains elements suitable to all running types and styles, such as nutrition, warming up, physiology and common injuries; and touches on all areas of running – middle-distance and long-distance particularly, but with specific chapters on sprinting and marathons too. There are also training programmes that will suit beginners, intermediates and higher-level athletes alike.

In short, if you're new to running this book should provide a great starting point for you. If you're a seasoned runner, then you'll perhaps already have touched on some of the areas covered, but I'd still urge you to read on, as you may find the very tip that will take precious seconds off your personal best.

I also think it's imperative to know that an author has a passion for the subject they're writing about. For me, if someone writes about a topic without any real passion for it the end product is often lacklustre. Well, let me put your mind at rest; this morning I ran for an hour in an altitude chamber supplying me with 14% oxygen (as opposed to the normal 21%); at school I won my first 400m County Championship at the age of 14; I ran in the National Schools Cross-Country Championship representing the South-West at the age of 16; and while serving in the Royal Marines I ran in the United Services Cross-Country League and represented the Royal Navy at Aquathlon, where on one occasion in South Korea I gained the fastest 10km time in a field of British, American, Australian, French, South Korean, Japanese, Egyptian and Russian competitors. I've been a keen runner for as long as I can remember. Running has helped me attain the levels I've wanted to in every area of my life – personal, sporting and career. I believe running cross-country races as a child gave me the strength of mind I have today, and enabled me to complete my Royal Marine Commando training.

Running itself

Although we may think that we can all run, there's actually far, far more to learn and understand than people realise. This is especially true for beginners, who need to precondition and gain a basic knowledge of running gait analysis in order to avoid simple overuse injuries. For seasoned runners too, an understanding of cadence and gait improvement could shave minutes off running times and personal bests.

→ The history of running

Establishing a timeline regarding when human beings first started to run seems slightly absurd – animals have always run through necessity, either to catch prey, avoid danger or escape predators. Think about it: running is simply the act of walking but faster. Once humans stood erect and learnt to walk on two legs instead of four running was just a natural progression – again either to catch food or to avoid becoming food ourselves. Of more interest, perhaps, is when competitive running was first introduced. No doubt man's competitive nature has been around since the Stone Age, but it's believed that the first formal races took place in Egypt around 3800 BC. These races of approximately 3,200m, performed by running four laps between two pillars 800m apart, are thought to have begun our obsession with race watching and competing to become the fastest human being.

Any history of competitive sport must centre round the Olympics, and the history of running is no different. Running was always one of the main focuses of the original Olympics, much as it is today – how many of us tune in just to watch the 100m final? In fact it's believed that for the first 13 Olympics the 'sprint' race was the only event. Soon enough, however, longer races and events concentrating on other disciplines were added. Outside of Europe, other cultures are also said to have raced in ancient times, but many started at the opposite end of the scale, concentrating on long endurance contests as opposed to the Greek sprint-based events. The Native Americans, for instance, are thought to have had races that lasted for several days at a time.

🏃 The Olympics

The first Olympics was held in 776 BC, the focus of which was a religious festival honouring the gods; it was believed that physical perfection would be the greatest honour to them. Soon enough, however, human nature took over and the games lost their religious focus as the competitors concentrated instead on the prize money and the prestige gained from winning.

Running's elite achievers,

Running has been an inspiration to people for many years, whether because of the perfect aesthetic physiques of the early Olympians, the huge sums of money collected from marathons via sponsorship, the records set by legends such as Michael Johnson and more recently Usain Bolt, or the incredible feats of regular people such as Eddie Izzard (43 marathons in 51 days) and Johnny 'Sticky' Budden (1,000 miles of Parkour from John o'Groats to Paris). People such as these have achieved something they can be proud of, and you should see them as an inspiration to you to get out there and run yourself. The following are a few of the people who've inspired me:

→ Sebastian Coe

British middle-distance runner Seb Coe won four Olympic medals during the 1980s, which made him a national hero. He won the 1,500m gold medal at the Olympics in 1980 and 1984, as well as setting eight outdoor and three indoor world records during his illustrious career. Modestly, Seb says he owes much of his success to his two closest rivals, fellow Brits Steve Ovett and Steve Cram, as their rivalry led to complete domination of middle-distance running by British athletes and provided him with the drive to train, work and run harder.

Running legend Sebastian Coe

→ Steve Prefontaine

American running prodigy Steve 'Pre' Prefontaine was an American long- and middle-distance runner who at one point held the US records in the seven distance track events from 2,000m to 10,000m. He was set to become a true legend of the sport but tragically died in a car accident at the age of 24 before he could really display his enormous talent on the world stage. A film made about his life, starring Jared Leto, also documents his large part in the founding of sports and running giant Nike.

→ Paula Radcliffe

Paula is an English long-distance runner, sports ambassador, national running hero and pretty much living legend. She's still currently the world record holder for the marathon, fittingly achieved in the 2003 London Marathon. Her time of 2:15.25 remains a very difficult target for the world's elite to beat.

Paula also still holds world road records for the 10km, 20km and 30km. Furthermore, she won gold at the World Cross-Country Championships in 2001 and 2002, and in 2003 became European Cross-Country Champion for the second time. Remarkably, Paula is the only woman to do this in the event's ten-year history.

Unfortunately for her and the sport Paula's track success has been somewhat hampered by injury and illness, her European 10,000m gold in 2002 remaining her greatest achievement. Showing her true ability for the sport, Paula's personal best at 5,000m is 14:31.42, which is only three seconds behind the world record and won her gold at the 2002 Commonwealth Games – a truly remarkable feat when you consider she holds the world marathon record. In 2002 she was awarded an MBE and was voted the BBC Sports Personality of the Year.

→ Eddie Izzard

Known primarily for his comedy, Eddie Izzard has demonstrated himself to be one of the UK's most amazing mentally fit runners. With only five weeks' training under his belt, and very little experience of running at all, Eddie began seven weeks of back-to-back marathon runs across the UK to raise money for Sports Relief. He ran for six days every week, only taking Sundays off to rest, though even then he apparently had to take short runs to ease his aches and stop his muscles and joints seizing. Eddie ran to and from London, Cardiff, Belfast and Edinburgh and then back to London. He completed the whole event on 15 September 2009, having finished 43 marathons in 51 days and run his last marathon in 5 hours and 30 seconds – an amazing feat for an unconditioned runner. He had run at least 27 miles each day, six days a week for seven weeks straight. During the entire event he had covered more than 1,100 miles. His achievement was recognised with a special award at the 2009 BBC Sports Personality of the Year ceremony. Eddie has now started training for Triathlon and Ironman events. When asked his reasons for this, he replied that he's simply caught the fitness bug and doesn't want to throw away what he's gained. That's an example many of us could learn from.

Eddie Izzard – a real running hero

→ Usain Bolt

Usain is a phenomenon. There's no better way of putting it. To look at him, the Jamaican-born sprinter is too tall to be able to run the speeds he can, but his achievements at such a young age speak for themselves. Amazingly he's three-times World and Olympic gold medallist and reigning world record holder and Olympic record holder in the 100m, 200m and 4 x 100m relay (yes, his team-mates play a part). On paper these don't sound as phenomenal as they are until you remember that the 100m and 200m have been THE most fought-over events since set distances became the Olympic mould. Yet despite that, since Usain bolted on to the scene he's dominated them in a way that no one ever thought possible. Truly remarkable.

→ Michael Johnson

As a teenager I was a 400m and cross-country runner (strange combination, but it seemed to work for me). At the time, Mr Johnson was a living legend. He won four Olympic gold medals and was World Champion eight times. Some of his records still stand: he holds the world record in the 400m and 4 x 400m relay (along with his team-mates). He formerly held the world record in the 200m too, his time of 19.32 at the 1996 Olympic games standing for over 12 years until it was beaten by a certain Usain Bolt.

Everyone should run

If you're reading this book, then the chances are that you've either already run or are planning to start running. Either way the following paragraph may be preaching to the converted. However, there may be a small percentage of readers who've been bought this book by a friend or relative in the hope it will inspire you to start a running/fitness regime. Either way, this section is for you.

Unless you have some form of injury, medical condition or disability that prevents you from running, then running is for you. It's cheap (besides clothing and kit it's free) and is good for you on many levels. These days we're unfortunately becoming an overweight, lazy, entertainment and fast-food addicted nation. We eat badly (wrong times of day, too much per sitting and the wrong types of food), sleep too little, work too hard, get too stressed and get too little exercise. Running can help with all of these. Don't get me wrong – running is NOT the be all and end all of fitness. Cardiovascular training (of which running is part) shouldn't be utilised in isolation. It's important to perform other fitness sessions too, encompassing weight-training and circuit-

training – running should be part of an all-round fitness programme, not its only constituent. Having said that, unless something prohibits it, it should definitely be an integral part of everybody's fitness programme.

Fitness

Your heart is like any muscle: exercise it and it gets bigger and stronger. Running makes your heart beat faster as your body needs more oxygen. The heart beats faster to pump blood to the muscles quicker, to enable them to complete the exercise being asked of them. The more you run, the stronger your heart gets. This means that when you aren't running (when you're working, sleeping, relaxing etc) your heart finds it easier to supply the body with all its oxygen needs. You've become fitter, healthier and stronger – you'll also most likely live longer and be healthier in later life than people who don't run or exercise.

Weight loss

Because we live in a world obsessed with the perfect body we all want to look like movie stars and supermodels. Unfortunately our lifestyles often mean this is near impossible, but running can certainly help, especially if simple weight loss is your goal. Combined with a balanced diet, running will lead to weight loss. In simple terms, if energy (food) taken in is equal to energy (calories) burned, then the body will stay as it is. If energy in is greater than energy burned then the body will gain weight; and if energy intake is less than energy burned the body will lose weight. As running burns far more calories than walking (or sitting on the sofa!), then as long as the amount eaten isn't ludicrous the calories burned by running will lead to weight loss.

Hobby

We all like to have something to do with our spare time. Often it's something that either de-stresses us, provides fulfilment in our lives, or allows us to interact with like-minded people. Well, running accomplishes all these goals. As a hobby running is relatively special, as it can be done both alone or as part of a group, so if you need to get away from every other human being you can; and if you want to run with a partner or friends you can do that as well. Even in Central London I've been able to choose a time and place where I can run and avoid human contact for at least 30 minutes. Alternatively, a running club or group of friends can provide great human contact, and sharing a hard run bonds relationships and make the 'social' (pub time!) after the run even more acceptable (it feels earned).

A personal trainer runs slowly in her 2nd trimester

Fun

When I was working for the Marines in London a few years ago, a fellow Marine PTI who was a Londoner would join me on hour-long runs around the city. We'd start at one bridge (Battersea, for example) and run all along the south bank of the river (where possible) before crossing another bridge (Tower, for example) and running back along the north side (where possible). We'd enjoy the sights, and in the summer we'd enjoy the weather and talk about everything and anything. We were running at a relatively slow pace (strengthening our hearts, as will be explained later) but we were also having fun. Running with a friend, with your partner or with a group can be a very rewarding pastime.

Discovery

Personally, whenever I stay in a new area for a few days or more I go for runs in different directions (I 'petal' the area – see diagram). This allows me to really discover my surroundings. It provides more information than going for a drive, a bus ride or studying a map, and is much faster than walking. The added bonus is the fitness training at the same time.

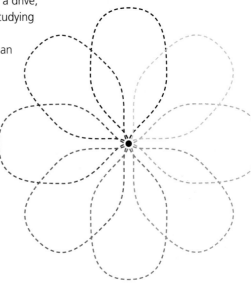

De-stress

We unfortunately live in times of great stress. We worry about everything: our jobs, our children, our bills, what people think of us, the weather – you name it, we worry about it. Ironically most of this stress is self-induced, but nevertheless it exists. Exercise in general is a great cure for stress, and running is a superb de-stressing tool. Personally I've used running to great effect during periods of indecision or stress: an hour's run, be it outside or in the gym, always gives me time to think and distances me from the problem itself. When I come back I'm relaxed and ready to refocus. Like me, many people find that while they're running they have time to assess and consider a situation without interruption, and following the run they have more clarity regarding a problem. I've always found that when faced with a difficult work or social decision, a long run (on my own with my thoughts) has always helped me to make the right decision.

⏱ Conclusion

Hopefully this chapter has inspired you to read on, whether you read from chapter to chapter or skip to specific sections you feel you can learn from. If you enjoy running, tell others. Inspire them to run with you. We human beings become unfit and overweight far too easily, but if we encourage each other to run we can combat this. Get out there and discover your surroundings, discover your running ability, discover which friends enjoy running, and most importantly discover yourself.

CHAPTER 1
TYPES OF RUNNING

Running can be separated into various categories depending on a number of factors. Usually types of running are sub-categorised by how they're seen in events such as the Olympics or World Championships, the type of surface they're run on, or their length and therefore the energy systems used when performing them. The following provides a brief description of each.

Sprinting

Sprinting generally refers to a short, sharp burst of maximal speed running. In athletics we normally think of the 100m, which really is the epitome of athletics – which seems fitting, as the original sprint of the Olympics (from one end of the stadium to the other) was the only running race.

The three sprint events of the Olympics and World Championships are the 100m, 200m and 400m, all run outdoors. There are also World Indoor Championships for all these distances plus 60m.

At competition level, the sprint events are the only ones to start from the crouch position using starting blocks. Furthermore, except for the indoor 400m event all sprint races require the athletes to stay in their own lane, and drifting into an opponent's lane leads to disqualification.

Whether racing or sprinting for fitness, the aim should be to reach the maximum speed possible as quickly as possible and maintain it for the length of the sprint. Individual abilities decide how long a runner can maintain his or her fastest speed. However, this can be trained (see Chapters 11 and 13).

Middle-distance

Middle-distance running usually refers to track races that aren't sprints, but also aren't long-distance. Basically we're talking over 400m (the longest sprint), but not more than 3,000m (3km is considered the longest middle-distance run).

As with sprint events, there are considered to be three standard middle-distance races: the 800m, 1,500m and 3,000m. The 1,600m is also run and trained for as it's almost exactly a mile (1,609m = 1 mile); although it isn't a standard event at the Olympics, due to the heritage of the four-minute mile it's often run by people training on a track (four laps) to see how they fare. The 'Mile' itself is also still run, but these days it's only raced at the top level at specifically laid-on events, and not at the Olympics or World Championships.

3,000m

The 3,000m is thought to be right on the borderline between middle and longer distances. Unlike the 800m and 1,500m, where a decent sprint/basic speed is essential, it's possible to be slightly lacking in this area yet still be very proficient at the 3,000m with good race tactics and excellent aerobic fitness (versus anaerobic sprint speeds).

The four-minute mile

It was long thought impossible to run a mile in under four minutes. Englishman Roger Bannister was the first to achieve it, in Oxford in 1954. Hicham El Guerrouj holds the record, however, with a time of 3:43.13, set in Rome in 1999.

The steeplechase

Likewise run over 3,000m, the steeplechase is also considered to be a middle-distance event. The only difference to the flat 3,000m is that after the first 200m five barriers per lap are placed en route which must be leapt over. Furthermore, one barrier per lap is placed in front of a water pit, ensuring the runners also get wet feet.

Long-distance

Long-distance races are generally anything greater than 3,000m up to and including marathons. Cross-country races are also included in long-distance running, as they're usually greater than 3,000m. Even if they aren't, the same attributes expected of a track/road long-distance runner are expected of a cross-country athlete: exceptional aerobic conditioning, immense endurance, a good level of stamina and, perhaps above all, huge mental resolve.

5,000m

The 5,000m is far more tactical than other long-distance events, and quite similar to the 1,500m and 3,000m in that sense. Believe it or not, training for top-level runners for the 5,000m (just over three miles) can require running up to 60–200km (37–124 miles) per week.

10,000m

The 10,000m is the longest standard track event. It requires competitors to run 25 laps of the 400m track. Tactics are less important, as runners tend to get more spread out than the shorter long-distance/middle-distance races. Unsurprisingly, many 10,000m competitors also compete at road races, marathons and cross-country events.

Ultra-endurance

Ultramarathons are considered to be events of any distance longer than a traditional marathon of 26.2188 miles (which is 42.195km). They can actually be split into two types: distance and timed.

Distance events are those that cover a specific distance, with the winner covering that distance in the quickest time.

Timed events are those that take place during a specified time, the winner being the individual who covers the greatest distance. Sounds horrible, doesn't it? It is!

The start of the Marathon des Sables – a true test of endurance

→ Distance events

The most common distances are 50km (31.069 miles), 100km (62.137 miles), 50 miles (80.467km) and 100 miles (160.934km). The 100km is an official world record event. Other common ultramarathon events are double marathons, 24-hours races and multiday races. At all these events there are aid stations every 5km to 15km so that runners can obtain prepared food, drinks and medical kits and can rest and recuperate where needed.

→ Timed events

Timed events are usually 6, 12 or 24 hours, but can be as long as three or even six days. The latter are often known as multi-day events, as obviously no one can run solidly each day without resting and sleeping. Painfully for the competitors, timed events are generally run on the track or a road.

→ Notable events

The world's oldest and largest ultramarathon takes place in South Africa – the 90km Comrades Marathon with approximately 12,000 runners competing each year. However, the biggy, the ultramarathon everyone seems to have heard of, is the Marathon des Sables, which takes place in the Moroccan Sahara. This is a hellish seven-day stage race that covers 250km through the desert sand and heat.

The Ultra-Trail du Mont-Blanc – a 166km loop around Mont Blanc involving 9,400m elevation gain – has also gained an incredible reputation in terms of its arduous nature. Not to be outdone, the 230km Al Andalus Ultra-Trail is a stage race over five days in the July sun and heat of Poniente Granadino in Andalucía, in Spain. The sparse mountainous trails and tracks have earned this race a reputation as one of the toughest Ultra races in the world.

The Spartathlon is Greece's most prestigious ultramarathon, covering 246km from Athens to Sparta. Due to the weather, the heat and humidity of the day, the cold of the night hours and the non-stop nature of the race it's up there with the toughest.

As you'd imagine, America hosts a number of ultramarathons, most notably the Self Transcendence 3,100 Mile Race, which claims to be the longest official foot-race in the world. Competitors run 100 laps a day for up to 50 days around a single block in Queens, New York, for an unbelievable total distance of 3,100 miles – yes, it sound horrendous to me too!

In the UK we used to have the London to Brighton Ultramarathon, thought to be the second oldest ultramarathon in the world and long considered to be the most prestigious until it was sadly retired in 2005.

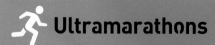

Ultramarathons

Ultramarathon events and courses vary hugely. Like marathons and cross-country events, courses can be single or multiple loops of a route. Incredibly, some ultramarathon events can be run on loops as short as a 400m track. Mentally this makes these long distance events even more astonishing. To make them all the more difficult, some ultramarathons are competed in horrendous conditions such as adverse weather or extreme terrain. Courses vary from dirt tracks to mountain paths, although some are still run on normal roads as well.

Various energy drinks are available. Try them out and find the best for you

Others

→ Triathlons

A triathlon is a 'multi-sport' race comprising three continuous and sequential endurance events. Variations do exist, but most triathlons consist of swimming, cycling and running over various distances, with each event following immediately after completion of the previous one.

Triathlons are split into three distances:

- Sprint distance: 750m swim, 20km ride, 5km run.
- Intermediate/standard distance (or 'Olympic distance'): 1.5km swim, 40km ride, 10km run.
- The 'Long Course': 1.9km swim, 90km ride, 21.1km run (also known as the 'Half Ironman').
- Ultra distance: 3.8km swim, 180km ride, and a marathon 42.2km run (also known as the 'Ironman').

Triathlons have become very popular in recent years, not only at the top end of the sport but for amateurs too, as a decent swimmer, runner or cyclist can have a go at training in the other disciplines and attempting a triathlon. As a runner, whether you start today for fun or weight loss, or whether you're already at a decent level, you'll find that the need to compete or achieve something in your chosen hobby often catches up with you. Once you've competed a few 10km races, a marathon may not float your boat and training towards a triathlon rears its ugly head instead. Often very time-consuming in terms of training, triathlons are even more rewarding once completed – a great place to take your running and fitness training if you so desire.

Personal experience...

I made the mistake of thinking that since I was a very strong runner and an OK swimmer, a triathlon would be easy. Don't underestimate how hard the cumulative effect of these events can be! Train and practice in order to make your life a little more comfortable on your first attempt.

→ Parkour

Parkour is a worldwide sport based around the swift and energy-efficient traversing of an urban or rural environment, using specific techniques and basic running to get from point A to B as quickly and directly as possible. Unlike other types of running, Parkour is non-competitive. Its origin lies in France, where founder David Belle (a French soldier, assault-course fanatic and gymnast) used skills such as jumping, climbing, vaulting, rolling, swinging and, of course, running to turn the urban environment into one big assault course.

Parkour is often confused with, or at least lumped together with, *l'art du déplacement* (the art of movement) or its competitive version, Freerunning, but the flips employed in these disciplines aren't considered Parkour by 'purists'. There have to date been two Freerunning World Championships, and the Red Bull Art of Motion is another world-class competition in which such athletes can display their art.

The author at the finish line of the Korean Aquathlon with fellow navy team members

Barefoot running

Barefoot running has leapt into popularity in the last two years, despite having been around for a long time before that (there was a time when we didn't have shoes!). Many Olympic runners ran barefoot around the 1960s but the movement didn't have the advantage of media coverage that it enjoys today, with magazines, newspapers and the Internet, not to mention Christopher McDougall's 2009 book *Born to Run*, which can perhaps be single-handedly praised for the significant increase in barefoot running. From articles in the *Times* and the *Guardian* to barefoot running courses organised by companies to encourage their employees to relax outside of work, it's become the new way to get fit and feel 'free'.

OK, so our ancestors ran for miles and miles without the use of fancy trainers and many of the world's top (African) distance runners hail from a background of running barefoot. But does that really mean that we should all put our trainers under the bed or in the loft? Perhaps it does. Let's look at the pros and cons.

Concrete world

The biggest and most obvious drawback is our surroundings. There can be all the argument in the world about our ancestors and the world's top long-distance runners, but the simple truth is they didn't have to worry about concrete! Pavements, roads, tarmac and the like are all too hard for our feet and bodies. The shock that goes through us when we run is about six times our body weight: now think about that on a paved road without the cushioning of a running shoe. Doesn't sound good, does it? Hence the increase in metatarsal breaks and Achilles and patella tendinopathies since barefoot running began. This doesn't mean you shouldn't run barefoot at all; it just means that a period of decent structured conditioning and an understanding of how to run barefoot properly must precede it.

The condition of the skin on the bottoms of your feet must also be considered. Our ancestors and those exceptional runners hailing from Africa had one thing in common: they didn't spend all day in nice comfy leather shoes or trainers with a pair of cotton socks to keep their feet warm. The skin on the soles of their feet was hard. Rock hard in places. Hard enough that walking on small gravel didn't hurt, thick enough that standing on a thorn would do little or nothing at all. We don't have this luxury. We don't spend enough time barefoot on hard surfaces to harden our skin, so if we go barefoot running (off the beaten track of course – no concrete!) we'll inevitably get cuts, grazes, thorns and in the end injuries as our gaits alter (even if ever so slightly) to avoid these little niggles.

So is the answer not to run barefoot? No. Not entirely. The answer is to either choose somewhere free from any potential hazards (like the local cricket square or bowls green, or even a beach) or to purchase one of the various very lightweight, almost glove-like shoes that encourage barefoot running. The Vibram FiveFingers shown here is a perfect example. However, although these alternatives may protect the soles from cuts and grazes they don't provide the cushioning support of trainers; hence the ligament and tendon injuries, not to mentions stress fractures, people suffer because most of them don't understand that they must run differently when barefoot. These injuries are a major concern, hence the need for preconditioning sessions to prepare the body for barefoot running, and a good understanding of how to run barefoot.

Why run barefoot?

This has to be the big question. Does it really offer any benefits? A small group of athletes have achieved success running barefoot over the years. These include Abebe Bikila and Tegla Loroupe, both Olympic Champions and world record holders, and British runner Zola Budd, who was famous for winning the 1985 and 1986 IAAF World Cross-Country Championships and competing in the 1984 Olympics, all barefoot. The simple fact is that the human mechanics of running are changed quite significantly when shoes are used: during natural, barefoot running it's the lateral edge of the forefoot that strikes the ground. However, running in trainers moves the strike point to the heel and the area towards the back of the foot. So the question is, is that a bad thing?

On meeting with the head of the company that imports Vibram FiveFingers into the UK, I was presented with a wealth of information as to why running barefoot is far more natural, why we should all be doing it, and why Nike, Adidas, Asics etc should all admit that cushioned trainers are a mistake and move on. The problem is that although Vibram can quote names such as *Time* magazine and Harvard University, no long-term private research has been conducted. Don't get me wrong, I like Vibram FiveFinger shoes, so I was disappointed that Vibram and their importer couldn't supply a pair for me to trial for this book; but it's still a fact that although super-talented runner Bikila won the Rome Olympic marathon barefoot in 1960 in 2:15:16, at the Tokyo Olympic marathon in 1964 he wore trainers and set a world record in 2:12:11. This is perhaps the most overwhelming piece of evidence to me that barefoot running, although freeing and natural to us once, is perhaps not as ideal as it was and is perhaps something we've evolved beyond.

Put it this way, wearing a bra is something most women in the Western world do. It supports them, makes them more comfortable and protects their breasts from sagging with age; but living naturally they wouldn't need such a thing. I see trainers for running in much the same way: we've designed, developed and perfected them to support us, keep us comfortable and protect us from the injuries age and overuse will bring. Why backtrack from this? Personally I believe we've moved on too far to go back. In the Western world we've evolved to rely on shoes and that's where we should stay.

Runner Rick Roeber has run in excess of 50 marathons, two ultra-marathons and an estimated 17,000 miles – all barefoot.

Personal experience...

Prior to joining the Marines I studied molecular genetics at King's College, London. Much of genetics is about evolution, how single-celled organisms became multiple-celled organisms, then larger organisms, then fish, birds, mammals, monkeys, chimps, humans etc. We're constantly evolving and mutating. We can't look back at what our ancestors did and say, 'That's natural, we must go back to doing that!' If we did it would be goodbye shoes, goodbye bed, goodbye car, goodbye sunblock, goodbye knife and fork and goodbye everything else – not practical is it?

Injury prevention by running barefoot

However, some biomechanical researchers argue that barefoot running is healthier for the feet and reduces the risk of chronic injuries, specifically repetitive stress injuries caused by the impact of heel striking, even in cushioned running shoes. If this is the case then perhaps reverting to our ancestors' running gait is the way forward. In truth, very little research has yet been carried out, but some initial results from limited studies seem to support the health claims of running barefoot. Having said that, barefoot running isn't advised by most mainstream medical or sports organisations, where the general consensus is to recommend decent cushioned (not too old!) running shoes.

Barefoot running shoes

The Vibram FiveFingers is the barefoot shoe we all seem to know and recognise, probably because it's such a different-looking piece of footwear that provides just a solid base for the foot (to protect the skin) and very little else. Unknown to most people, though, is that Nike preceded Vibram by some years with their Nike Free range, which features a segmented sole that supposedly allows the foot to move naturally while still having an amount of cushioning to protect the ankles, knees and joints etc. Cleverly, Nike designed the Free using a scale from 1 to 10, where 1 is barefoot and 10 is a normal running shoe, the idea being that an individual could start with a high number and over time drop to the lower numbers, allowing for the conditioning and slow build-up to barefoot running that I mentioned earlier, thereby hopefully reducing the chance of injury.

Saucony and New Balance have now jumped on the bandwagon, with Saucony's Kinvara line of shoes having a dropped sole, halving the thickness of the sole and removing much of the heel cushioning which in turn encourages the midfoot as opposed to the heel of the foot to strike. The New Balance Minimus is very similar to the Vibram FiveFingers but without the individual toe pockets.

Barefoot running and injury relief

Evolutionarily speaking, our feet and lower legs are designed to absorb the shock of running and turn the energy into forward motion. This is made possible, without injury, by the spring action of the foot's natural arch. The trainers we've designed for running allow us to run on our heels by placing large amounts of padding under them, so we can land on the heel rather than the ball of the foot. The downside is that the foot's 'natural motion' is prevented, so the arch and lower leg can't absorb the shock of landing. Instead the shock is sent up through the heel to the knees and hips, hence some of the chronic ankle, knee, hip and back injuries we see in runners.

The studies of barefoot running done so far aren't extensive, and it will probably take several years, perhaps decades, to understand the long-term effects of throwing away our trainers and running barefoot. However, the studies that have been done suggest that running in trainers increases stress on the knee joints by up to 38% compared to running barefoot. The question is whether this leads to higher rates of heel injuries instead. They also suggest that the energy cost is reduced by about 4% when running barefoot, but this is likely to be the lack of extra weight on the foot.

In conclusion, then, the simple truth is that people running barefoot have a completely different foot strike to those who run in trainers. This is fine if they've been running barefoot all their lives, but if someone who's always run in trainers suddenly starts to do all their running barefoot the change in footstrike will most likely prove a recipe for disaster. As stated above, start slowly, condition, run on soft ground (not concrete), and if you have any worries seek the advice of a professional podiatrist. Having said that, people who run barefoot naturally and 'properly' (by landing on the middle or front of the foot) do seem have almost no shock through the feet and lower legs, or at least much less than a runner in trainers using a conventional heel strike.

⏱ Conclusion

As human beings, running comes naturally to us. From our need to hunt and escape predators to our desire to compete and prove who's top dog, we've been running for centuries. Today running can be seen on the world stage and in the local park, and whether you choose to sprint, jog or swim/bike/run, just enjoy it. Take inspiration from following your favourite races on TV or the Internet and do everything you can to inspire others.

CHAPTER 2
GETTING STARTED

For some reason the majority of us find that getting started, at almost anything, is always the hardest thing to do. But once we've started, no matter how much we'd worried about it, the reality is never as bad as we'd imagined, be it a piece of course work, quitting smoking or the first day in a new job. Starting a running programme or regime is no different: the first session is never as bad as you thought it was going to be, and after that things get steadily easier.

Who are you?

Whether you're young or old, a seasoned sportsperson or a couch potato, running is for you. You need no special kit or equipment other than a pair of running shoes and some comfortable clothes. If you start slowly and build up sensibly, running is for all ages, all fitness levels and both sexes.

Medical advice

Every fitness professional is taught to advise that anyone who's beginning an exercise programme but hasn't exercised for some time should consult a doctor prior to starting. I always ask them if they've consulted their doctor and if there's any reason they shouldn't be exercising. Old injuries and operations, current medication, family traits, the possibility of pregnancy and any medication being taken should all be considered. Life's too short and too precious to take chances, so safety must always come first. It'll give you more confidence if you know that your body is healthy and able to undertake the exercise you're going to ask of it.

→ **Checklist before running**

Before you start running, it's advisable to:

- Consult a doctor.
- Consider some personal motivational goals (see Chapter 7).
- Ensure you have sensible clothing, trainers and kit to run in, that won't rub or injure you (see Chapter 3).
- Ensure you have a means of taking everything you need on your run: essential medication, mobile phone, water, keys etc.

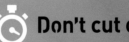 **Don't cut corners**

An old mantra taught to me by a legendary Royal Marine PTI was 'That'll do will never do.' Think about it. It's true. Don't take short cuts; do things properly.

'Worrying is like a rocking chair: it gives you something to do, but doesn't get you anywhere' – Van Wilder

Individually, with a partner, or in a group?

Personally I love running on my own. I find it gives me time to clear my thoughts, escape reality, listen to 'my' music and make decisions I've been struggling over. Furthermore, I'm pretty serious about my running and find that most of my training partners tend to hamper my speed and goals, unless we're running side by side on treadmills (a good point here, though, is that if one of you is far quicker than the other you can use treadmills to co-train and co-encourage, and both get the required workout).

The problem with individual training is that you can lose focus and easily avoid a session due to feeling tired or working late. If you're a very focussed, almost obsessed person you'll probably get past these feelings on your own. If you're not, then perhaps a partner is better for you.

A running partner (or selection of partners) is great. Firstly, you know that if you miss a session you're not only letting yourself down you're letting your partner down too, so you encourage and motivate each other. Furthermore, when you have a bad day (or days!) your partner will pull you through it, and on their bad day you'll be able to do the same. It's a perfect recipe for getting through those cold winter months and early starts.

Some partners I run with are faster than me and some are slower, but both are equally enjoyable. When I'm the more accomplished runner I enjoy a slower tempo run where I can allow my heart to beat steadily and feel relaxed even though I'm still working out. Equally, I can use my experience to help my partner and try to encourage and enhance their performance. That can be very rewarding, and often helps my running too.

When running with a quicker partner I enjoy the harder workout involved in matching their pace. The challenge is a welcome addition to a normal run. Furthermore it's a good opportunity to analyse their running gait and ask questions. They may just be fitter and better trained at that point than you are, therefore they provide a challenge for you the next time you run together: if three months down the line you're beating them, then you can be assured that you're doing something right.

Running with a group or club is also great. It has all the benefits of running with a partner, but multiplied. At the

beginning of each run you can choose whether to train with those better, equal to or worse than you. It's therefore a great way to learn and progress. Equally, you can get all the advice you need about trainers, kit, local runs etc. However, be sure to check their facts – some people 'have all the gear, but no idea'!

A running group is also a good way to socialise and meet other runners with similar interests. Before you know it you'll be meeting them at weekends, either for a cross-country run or some laps of the nearest track. Either way it can only improve your running and allows you to befriend like-minded people.

Some people surround themselves with training partners who are weaker and less fit than they are. This may make them feel great, but without competition they'll struggle to improve.

Safety

Road safety

Road safety is common sense and is the same as you learned as a child. Primarily, remember that cars generally have the right of way, except at zebra crossings. However, they're not used to pedestrians moving as fast as you, so be aware of that. Never try to beat a car to a junction to cut in front of it, and never run across as a speeding car comes towards you. You're moving faster than when you walk and this can affect your judgement and perception. Safety first, not personal best first!

If there's no pavement, run facing the oncoming traffic, so that even if they don't see you, you see them; and wear something reflective or bright – either special reflective vests/jackets, or the gloves and hats in luminous colours that are now made by running kit companies. You may feel silly, but it could save your life. You can also attach lights to yourself like those cyclists have on their bikes (Adidas do a great range of products for runners). A head-light can be a useful tool too, especially if you're running down country lanes at night – make sure to take spare batteries, and remember to switch it off when running towards other people or you'll blind them!

Running with a partner or group is great for safety. This is especially true in the evenings or early mornings when it's dark. If you're running alone (like 90% of runners do, apparently), call a friend and tell them your route and when you expect to be back. When you're home, drop them a text. Tell them to call you if they don't get one by a set time, and if you don't answer, to start looking for you. In the winter (and even the summer in the UK) it's easy to slip on a wet pavement or even trip over a tree root. So if you can't take a phone with you, always make sure people know your route.

For women (and even men) a rape alarm or a whistle around the neck is a great piece of equipment, better to have and never use than to need and not have.

Again, running with a group or partner makes the sport a little safer and perhaps more enjoyable. If you do have to run on your own, vary things. In the military we get taught to watch 'patterns of life' to learn when and where to attack, so if someone varies their pattern of life its very hard to know when to strike. Don't be an easy target – don't become habitual. This is not only for your personal safety: if you live alone and run at the same time every day, people will know your house is empty at certain times and that you're unlikely to return if you're on your usual 30-minute run starting at 05:45, when it's nice and dark to steal you car... You get the picture.

Medical details

If you have any specific medical conditions, make sure you get a medical card with them printed on it and carry it with you. In the Marines we had 'dog tags', which apart from our name and personal details gave our blood type and medical details such as allergies etc. Obviously if you're diabetic or allergic to anything in particular then carry the necessary information with you.

Running alongside water

Firstly, never ever be tempted to jump in for a swim to cool off. It's far too dangerous, even if you do consider yourself a great swimmer. You'll be tired from running and there are hidden dangers such as strong currents, the cold and underwater debris.

Never run too close to the edge in case you fall in; and it goes without saying that you should never run across frozen lakes or rivers.

A flourescent or brightly-coloured top is a great idea if running at dawn or dusk

New routes

It's best to try new routes in the daytime, or at least walk them at the weekend in the daylight. You never know if roads are closed, rivers are flooded or the tunnel under the motorway no longer exists. Whatever happens, don't try a new cross-country route unprepared – that could mean you'll get lost. If you're attempting an off-road route take a map and maybe a GPS. Furthermore, try to pick out landmarks, just in case you need to retrace your steps.

Sensible choice

In the Marines we were taught an 'A–H' for describing someone:

A – age
B – build
C – clothes
D – distinguishing features
E – elevation (height)
F – face
G – gait (how they walked/ran)
H – hair

Follow this to describe people to the police.

Personal experience...

In the military we were taught to look at the landmarks we passed from behind as well as in front, as this is how you'll approach them on your return journey, and they may look different to how they did from the front.

Walk away

It's an old mantra, but a good one. If people mock you or run alongside you, be the bigger and smarter person and walk away. Make eye contact if it's normal to do so, but don't be aggressive; equally, don't sprint away unless it's vital to do so. Just carry on running at the same pace. If something does happen and you felt victimised or scared, report it to the local police with as many details as possible.

If you're attacked

Try to avoid this at all costs. If you have no choice, try not to escalate things by responding with violence, but protect yourself if you have to. If you can use your running prowess to reach the safety of other people or a populated area, do so, but only if you know the area. If you run the risk of getting lost, then keep to your route or retrace your steps. Scream and shout, as this attracts attention and will put most attackers off. I tell all my female relatives, friends and clients the same thing: 'Go for the eyes,' since no one will keep holding on if you jab your fingers into their eyes or, better still, get your thumb in behind one. Failing that, go for the windpipe or crutch, although many attackers are expecting this and may wear a cricket box.

What type of training and where to do it?

These questions are answered in detail later in this book, but in short there are four types of running you can try:

→ Continuous runs (long and short)
→ Interval training
→ Fartlek training
→ Sprint training

The type you choose will depend on a number of factors, most importantly your current fitness level and your long-term goal.

Continuous training

The chances are that you won't be able to run for 30 minutes straight away, so start with far less. See Chapter 9 for a programme to match your level. However, as a start you could either walk or run for five minutes, if that's all you can do, then the following week increase this to seven or ten minutes, then the next week to 12 or 15 minutes and so on. This will enable you to progress. The most important part of running is to gain a base level of endurance fitness. It may be that even five minutes is too much in one go. If that's the case, then jog for one minute and walk for one minute and repeat this five to ten times. Again, increase these sessions progressively each week. Eventually you'll be able to run for 20–30 minutes without stopping. Then you can work on improving how far you run in that time or for how long you can run continuously.

Interval training

This is a running technique where you raise and lower the intensity and therefore your heart rate, with the idea of drastically improving your fitness, calorie consumption and the rate at which you recover. To perform an interval session, choose a certain distance (if outdoors) or a set time or distance (if using a treadmill). Outdoor examples are all the way round a football pitch (300m) or across a large playing field (100m); examples on the treadmill are 300m or one minute. Warm up as normal, then sprint the set distance as fast as you can. To recover following this, walk/jog back to the start (if outside) or walk/jog the same or double the distance/time (if on a treadmill).

Timed recovery is best as it ensures that the repeats are the same and you don't take too little or too much rest – ie give yourself a minute or two minutes between intervals depending on your fitness. Try to do at least four intervals on your first attempt, then add one or two each time, aiming to reach ten eventually. Then you can decrease your rest time as well, from a minute down to 40 seconds etc.

Fartlek training

Fartlek is a technique used for increasing stamina as well as endurance. It can also make running a little more interesting if you're someone who finds that it bores you. You can perform a simple Fartlek session on a treadmill or outside. To do so, set off at your normal running pace and after five minutes or so run almost as fast as you can for a short distance, say from one lamp-post to the next or one tree to the next. Then carry on at your normal pace and let your heart recover. After a couple of minutes repeat this process and run fast to another specific point. On a treadmill you could perhaps increase the incline but hold your speed for a minute. The idea is to change your pace, the gradient etc, to work your heart and improve your fitness instead of just running for a set time. Your imagination and ability to try new things is imperative to Fartlek training.

Sprinting

Sprinting is much like interval training but the distance is far shorter – anything from 10m up to 200m, but rarely more. Furthermore, the focus must be on technique, so it's more important to recover completely before the next sprint than when performing intervals, where the focus is on fitness/speed increase. For sprints long rests of a few minutes are usual. In fact the use of a heart-rate monitor to return the heart rate back to at most 120bpm or less than 100bpm is common.

Realistically, unless you're very fit and just looking to change your goals and type of fitness with intervals and Fartlek sessions, the chances are you'll be starting with continuous runs. Make sure you look at the beginners' programme in Chapter 9. Also, if you're going straight into Fartlek and interval training it's important not to overdo them. Start with them once a week initially, to ensure you build up a base level of fitness first.

If you find them particularly beneficial and that your fitness has increased to a comfortable level, then you can increase their frequency to twice a week.

When to run

A lot has been written about the 'best' time of day to run. Yes, there are advantages and disadvantages to running at different times of the day, so if you've all the time in the world then pick the one that suits you and do it then. However, for most of us it's not that simple. We have to run when we get the chance, be that before work, at lunch, after work or perhaps only at the weekends. My belief is that you should run at the times that are most convenient to you, as this will make things easier and mean that you're more likely to stick to it.

⏱ Running on empty

Interestingly, research suggests that no matter when we think we're best suited to exercising, almost all of us are, in fact, physically stronger and have more endurance in the late afternoon, when we've fuelled our bodies for the day.

Circadian rhythms

Research suggests that we have semi-regular sleep/wake cycles that attempt to follow the same pattern daily, called 'circadian rhythms'.

The circadian cycle supposedly regulates a huge number of our physiological functions, from blood pressure to metabolism. Studies indicate that our individual rhythms conform to our individual activities – daily alarm clock, meal times, bedtime and exercise times. Furthermore the studies indicated that we can teach our bodies to be 'good' at exercising in the morning, by consistently exercising in the morning. The same is therefore true of exercising at lunchtime or in the evening. Regularity seems to be the key.

This doesn't mean that you can't train at different times; it just means that if you always train at a similar time your body will be expecting it and therefore perhaps perform better. For most of us just getting the run done is enough, if it's about the exercise itself. However, if you're competing then it might be beneficial to train at the same time of day that the event will occur, therefore allowing your rhythms to adjust to this time and therefore, hopefully, perform better in the race.

Humans are the only animals to use alarm clocks. Except when threatened, all other creatures wake when they wake, meaning they get a better, more natural sleep.

Larks and owls

Some people are better in the morning and some are better in the evening. Often we describe these types of people as larks and owls respectively. Although this generally refers to their ability to be productive, friendly and get things done, it's also true of their ability to exercise.

Some of us have no trouble exercising first thing in the morning, while others feel like exercising much later in the day and the thought of exercising in the morning makes them feel quite nauseous. Yes, these things are possibly due to circadian rhythms. And yes, from what I've written above they can possibly be changed. However, if your lifestyle means that you have a very obvious preference then go with that and exercise when it suits your lifestyle to do so.

Chopping and changing

Believe it or not, apart from when we were in the UK exercise schedules in the Marines were pretty haphazard. Marines would train as and when they could, even if that was in the middle of the night. The simple fact is that not all of us are lucky enough to be able to exercise when we'd most like to, so the best thing to do is be as regular as you can with the time slots available around your work and family commitments. You'll be surprised how quickly you adapt to running at 05:45 every morning! Just make sure that if you do become a morning runner you get to bed early and have a quick bite before hitting the road.

 # Commitment

Beyond having a goal you must also have commitment, which will help you in the early stages of a running programme. Keep your goal at the forefront of your mind and stay committed to it. Don't be one of the thousands who start something new every year and soon give up, making one of the myriad excuses I hear as a trainer. In the Marines we had a saying 'Excuses are like assholes, everyone's got one.' If you want to quit, quit. Quitting is easy, finding an excuse even easier. But commitment makes you say no to that nagging urge to give up when things get hard. Commitment requires you to focus on your goals. If you stay committed, you'll make yourself, your friends and your family proud of you, which in turn will add to your self-confidence in ways you never expected. If you're lucky you'll also inspire the people around you. Commit to being committed now.

By purchasing this book you've already shown that you want to find out more about running.

Essentially, it's my job within these pages to convince you that running is for you and will change your life. It will, I have no doubt. By reading this far you've already taken the first, most difficult step – you haven't got to get started at all, you already have. So why stop now? Go out this weekend and buy some good trainers, dig out the running shorts you bought when you thought of doing the local charity run, choose a goal to achieve, and then start planning. Draw up a week's training programme, ring up your best mate and tell him/her that you're training partners for the foreseeable future until you reach your goal (and beyond?). Commit to all those things right now. Remember, you need no real kit and your environment is your treadmill. Get out there and start running! Stay committed, stay focussed, and believe in yourself. Your mind will be your greatest weakness, but it can also be your most powerful weapon. Use it to ensure you attain your running goal, whatever that may be.

Morning, noon or night?

Morning

A huge percentage of runners run in the morning, often before breakfast. They do so because it's a good way to begin the day; not only does it help them wake up for the day, it also gets the day's run over and done with. It avoids having to run at lunchtime or the end of the day when they're tired, or having the run hanging over their heads all day so that it becomes a chore.

The problems with running in the morning are that in the winter it's likely to still be dark and reflective vests etc will have to be worn, and the rain and wind banging against the window when the alarm goes off is often enough to put you off.

Studies have shown that proportionally more morning runners pick up injuries than daytime/evening runners, probably because our bodies are stiff from sleep and we're sleepy ourselves and therefore less careful. By contrast, being up and around all day before we run is like an extra-long warm-up, so the obvious answer for morning runners is to perform a long warm-up and dynamic stretch before the run, or to start very slowly and build up as they warm up. Furthermore, due to logistical problems and being pushed for time most people find that they run alone in the mornings, meaning they miss the benefits of running with others. For those who like to be alone with their thoughts, however, this isn't such a downside.

My main piece of advice is to ensure that you ingest something before a morning run. You may think that by running on an empty stomach you'll encourage your body to lose more weight, and this is true – sort of; the problem is it's muscle you'll be burning, not fat. Overnight our bodies have been essentially starved, and in times of starvation we store our fat, as we may need it if the starvation continues, and our bodies therefore break down our muscles for fuel instead. None of us actually wants to break down our

If you struggle to run in the morning, lay out your running kit the night before. With your kit already sorted it will be much easier to go out for a run.

 Personal experience...

If you can, arrange lunchtime sessions so that you can catch up with friends while you run. These are like lunch meetings, but while you're exercising! By contrast, morning running is often an isolated, solemn experience.

muscles, since they allow us to run faster and more efficiently, and the more muscle tone we have the more energy we burn when sleeping, working and relaxing. Hence our muscles help us lose weight even when we aren't training.

By simply having a small bowl of muesli or porridge or at worst a fruit juice or smoothie before running, our bodies will have high and low glycaemic fuel to burn during the run and thus won't break down our muscles. Furthermore, once the fuel from your small breakfast is used up, your body – since it's been fed – is more likely to turn to your fat stores for fuel.

On returning from your run have a breakfast before heading off to work, such as another small bowl of cereal or some eggs etc. But make sure you eat something!

Midday

Most of us are entitled to take an hour or so for lunch when at work. This can be a perfect opportunity to get out for a run. If you're lucky enough to work in an office that has a gym or at least shower facilities, then this makes things even easier. If not, you need to look for a gym close to work to allow you to shower afterwards.

Running during my lunch break was always my preferred option. It gave me time to wake up and not have to worry about exercising in the morning. It also allowed me to eat breakfast and a mid-morning snack to ensure that my energy levels were high enough to complete the run. I never felt my early morning performance was as good as during the day. However, the trick is to manage your time effectively to enable you to eat prior to and following your run. Either take a prepared lunch into work so you can eat a snack two hours before your run and then eat something at your desk afterwards, or ensure you have enough time to go and buy something after showering.

Midday is also an excellent time to run outside, all year round. During the winter it's light and the temperature is far warmer than in the morning or early evening. In the summer you can get a tan and that all-important vitamin D in just 30–60 minutes out of the office. Furthermore, the local park will often be full of people, making you feel glad to be alive,

If you find it hard to get motivated at any time, plan your run around a chore, eg picking up some dry cleaning – anything that will make your life easier and get you out on a run.

and you might even be encouraged to run that little bit faster in case they're watching.

Finally, many people find that after training at lunchtime they're more productive in the afternoon – but only if they eat after their run. The change of scenery, use of the body instead of the mind during the session and the simple fact that it wakes them up and breaks up the day means that they're more able to complete tasks and concentrate. I've definitely found this is the case for me when I've been deskbound for nine hours a day.

Evening

For many people this means running home from work, stopping off at the gym on the way home, or going out as soon as they get home. If you love your run and find it's a de-stresser, then this can be a perfect way to relax at the end of the day. This is especially true in the summer when the sun is still up and it's warm – the feeling of relaxation and enjoyment after another escape from the office is elating.

Contrast this with the same run in the winter. It's already dark, the wind and rain are howling at the door and the thought of taking off soaking wet trainers in an hour's time is slowly putting you off. Obviously there are alternatives; running on the treadmill at the gym is one. But whatever your decision, commitment is the key.

Studies indicate that the sooner after finishing work the run is planned, the more likely it is to actually occur. To make this more likely, have a snack or small meal at work around two hours before the run is due to start. This will stop you needing to refuel at home before running, and in the process losing interest or finding something distracting on TV.

For many people with a family the option of evening running is just too difficult to contemplate. Perhaps the only way round it is to negotiate with your partner to alternate running and

homemaking days, thus allowing running to take place every other day. The only other option is to run much later, after the kids are in bed, but this time is generally needed for relaxing and preparing food and clothes for tomorrow.

Weekends and days off

The weekend is the runner's (especially the marathon runner's) godsend. Unless family issues are pressing or your job requires you to work the whole weekend (in which case I'm assuming you'll be granted other full days off), the weekend allows runs to take place at any time and without any pressures on length.

This means that the long runs of a training programme should be left for weekends and days off. At the weekend a ten-minute warm-up followed by an hour's run, then a 15-minute cool-down and stretch should be nothing to worry about – a quick break from the day's chores or time with family and friends.

Running at the weekend, especially in the summer, can also be a great way to see your local surroundings, run with friends, share a hobby with your partner or perhaps review the week's events.

⏱ Committed or addicted

Be careful not to organise your life around your training. It's great to make training a priority, but don't be too inflexible; if you get invited out on Saturday night but you usually run at 11am on Sunday morning, do the run on Saturday afternoon instead, and then make everyone feel bad when they ask what you've done today!

Treadmills

Treadmills are a controversial piece of equipment. Runners either love them or hate them, use them frequently or never use them. But in truth it's probably not quite that black and white. Although some runners (including myself at various times) do about 90% of their runs on treadmills, and others wouldn't touch them with a bargepole, most people sit on a fence somewhere between these standpoints. Whether you prefer treadmills or running outside, use treadmills only on rainy days, only avoid treadmills in the summer or only use them when the pollen count is high ... wherever you stand, I urge you to read on – I might just persuade you to change your opinion.

For most people a mixture of the two is the preferred choice. Running outside is more refreshing and freeing, and time tends to pass more quickly, but running indoors allows the joints to rest while also avoiding winter weather for at least one or two runs a week. If we're honest, a treadmill is just a moving platform – a simple conveyer belt that, if used correctly, can vastly improve any able-bodied person's fitness, weight loss and running times. But inevitably there are a number of pros and cons to using them.

Advantages

→ Weather

Treadmills allow a run to be completed regardless of weather: snow, rain, heat and pollen have no bearing on running on a treadmill.

→ Onlookers

Other people can be a real double-edged sword, dependent on your viewpoint. For some they're a disincentive to run because the thought of others watching causes feelings of self-consciousness. For others, the thought of being watched as they eat up the pavement is inspiring and leads to a faster pace. Treadmills, either in the corner of the gym or your own home, allow you to hide away.

→ Embarrassment

That sense of being watched is something felt by all new runners, and runners returning from injury. We feel we should be doing better, and that everyone watching is thinking the same thing. In truth, no one really cares what you're doing – they're all too self-involved, worrying about what people are thinking about them. However, if you can't escape the feeling a treadmill minimises it, particularly if you have one in your home. Even in the gym, though, everyone is there for exercise of some sort, and most are more interested in what they're doing than what you're doing.

→ Interval training

A big mistake by many is slowing down on each successive interval. When training alone it's difficult to run the interval and use a stopwatch accurately, so many of us perform our intervals without timing them.

Without realising it, we slow on each successive interval quite drastically when running outside, which isn't a huge problem if you're running for weight loss. However, for fitness or competitive running successful intervals should be performed at a fairly precise speed and a precise distance, and a treadmill allows both of these to be set precisely: you can't speed up or slow down, your pace must be maintained.

→ Consistent pacing

Just like interval training, we all slow down during runs. We don't realise we're doing this, as our 'perceived exertion' (how hard we believe the run is) stays the same because the longer we run, the harder it is. In other words we believe we're still running at our target pace. The beauty of a treadmill is that it stays at a constant pace and therefore forces us to stay at the pace designated by the session, or at the very least forces us to slow down in which case we have to acknowledge that we haven't kept to the session pace. For that reason, consistent pace training is better on a treadmill, where the speed remains constant for the entire session, than on a track or road.

→ Easy runs
You can also use the treadmill to ensure you have an easy run. It's often difficult to run an easy pace that will allow muscle recovery. Easy runs often feel too slow, meaning many runners tend to perform them too quickly. Although this can occur on treadmills (by just upping the speed) it's far more obvious, as it's a conscious decision. Outside it's difficult to ensure you run at an easy pace; often the lure of catching the person 100m in front or speeding up as you go through a populated area is just too great. Furthermore, for many of us the need to feel we've worked hard is too overwhelming, and a faster pace is inevitably run. The problem is, our muscles need to rest and recover after hard runs, as without recovery time we'll be unable to complete harder future sessions or improve. If running outside, the use of a heart-rate monitor to ensure the pace isn't increased can be beneficial, but a treadmill – where the pace is selected then forgotten about – is far simpler and more effective.

→ Hill training and hill sprints
To seasoned runners those two terms will probably have given them that little butterfly in the stomach that precedes any really intense session – the type of sessions that you loathe prior to doing them, but feel elated about afterwards. Simply put, hill training is one of the most efficient methods of building running strength, perfecting running economy and improving uphill running. Furthermore there's little that's better for promoting weight loss, due to the intensive nature of the training.

But what do you do if you live in a place with no hills, or where you'd have to run a considerable distance to reach a decent hill? The answer (of course) is jump on a treadmill. Treadmills can be inclined from 0.5% or 1% up to 12–15% in either 1% or 0.5% increments. This means that any type of hill training can be completed using a treadmill.

♥ Personal experience...

The treadmill is great for new runners. When I have a client who hasn't run since childhood, or is returning from a long-term injury, I use the treadmill prior to outside running. It not only allows me to dictate the speed and ensure the runner doesn't go too quick too soon, it also allows underused tendons and muscles to gradually strengthen prior to more intense training.

♥ Personal experience...

I used treadmills extensively when recovering from severe patella tendinitis. Not only did it allow me to walk or run for a good amount of time, it also allowed me to run backwards safely, which I couldn't have done outdoors despite it being something that's highly recommended when recovering from such injuries.

→ Injury prevention
Running on concrete and tarmac places considerable stress on the body's connective tissues, specifically the tendons, ligaments, muscles and even the bones of the legs and feet. Believe it or not, each step puts around six times your body weight through the legs and feet – a considerable amount when you consider how many steps we take during an average 30-minute run. Therefore running on such hard surfaces every day (especially in worn-out trainers) leads to injuries. Treadmills, however, all offer some form of cushioning, anything from 'suspension' to simply a softer surface than the side of a road. In short, however low-tech the treadmill it will offer more cushioning than a road.

→ Rehabilitation
Treadmills are an excellent place to start if recovering from injury. Unlike outside, you can dictate the speed, incline and timings you want to run/walk at over a series of sessions. This allows us to test, strengthen and get over our injuries. The treadmill's more forgiving nature compared to roads is also perfect for 'breaking in' the injury site slowly. To me, this is the reason why almost everyone, even the severest anti-treadmill campaigner, will eventually give in and use one. Furthermore treadmills are very useful in posture training, as they encourage the runner to settle into a rhythm, both physically and mentally, thus protecting the back and core more than running outside does.

→ New runners
On the one hand treadmills are a new runner's best friend: great to ease in and control the pace, incline, time, distance and environment. On the other hand, unless you're lucky enough to have a treadmill in your house you'll be running in a gym, with lots of other people in the same space; not necessarily watching you, but there may still be feelings of intimidation. Whatever your viewpoint, I promise that the treadmill is a perfect way to gain confidence in your ability to run.

→ Structured programme

As you'll be aware by now, I'm a real advocate of the treadmill, both for personal use and for the clients and friends I train. It's an incredible piece of training equipment; since nearly everything can be adjusted and maintained (speed, time and gradient), very specific and structured programmes can be put together both for beginners and seasoned runners, to see and ensure improvements quickly and safely. Each session can be controlled by the second, meaning the pace or gradient can be adjusted at any point in the run and for as long as the runner or trainer requires. This means that a runner can train specifically for a particular event, mimicking the type of course in terms of pace, hills and distance. Furthermore, most treadmills have cross-country, interval and hill modes to allow anyone to test themselves with an unknown and highly challenging run.

→ Personal preference

There's no real reason why someone couldn't do all their training on a treadmill – I've personally done just that for a number of reasons, from being on board a ship to being in an incredibly hot environment. I actually find completing certain distance runs in specific times easier on a treadmill than on roads, as I can't slow down as I would outside. Furthermore, I've recently been doing all my treadmill running inside the Hypoxic Chamber of London's 'The Third Space'. This provides a room where the oxygen content is only 15%, instead of the normal 21% outside. Hence my ability to run has improved drastically as my body has become used to running at a lower oxygen content (hence my red blood cell count has increased and thus my ability to carry oxygen to my muscles), which is next to impossible outside unless you live on a very tall mountain!

→ Weight loss and general health

Last, but by no means least, there are no disadvantages to treadmill training when it comes to health, fitness and weight loss. A calorie burned on a treadmill is the same as a calorie burned running on the road or in the park, and cardiovascular fitness is improved just as much.

Disadvantages

→ Competitive runners

The only real disadvantage for a competitive runner is the lack of specificity for a race. Although a treadmill can be used to mimic a course or race, this is only possible to a certain point. A rule exists in the sports conditioning/training world called the 'rule of specificity', which suggests that training should mimic the activity being trained for as closely as possible. There are very definite differences between treadmill running and free range running that violate this rule in terms of proprioception of the knees and ankles and length of leg stride, to name but two. Therefore if the goal is to lose weight, then a run is a run, whether outside or on a treadmill. However, if the goal is to race on the road, trail or track, then training on a treadmill alone isn't specific enough.

→ Wind resistance

Running on a treadmill is stationary – there's actually no real forward momentum, therefore no wind or air resistance. Running outside creates wind resistance; in fact the faster you run the more wind resistance is created, and the bigger effect it has on the runner. I ensure all my clients always run at a gradient of at least 1%, 1.5% or 2% to mimic this as much as is possible.

→ Biomechanical differences

Without getting too technical, it's thought that there are very subtle biomechanical differences when running on a treadmill compared to running outside. These are:

● **Stride length** – All runners alter their stride on a treadmill compared to running outside. As we're running on a belt with a computer terminal (of sorts) in front of us, some runners (particularly the more experienced) lengthen their stride on the treadmill whereas others (usually less experienced) shorten their stride. Both obviously affect the runner once they return to running outside. Though these changes may not be all bad, as shortening their stride may up their cadence, the bottom line is that differences occur.

● **Forward lean** – Some runners lose some forward lean when using a treadmill. So what, you may ask? Well, when put into conjunction with less wind resistance (which would cause a forward lean) it can mean energy is wasted on up and down motion because less energy is focused on momentum. This can again change a runner's normal outside running gait, which isn't beneficial at all.

● **Running surface** – It may seem that the repetitive, predictable surface of a treadmill is an advantage. For injury rehab, track running and avoidance of uneven surfaces this is true. However, the uneven surfaces encountered when running outside improve proprioception and therefore help avoid injuries. Again, it's all about specificity. If you're training to run on a treadmill, then it's not a problem. But if you're training to run cross-country, a treadmill isn't the place to do all of it.

● **Visual stimuli** – If you've ever sat on a train in a station and seen the train next door move off, for a split second it seems as if your train is moving. When running, seeing everything rushing by signifies to your brain that you're moving and gives an indication of speed. On the treadmill this visual stimulus is absent. You're essentially stationary. Psychologically this can lead to confusion and a lesser performance, especially when you then go back to running outside. Admittedly, however, this is all down to the individual. Everyone is affected differently.

● **Space limitation** – All good treadmills have enough room for even the tallest, longest-striding runner. However, the limited length of the running surface can still give a perceived feeling of running into the console or falling off the back of the machine. What happens, therefore, is that most people shorten their stride as a result, or develop a more vertical stride, which is energy-wasting and less efficient. Whichever occurs, it can be detrimental to the natural running gait.

→ Lack of confidence

This is a very common consequence for runners who've spent all their running life outdoors and aren't used to running on a treadmill. They feel their gait changes, they lose the visual stimuli so feel a little disorientated. Therefore they lose confidence in their ability. Furthermore, the feedback a treadmill gives in terms of speed, gradient etc for the entire run can lead to the realisation that the outside runs undertaken by the runner throughout their running 'career' were perhaps not at the constant speed and perceived exertion that they originally thought.
Again, this can lead to a slight lack of confidence in the runner's abilities.

→ Boredom

The last item on my list, but probably at the top of most people's, is something nearly every (unseasoned) treadmill runner complains of. Agreed, it's one of the biggest of all the mental barriers of treadmill training, but running is itself a mental pastime. The strength of mind a competitive, fitness or fun runner needs is far greater than your average squash or golf player. Although running 'on the spot' can be boring and tedious it's up to the runner to occupy their mind: listen to music, watch the football (many treadmills have little TV screens attached) or review a work problem. As my mother taught me, boredom reflects more on the bored person than the activity.

A series of stretches can be completed on the treadmill

⏱ Conclusion

It's best to run when you can. It may be that twice a week you run before work, because that's your only opportunity, once a week you run at lunchtime because that's the afternoon you never have any meetings booked, and then once a week you run in the evening because that's when the local running group tries a new route they've come up with.

There's something to be said for regularity, and if you're a serious runner that's something you'll eventually have to consider perhaps, but for most of us – running for fun, fitness or weight loss – as long as you're getting the runs done, staying committed and seeing results, when you run has little overall bearing.

CHAPTER 3
KIT & EQUIPMENT

I'm not expecting you to read this chapter then rush out and buy all the latest kit. However, it's worth spending a few pounds if you're completely new to running. There are two reasons for this: firstly, to ensure that your kit won't cause you problems, such as rubs, blisters, overheating or feeling self-conscious; and secondly, because some people find that if they've spent hard-earned money on running kit, that in itself is sufficient motivation to go out and run.

You only need to look at the streets and local gyms to see that many people are happy to exercise in old T-shirts and jogging bottoms and a pair of squash shoes or football shoes that they've had longer than they can remember. This may not seem like a problem; at least they're getting use out of them. However, running home from work in old squash shoes isn't a good idea. They have little grip, no shock absorption and just aren't designed for pounding the pavements. This subject is covered in detail in Chapter 3, but a basic maxim is 'Use things for the purpose they were designed for'.

Clothing is perhaps a little more forgiving and a little more personal. However, a very similar logic prevails – when setting out on a run, be it outside or on the treadmill, you need to feel comfortable and stay comfortable. An old paint-splashed pair of cotton jogging bottoms may be fine at first, but as you train harder you'll find them too hot; they'll soak up sweat, become heavy and either slow you down or fall down! A couple of pairs of sports shorts will be better – they don't soak up sweat and are very quick to dry after washing, so can be turned around day to day. There's no need to buy lycra shorts and lycra leggings unless you really want to – simple black running shorts are cheap, understated and available for both sexes.

In a similar vein, you may feel that a baggy old T-shirt or rugby shirt will suffice at first, but the problem is they soak up sweat, smell after washing, and in the case of rugby shirts and many cotton T-shirts will start to rub and chaff in the wrong places. Simply purchase a couple of sweat wicking T-shirts or vests that will wash and dry quickly, as they're designed for purpose. They're soft to the touch, wick away sweat, remain cool as you heat up, and when washed don't retain a stale sweat odour.

The Internet is a great place to start for kit and equipment. Failing that, many sports shops have sales throughout the year, and most brands do bottom-of-the-range running trainers for about £30. Shops like Decathlon and even some supermarkets have their own brand sports kit: very cheap, but hard-wearing.

Huge sums of money are spent on sports products every year. The running shoe industry alone is worth billions, let alone the money spent on running watches, drinks bottles, compression tights, backpacks – the list goes on and on. However, all that you need when you start is a pair of good trainers, a top, some bottoms and perhaps socks (plus a sports bra if you're a woman), though you'll soon find there are other bits and pieces you want: gloves and hat for cold winter mornings, a reflective windproof jacket for dark, traffic-filled evenings, a pair of off-road trainers for weekend runs in the woods and even a special baby-stroller that allows you to run while your firstborn catches a few zeds. The list below is by no means comprehensive, but I've tried to include what I've personally bought and used, what my clients recommend and what the industry is now promoting.

When setting out on a run you want to feel comfortable and stay comfortable. Cotton items soak up sweat, become heavy and retain odour.

Footwear

I'm going to start by reiterating something I've already said in this book: only run in running shoes. You wouldn't go fishing in football boots, scuba diving in wellingtons or dancing in flippers. So don't run in football astro-turf shoes or skateboard shoes. Buy footwear specifically made for running. Yes, I understand that these days it's not all about the gel or air cushion, and a lot of research suggests we should actually run on our fore or mid-foot in shoes that just about provide protection against small thorns. I'm not disputing this. However, at least run in new(ish) trainers or shoes designed for their purpose. If you choose to run in supportive gel/air-cushioned shoes, then heel strike to your heart's content; and if you choose to run in very lightweight road shoes or barefoot-style shoes, readdress your running gait and run accordingly. But whatever you do, don't start heel-striking four miles to work and four miles back in your old footballing astro-turf shoes. You WILL end up injuring yourself.

The running shoe

There are a number of brands that consider themselves to be at the top of the tree when it comes to running shoes. They believe they're at the forefront of technology and have the market cornered. My only issue with this would be that the same companies produce a lot of fashion shoes as well. To avoid purchasing one of their fashion shoes by mistake (these are usually in garish colours and have some huge form of air bubble or the like visible on them), go to a reputable running shop and look at the models they stock. They should only stock actual running shoes, not their fashionable alternatives.

My personal favourite, and the brand of choice for 90% of the best personal trainers I've worked with, is Asics, who were also kind enough to supply the trainers used in the photos in this book. I started wearing Asics trainers after developing jumper's knee and a collapsed arch (possibly through overpronation), and I've never looked back.

Regardless of brand, I consider there to be six types of running shoe:

1 Stability shoes
2 Trail shoes
3 Shock-absorbing shoes
4 Motion-control shoes
5 Barefoot running shoes
6 Spikes

1 Stability shoes

These are designed to offer increased support to the inside of the midsole specifically to stop the ankles turning inwards. Generally speaking, running coaches consider these shoes to be good all-rounders and therefore suitable for beginners and seasoned runners alike, as they provide a good level of cushioning, good grip, and are neither overly heavy nor too light.

2 Trail shoes

These are designed specifically for running off the road or treadmill. They generally have a more rugged design to ensure they can withstand the abrasions that occur running off-road. Road trainers often have more mesh to make them breathable and lightweight, but one simple thorn leaves your toes seeing the light of day and your £80 trainers seeing the inside of a bin. Trails shoes don't usually have as much cushioning as other trainers as the terrain they're used on is generally more forgiving than a road. Although they're good for new and seasoned runners alike, ideally a period of running on level ground like roads should precede running on uneven surfaces.

3 Shock-absorbing shoes

These are best suited to seasoned or efficient runners whose feet, ankles, ligaments and bones are more used to running compared to those of new runners. Despite their shock absorbance such shoes have the least added stability, as they're aimed at neutral runners who are unlikely to pronate.

4 Motion-control shoes

These are the most rigid of road-running trainers. They're specifically aimed at runners who collapse in at the ankles, known as overpronators. Motion-control shoes are often heavier than other running shoes because they contain a 'medial post' – basically a hard area under the arch to provide support. Don't let their weight put you off, however; if you're an overpronator these shoes are for you.

5 Barefoot running shoes

These are supposed to mimic running barefoot as closely as is possible. For this reason they generally have little or no stability, arch support, motion control or shock absorbance. Most are literally a sole that protects the bottom of the foot and that's all. Some offer a very small amount of cushioning across the mid/forefoot (the ball of the foot area), as these shoes are designed for mid/forefoot runners only.

6 Spikes

I haven't spoken about spikes in this book, as they're not something most of us will ever run in. I hadn't run in spikes since school, then in the Marines needed them for a couple of cross-country runs and now have them sat in a cupboard, pulling them out every so often if I feel like hitting Dartmoor on a very wet day.

Spikes come in three major types: sprint, track distance and cross-country. All have interchangeable metal spikes, meaning you could actually use a sprint spike for cross-country by simply putting in longer spikes. However, this isn't really advisable. My advice would be that unless you're going to be a regular at your local track and think about competing, stick to trainers. If you really get bitten by the track-running bug ask the specialists in a running shop and they'll help you pick the right pair for your event. If you're running a lot of cross-country events and find you're slipping and sliding all over the place, then by all means buy a pair of cross-country spikes. Always check the course and change the spikes accordingly; also, like your trainers, wash and dry them after each use, or the spikes will rust into the shoes.

Picking the right shoe

N ow that you have a good idea of the types of running shoe available, it's worth working out which are best and most suitable for you by considering the following:

→ Any previous injuries
What injuries have you suffered? – specifically collapsed arches, patella tendinitis, overpronation, Achilles tendinitis or shin splints.

→ Running surface
The surface you'll be running can make a huge difference to the shoes you require. Running on roads means more impact, so a more cushioned shoe will be needed. Running on sand could need less cushioning, but the uneven surface may require more stability or even motion control. Consider off-road versus grip versus cushioning etc.

→ Running gait
Get yourself tested to see whether you supinate or pronate – whether you need motion-control shoes or stability shoes – or if you're a forefoot runner and can use barefoot shoes.

→ Length of your run
Most running magazine and running shops will encourage you to get trainers with a thumb's-width gap at the toe. However, whereas this may be true for a long-distance/ marathon runner whose feet will swell during a run and will need a bit of room, a sprinter running for as little as ten seconds or perhaps a minute should perhaps get a pretty snug fit. Remember also that friction leads to blisters, and a loose fit will mean your feet slide about, hence more friction.

→ Climate
If you run in the heat your feet will swell, if you run in the cold they probably won't swell as much. Are you running near snow or ice, or dust and hot tarmac? Just consider the use of your shoes.

→ If you like them
It may sound stupid, but if you buy a pair of shoes because you're advised to or think you should, but don't actually like them, you'll end up leaving them in the closet and wearing your old shoes or buying another pair. Make sure there's at least something you like about your shoes, even if it's just the colour of the laces!

→ Where you'll run
If you're running on roads and pavements you need more cushioning but less grip. If you're running off-road cushioning isn't as important as grip.

→ Take advice
A good running shop will have trained staff who'll watch you run on a treadmill before they advise you on the best option for your running gait. Most of the time they'll just be looking for pronation (collapsing in of the ankles), and if they see it they'll recommend motion-control shoes.

→ Personal preference
This doesn't mean picking shoes because they look good. However, if you feel good then you'll want to go running. First ensure that they'll do the job, then decide between those that are suitable by price and look. If you don't like something about a shoe, be honest and get advice on anther brand that may suit you better.

The wet foot test

Before you buy shoes, tread on some card or dark paper with a wet foot to establish the type of arches you have.

Normal print:
normal arches

You're likely to have normal pronation, as it appears you land on your heel and the foot rolls only slightly inward. Buy neutral shoes or perhaps stability shoes to prevent rolling occurring.

Narrow print:
high arches

A narrow print indicates underpronation, which means you run on the outside edge of the foot and get little or no shock absorption. Buy flexible shoes that cushion to promote movement.

Wide print:
low arches

A wide print indicates overpronation, meaning the feet roll in too much, which can lead to injuries because you're pushing off with your big toe, not all your toes. Buy stability shoes. Lace them up well and ensure the rigidity stops your foot from rolling.

Making your trainers last

Trainers need to be replaced every three to six months, dependent on how much use they get: a seasoned runner will complete more miles per week than someone training for weight loss and will therefore need to replace their trainers earlier. However, it's important to look after them properly if you want them to last. Always wash off mud, dog's mess or anything else straight after your run, even before you shower. You can't run without your trainers, so look after them first.

Don't use a washing machine unless absolutely necessary – with most trainers this will warp them or melt the glue used in their manufacture. In short, it's not good for them. Use warm water and a little soap with a medium hard-bristled brush. Remove the insoles to help the shoes air so they don't smell. If wet, fill with scrunched up newspaper and replace the newspaper as it becomes sodden until the shoes are dry. Never dry your trainers using an airing cupboard, tumble dryer or radiator – it's too hot and too quick, and the trainers won't last as long.

Store your shoes indoors, but not in real heat. If you store them outside they'll decay quicker than they should.

Don't use them for anything else EVER, not even a quick kick-about with the lads you see as you run past on your five-miler.

The best piece of advice I've received regarding footwear is buy two pairs – exactly the same if possible – and use them equally. Both will last longer than either pair would on its own because they'll always have a chance to dry out & be cared for.

Fashion shoes

Running in the correct footwear is a huge bugbear of mine. There are far too many people running to and from work every day in completely the wrong shoes and potentially doing themselves a lot of harm. A superb personal example of this is seeing young men trying to join the Marines. To obtain a place in Royal Marines Recruit Training, potential recruits have to pass a multi-stage fitness test, more commonly known as the 'Bleep Test'. This requires the individual to run between two lines 20m apart and arrive as a bleep sounds. The bleeps get progressively faster and faster until the individual drops out and is given a score. This test is relatively important, as passing is a big step towards obtaining a place in the Royal Marines – there are a large number of other tests, but this one is highly important; failing it pretty much guarantees a train-ride home. Considering the importance of the test, the types of footwear the young men would turn up in always astonished me.

Now, I appreciate the cost implications of buying expensive running shoes, and I'm certainly not advocating that we need to part with £100 for our new hobby, mode of transport or ticket to a specialist lifestyle. However, with the Internet and high street discount stores like Sports World or even Decathlon

it's possible to get bottom-of-the-range running shoes for around £25. Thus it constantly amazed me to see individuals turn up in basketball boots, football AstroTurf shoes, skateboard shoes, tennis shoes and even fashionable Velcro 'pumps' (all probably costing well over £50).

First of all, these shoes are not designed for running. You think that a trainer is just a trainer? Wrong. A tennis shoe is a tennis shoe, a squash shoe is a squash shoe, and a running shoe is a running shoe. No one would run in motorcycle boots or a pair of flippers. Why? Because they're designed for a completely different use. The same is also true of skate shoes and football trainers: they're not designed for the constant pounding in one direction of a running shoe. At best they'll result in a bad performance, at worst they'll lead to an injury.

Think of it this way: if I said 'Let's go for a run – it'll be cold, so bring trousers', what would you bring? The majority of you would bring tracksuit bottoms. Some seasoned runners might bring lycra leggings, and some outdoor pursuits-minded individuals might bring trail pants. Nobody would bring jeans or a pair of suit trousers. Why not? Because they aren't designed for running in? Because they'd be uncomfortable? Because you'd look stupid? Yes. All of the above. And this is also true of going for a run in anything but running shoes. Other shoes aren't designed for running in, are far more uncomfortable than running shoes and will often affect your running gait, which will eventually cause injury.

There are a few exceptions to only running in running shoes, I'm aware of that – don't forget I spent a number of years in the Royal Marines, where we'd run in combat boots all the time. However, we also conditioned ourselves to them over time and ensured our insoles provided cushioning and arch support. But even so, plenty of Marines got foot, ankle and knee injuries. I personally have a knee injury and wear orthotics to combat a foot injury I picked up running and jumping in the wrong footwear, so I speak from experience when I urge you to only run in trainers designed for running.

It is obvious which shoes are for running and which are for fashion. Look after your feet and wear appropriate footwear

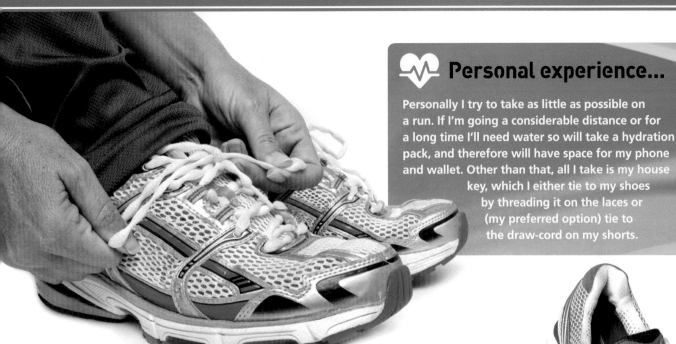

How to lace

Different people lace their shoes in different ways. It seems to be a mixture of ease, use and comfort, which is fine, as long as it's never fashion. Personally I find a criss-cross system is best as it allows quick tightening and loosening. I sometimes tie a knot at the end of the lace to allow me to loosen all the way to the knot without unthreading the lace. Some people like to miss lace loops if they feel those parts of the lace put pressure on their foot. This is especially true of people with high arches. Do whatever works for you and whatever you're used to.

Socks

Socks come in various lengths, thicknesses and qualities. The type you'll need depends on the type of running you'll be doing. Most brands do regular ankle socks in thick and thin materials, trainer socks (smaller than ankle socks) in thick and thin materials, and calf-length or up-to-the-knee socks offering some compression and warmth. Don't think that if you've spent a lot of money on your trainers any old socks will do (or, for some people, no socks): you need to have a reliable, well-made pair that won't slip down and will help avoid blisters and chaffing rather than cause them.

Cotton should be avoided in favour of the wicking materials which most sports brand socks use. Many also offer cushioning. Like trainers, when they look old they probably are and should be thrown away.

All running manufacturers seem to make their own socks; try them, figure out what type works best for you and stick with it. Personally I'm a fan of thick trainer socks. Although thicker and therefore a little more sweat-inducing they're more comfortable on longer runs and I find they last longer over multiple washes.

Triathletes often replace laces with elastic or some form of draw cords that allow them to pull their trainers on more quickly and not have to waste precious seconds doing up laces during a changeover.

Bottom half

Shorts

Shorts aren't just shorts. What I mean by this is you can cut the legs off a pair of combat trousers and make shorts, but they're not going to be any good for running in: the length and hard cotton material will chaff and they'll become heavy with sweat and most likely fall down. So buy some proper running/sports shorts.

Whether male or female, buy gender-specific kit – the cuts are slightly better for your sex so the likelihood of rubs and chaffing will be less. All running shorts come with a built-in liner, which is generally very soft, made of wicking material, and (certainly as far as I'm concerned) good enough in terms of support that underwear isn't required. However, if you feel more comfortable wearing it that's your call. Apparently underwear is unnecessary for men, but sports manufacturers still expect women to wear it.

Running shorts are generally short to allow better freedom of movement and many have splits on the outside to allow the legs even more freedom. Some splits go all the way up to the seam, and generally the longer the split the shorter the shorts. The shortest shorts with the largest splits are generally for sprinters and faster distances, whereas those with no split or smaller splits and slightly longer legs are fine for longer distances. When running in very short shorts for long distances I found that my thighs would sometimes rub together (Vaseline helped), whereas longer shorts alleviate this.

The bottom line for everyone should be to run in whatever makes you comfortable, and for most of us wearing very short, large-slit running shorts would make us feel a bit 'on show', and it's important to not feel embarrassed as it will put you off your running. In general pockets aren't included in the normal sense as they tend to rub and bump the thighs, but a small hidden pocket is often included in the seam or at the back for a key or credit card.

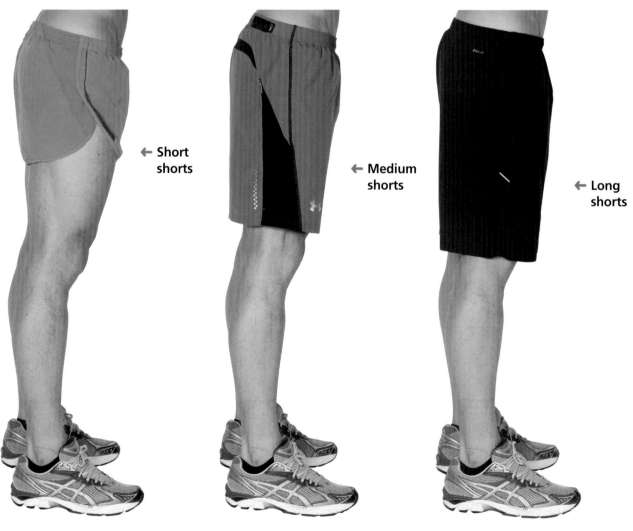

← Short shorts

← Medium shorts

← Long shorts

In terms of materials it's more sensible to tell you what to avoid than what to buy, as every decent sports/running brand has developed its own fabrics, which essentially are lightweight, wick sweat away and dry quickly. Personally I always buy kit from a good sports brand, as you know it'll be hard-wearing and fit for purpose. In terms of what to avoid, nylon and cotton are the only real no-nos as they tend to chaff badly and soak up sweat, becoming heavy, flappy and saggy.

Leggings

Although these were originally just for sprinters and women they're now worn by everyone. They're perfect for cold winter nights and even better when a small case of DOMS (delayed onset muscle soreness) is felt, as they provide compression. There are many different types and brands, all meant to provide different qualities and functions. For example, I own a pair of Skins leggings designed specifically for compression. I bought them while on a military course, where I had the worst DOMS I've ever experienced. However, they're also stated to be perfect for flying, as they help lower the chance of DVT. Other leggings offer warmth or claim to help you run by activating muscles

that occasionally fail to fire correctly. Personally I prefer to wear a pair of shorts over the top, but this isn't necessary and sprinters wouldn't do so.

Like shorts, it's personal preference whether underwear is worn. For women it's apparently recommended, whereas for men it's a matter of choice. However, unlike shorts leggings don't come with built-in underwear, but their tightness offers support anyway. The only downside is you may feel a little on show. If this is the case, wear shorts over the top.

Leggings generally have two functions: to provide warmth and compression. However, these days, manufacturers have produced many different types for a myriad of functions: compression, speed, warmth and even special types for DVT and to reduce DOMS. Top manufacturers have developed fabrics offering windproof properties, cooling properties, waterproof qualities and warmth. Personally, rather than having three or four different pairs I tend to stick to the wicking/breathable versions, which work well whether it's cold or hot. Most are designed ergonomically so that they're more suited to either men's or women's running gaits, so always buy the right type.

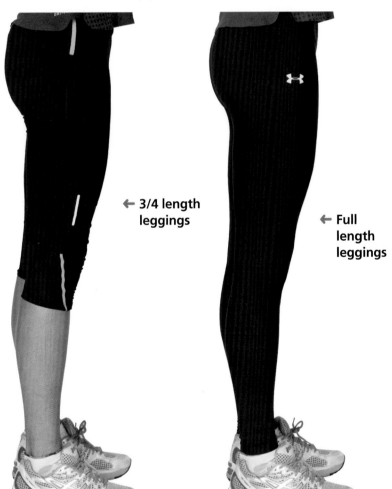

← 3/4 length leggings

← Full length leggings

○ Underwear

As already mentioned, chaffing is common to runners and therefore underwear should be designed for purpose. If you're like me you'll use the built-in liner in your shorts and 'go commando', but women and those of you who find that uncomfortable should choose something that provides support, is comfortable and won't ride up. Cotton should be avoided and men's boxer shorts are a big mistake. Apparently Bridget Jones knickers are better for women than thongs in the support, health and fitness sense, but thongs are less visible when wearing leggings and cause less embarrassment when exercising, and consequently encourage training to take place.

Top half

These days fabric seems to be the important factor in a garment, or at least as important as style and fit, and the important thing to look for in a fabric is its ability to wick. Wicking, whether made by UnderArmour, Asics, Adidas or any other sports goods manufacturer, should keep you dry and cool and take the moisture away. All manufacturers now make their kit from their own wicking material, but to be honest they're all a much of a muchness and basically work the same way. They're generally made using a three-layer approach, so that the material takes sweat away from the body to the garment's outer surface so that it can evaporate (which helps cool you down as well), thus preventing the soggy, flapping material associated with cotton.

Vests, singlets and T-shirts

As long as they're made of a decent wicking material there's little difference between a singlet and a T-shirt apart from personal preference. Personally I find a T-shirt is fine if I'm doing a long, slow, continuous run, but if I'm doing a fast pace or interval session I overheat in a T-shirt and much prefer a vest or singlet. Having said that, you need to consider the climate: will you get burnt shoulders in a singlet where a T-shirt will protect you? Are you running in the evening when the temperature may drop suddenly? If so a T-shirt may be better. Personally again, if I'm running in a singlet I'm trying to run fast and my body heat should keep me warm, despite weather changes or nightfall.

Sports bras

These are covered in depth in Chapter 14, but the bottom line for women is always wear one, get fitted for it, and be refitted periodically, especially if you change size or weight. Try different brands and if you find one that fits well and works for you, buy a few and alternate them. Replace them periodically, as the elastic 'suspension' gives over time. Wash as per instructions to prolong their life. Remember, *always wear one!*

Warmth

Once you start running you'll heat up very quickly. For this reason you don't want to start off like Michelin man, in layers and layers. The best advice is to start off feeling a little cold – not unbearably, but certainly chilly! The trick is to get it right, so that when you're running you don't feel cold and don't feel hot. So the best advice is not to start out warm.

Most clothing manufacturers produce clever materials that provide warmth without needing to be thick and baggy. Look at runners around your area, specifically the more proficient ones, on a colder day. What are they wearing? Most will probably have the following:

- A long-sleeved wicking T-shirt, long enough to tuck in to keep the core warm.
- A pair of full-length running leggings to keep the legs and ankles warm.
- A windproof/showerproof soft or hard shell jacket of lightweight breathable material.
- Possibly a hat, gloves and a pair of breathable shorts over the leggings.

→ Base layer

Base layer tops are always made of wicking material and are generally quite figure-hugging. The higher-end versions are seamless to ensure there's no chance of chaffing. The cold-weather variants are often overly long, to enable them to be tucked into shorts or leggings to prevent cold air entering waist-level gaps.

Long sleeves can be great for a number of reasons: firstly during the winter when it's cold, obviously; secondly if you're prone to sunburn and want to cover up; and lastly, when teamed with leggings, for protection from brambles and stinging nettles on cross-country runs. Summer versions are often sleeveless and very tight, wicking the sweat away and holding the muscles to aid running technique.

→ Jackets

Running jackets are a relatively new concept spawned from the need to protect yourself against showers and wind when training in all weathers. There are generally considered to be two types: soft shell, which includes a warm fleece-like lining; and hard shell, thin and breathable but providing protection from wind and rain.

Soft shells are great for protection from all weather types and avoid the need to layer and layer, but if you overheat they're more bulky to carry. With hard shells you'll need to add layers in the real cold. Both jackets can be bought in bright colours to increase visibility in the dark.

→ Gilletes

A personal favourite of mine, these provide warmth to the core, which is where it's most important, but allow cooling and breathability in the arms. Some jackets are actually available with detachable sleeves.

→ Hats

Did you know that around 40% of your body heat is lost through your head? This can be a good thing and a bad thing. On cold, early morning winter runs it may be necessary to don a woolly hat. Many sports brands offer running-specific versions that are made of the same wicking material as their shirts. These are designed to keep the ears and head warm without becoming soaked with sweat. Earmuff variants provide warmth for the ears but allow heat to escape from the top of the head during a run. Many companies also offer hats made of high-visibility material or with reflective strips, which can be of benefit during road runs.

→ Caps

These are a good alternative to woolly hats, whether in summer or winter. They can still insulate the head somewhat, yet in the summer can provide shade for your face and keep the rays off your head. (This is especially important if you're somewhat lacking in hair and your head is prone to sunburn.) Running manufacturers make their caps from high-tech materials to keep you cool and stop the sweat.

→ Gloves

Just like hats, the top manufacturers produce gloves that keep hands warm yet wick away the sweat. They may also be reflective and/or bright for additional visibility. With the major muscles of the body using all the blood, the extremities often have restricted blood flow and become cold. Gloves combat this. As in the neck, the proximity of blood vessels to the surface in your wrists causes the blood to cool quickly, so gloves will help keep you warmer overall.

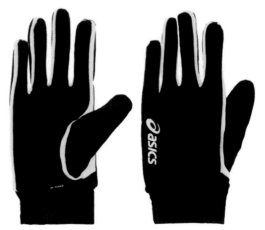

→ Scarves

Brands such as Buff, North Face and even Adidas make snoods (basically tubular scarves) that can be pulled up over the mouth and ears when running if necessary. These are particularly good if you're running in extreme cold, as they can protect your lungs from very cold air somewhat, as well as keeping your neck warm, where heat is lost due to the proximity of the carotid and jugular to the surface.

Wearing a hat over the ears can obstruct your hearing, so be careful when running on roads. Obviously other safety issues arise when you can't hear, so running with friends is advisable.

Special items

Ankle/wrist wallet

Pieces of kit are available that allow you to carry a few small items on your run. These are usually in the form of a wrist or ankle wallet, with probably enough space for keys, a phone and a credit card or a few notes. There are larger items that fit around the waist, but these generally include some form of hydration system (water bottles) as well, and if you're going to carry that much (which will change your running gait) you may as well carry a backpack. A recent addition has been a small lace pocket that allows a key or a few coins to be carried on the front of your shoelaces. However, personally I'd just tie your key to a shoe or the waist-tie on your shorts.

Compression wear

The basic idea behind this gear is that the material – which generally contains spandex or lycra in some form or other – separates and compresses your muscles, making them more efficient and warmer while providing support and preventing chaffing. By compressing the body the clothing constricts the blood vessels in the muscles, thus maintaining the heat in them. Not only does this aid warming up and prevent strains, it also helps recovery from DOMS. Like running tights, most compression gear is sex-specific: whether ergonomically designed for fit, or just in terms of comfort, it's worth buying compression gear that fits and is made for you, whether you're male, female, young or old.

Sunglasses

Sunglasses aren't simply to protect your eyes from UV rays, they're also perfect for protecting them against rain, flies, dust and even strong winds. Many top manufacturers produce glasses specifically for running that have interchangeable lenses to work in any light conditions, including clear lenses for rainy days.

⏱ Energy saving device

Some manufacturers claim that by preventing unwanted (eg lateral) movement within muscles, compression gear can prevent them from wasting energy and maintain forward momentum better. This saves energy and thus allows us to run for longer.

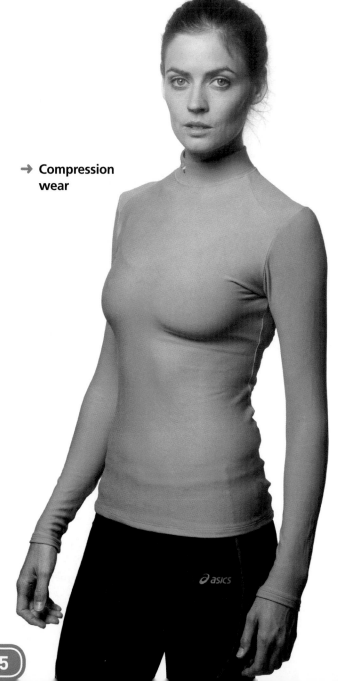

→ **Compression wear**

Watches

Running watches have become big business. For many years the only real variant to the sports stopwatches produced by Casio or Timex was the heart-rate monitor, and Polar had the monopoly on those for years. The main functions they need to have for any weight-loss or fun runner are:

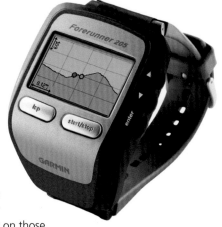

- Time (so you know what time of day it is and can ensure you get back from lunch on time etc).
- Stopwatch (to time your run/intervals/rest etc; this should be in 1/10-second splits).
- Countdown timer (to keep track of intervals between rest or work periods without constantly needing to look at the watch).

Stopwatch-wise it's also nice if you can record splits to look at later. This is especially useful if you have mile markers or are running time trials of a certain distance.

In recent years brands such as Nike, Suunto and Garmin have released watches. The big difference with these is that although they provide stopwatch and heart-rate facilities, most usually offer something else as well: a way of giving you feedback regarding pace and distance covered. Nike originally did this using a 'footpod', now replaced by their Nike Plus system, both being similar to a pedometer in that an accelerometer is used to measure your pace and distance once you've calibrated it. Now that it's become more readily available GPS technology has largely replaced accelerometer technology, and provides instant and accurate feedback in terms of speed, distance and time.

Heart-rate monitors

These allow the heart rate to be viewed on a screen in beats per minute (bpm) at any point on a run simply by glancing at a watch, which displays the heart rate registered by a belt around the chest. All models come with a watch and chest-belt, but features within this setup vary wildly. At the bottom end of the market the watch simply provides your heart rate (HR), with very little input regarding its relevance. In mid-price-range types a heart-rate zone can be set (eg 140–150bpm), and if you exercise above or below it the watch beeps and you have to speed up or slow down to stay in the zone. At the top end the watch saves each run, the average HR on a run and the highest heart rate. These days many also have a computer interface embedded so that you can see at which points on a run your HR was high or low. An amazing training tool, regardless of your level.

GPS

The best things about a GPS watch system is that once you're home you can plug it into your computer and see the route taken and what your heart rate was doing at every point along the way. This allows you to examine see what it was doing on a big incline or if it jumped to an all-time high at mile four and failed to drop until you stopped, enabling you to make the necessary changes to your training to ensure you're not hitting any sort of wall too early.

The sort of feedback and information gained from GPS watches is second to none and makes their hefty price tag well worth it, whether you're running for fun and weight loss or are a competitive runner or building up for your first marathon attempt.

Running buggies

I should probably start by saying I don't have children and have never actually used a running buggy. Consequently the cost of an addition to the family seems astronomical to me, especially the thought of spending between £250 and £500 for a basic pushchair with small BMX wheels when I could buy a large widescreen TV or pretty good mountain bike for the same money.

Having said that, I'm also an exercise addict, and if a running buggy meant I could start running again sooner than if I didn't have one I couldn't put too high a price on that! Furthermore, a running buggy will be a chance to get your baby out in the fresh air and allow them to start experiencing the real world (albeit flashing by) sooner rather than later.

There are so many different types of buggy with different functions that I'm not going to expand on the subject too much. However, wheels come in sizes from 12 to 20in, and the larger the wheel the more comfortable the ride. Large wheels would also mean you could go on trails and tracks, whereas with small wheels you'd need to stick to pavements. Wheels and frames also come in different materials. Steel variants are heavy and prone to rust, alloys are lighter and more expensive. Tyres on the wheels are an added bonus, but

← **Running buggies**

are more expensive and need more maintenance. Having said that, a real tyre will be less bumpy and hopefully keep the little'un asleep as you run.

Adjustments are really important. If you share the buggy with your partner, chances are you won't both want the buggy at exactly the same height and angles etc. By buying an adjustable version you can set it up specifically for you. Equally, if your wrists or shoulders ache during the run a quick change will alter the angles and hopefully ease things. Lastly, check a decent 'safety harness' is in place – a five-point version is best and will give you peace of mind when you really push the pace.

 Buggy build

Top buggy tip – get an aluminium frame for light yet sturdy build and ensure suspension is built in to guarantee the new addition is kept safe, as at the end of the day that's far more important than your run.

Music players

Gone are the days of cassettes, CDs and minidiscs. We've moved on amazingly in terms of portable music. My recent iPod was 160gb and I only managed to fill 75gb, yet still had all the music I wanted with me at any one time. If I needed a specific song, to give me an adrenaline kick, I had it; I just had to spin through the menu system to find it. Added to which the ability to create playlists meant I had running, circuits, inspirational etc playlists for different runs and sessions.

The only drawback that I can honestly see to the accessibility of music these days is how it cuts you off from everything else on your run. Yes, there are some wonderful things to be gained from running with music – relaxation, adrenaline, inspiration, a beat etc – but sometimes the sound of the countryside or even the city can be just as inspiring. Also, remember that by listening to music you're cutting off one of your senses, meaning that traffic, muggers, dogs or anything else are inaudible to you. And listening to music while cycling or running along roads certainly isn't a good idea. Being able to hear the sounds of sirens, horns and vehicles could give you a split-second advantage that might just save your life.

Choosing an MP3 player is a matter of taste, brand preference and usage. Apple's iPod seems to have cornered the market and for usability I'd have to agree. However, if you also enjoy swimming Speedo do a waterproof MP3 player that can also be used when running. All the top electrical brands do their own players, with different functions including radio, pod cast and audio books rather than music. Don't forget as well that many mobile phones can also be loaded with MP3s and act as music players. This gives you the added security of having a phone should you need it. Don't be tempted to answer business calls when exercising though – this will defeat the object of its de-stressing nature.

Water bottles

As with all sports equipment, water bottles are big business. A large number of companies make their own, and there are even companies that only make water bottles. All I'd advise is exactly what we told recruits going through Marine training: when you're exercising, always have a water bottle with you. If it's possible to have one with you at all other times then do so.

There's a wide variety on the market, from simple branded water bottles like that provided by MaxiNutrition, to bottles with built-in filters from Water Bobble and specialist bottles like the HydraCoach, which actually tells you when to drink, based on the information you input when setting it up. Other hydration systems like the North Face/Nalgene hydration pack provide a means of drinking while running. These are especially useful during long marathon sessions or when running in particularly high temperatures where dehydration is more likely.

⏱ Inventive drinking

Bottles such as Waterbobble and HydraCoach are an excellent addition to your running kit. Waterbobble allows you to take your running abroad and not have to worry about the water making you ill, as the built-in filter will do the necessary. As for HydraCoach, if you get to half an hour before your run and realise you've drunk nothing but coffee all day, HydraCoach is the answer: it will literally nag you to drink – all you have to do is take it with you.

I personally love running with music. I have five or six songs that I play when really working hard on the treadmill – they give me such a boost of adrenaline that I complete my run faster than without them.

Rucksacks and backpacks

Running with a rucksack or backpack is something that's become increasingly more popular. Living in London, I would say that over 50% of runners I see in the morning and early evening run with a backpack. On the one hand this is great; they're running to and from work and maximising their time to fit in their fitness and healthy lifestyle. However, on the other hand around 90% of them are running badly because of their choice of rucksack.

From my background as a Royal Marine PTI I know a bit about running while wearing a backpack. So let me put it this way: in the same way that bad trainers can change your

running gait, give you blisters and cause you injury, a rucksack not designed for running can do the same.

A decent backpack for running should be stable and not swing from left to right while you run. It must therefore have a waist strap, possibly a chest strap, and be padded and ergonomically designed to take up-and-down movement without swinging from side to side or bouncing up and down, which will give you rubs, chaffing and blisters and may lead to back and core injuries.

The picture below shows the North Face/Nalgene pack and a Karrimore SF 45-litre daysack. Both are designed for walking, running and trekking. They're ergonomically designed, padded and have added straps for comfort and support and should be the sort of rucksack you purchase if you need to carry things to work when running.

Medical kit

Whether we're talking about tape and plasters to cover up blisters or suncream to stop your shoulders burning, medical supplies are very important to a runner. For women some spare tampons or towels may be advisable, and for men, with no sports bra to protect us, some Vaseline for the nipples, the backs of the arms and between the legs. In short it's all a matter of personal preference. I'd advise finding a suncream and sunblock you prefer and make applying it a ritual before a summer run, likewise whatever lubricant – Vaseline or otherwise – that works for you for your feet, nipples and other areas prone to chaffing. And then there are anti-inflammatories and painkillers. Be wary of masking pain or injury, but have a cupboard with some anti-inflammatories ready to go, just in case you pull a hamstring or sprain an ankle; taking them combined with PRICE (see page 184) can take days off the healing process.

CHAPTER 4
HOW TO RUN

As a personal trainer, Royal Marines PTI or in my own training, I'm a great advocate of the adage 'If it ain't broke, don't fix it'. What I mean by this is that although somebody may seem to run 'differently', if it works for them and they're not looking to break any records or compete, and it isn't causing them any issues or injuries, I don't change it. I leave it and work with it.

Once a friend or client decides to take their running to the next level and their particular style needs adapting, *then* I'll make little tweaks and changes. However, the majority of you reading this will be running simply to get fit, so unless your gait is going to cause you injury there's no need to alter it.

In short, there's no perfect running technique. We're all different and so are our running techniques. Look at Paula Radcliffe, who nods her head as she runs, something that most coaches would have tried to stop because of the unrelaxed nature it leads to. However, to her it's natural, and not only led her to a record-winning time (around three minutes quicker than anyone else), but a time that no British man came close to the same year – so she must be doing something right. My point is, it's natural to her and you should also run naturally, as you learnt to do as a child.

Nevertheless, despite what I've just written there are certain key factors that can help and could lead to a faster or longer run using less effort.

Biomechanics of running

Most people's running techniques can be improved vastly by training. Training doesn't just mean repeatedly running. In the same way that David Beckham kicked thousands of footballs as a child to perfect his cross/delivery, running can be improved with perfect practice. However, it is, of course, necessary to know what makes a 'perfect' running style (does it exist?).

Obviously, running is slightly different to kicking a ball. Although technique can be improved through a series of small pointers, it's difficult to teach; it's more something that becomes easy, economical and comfortable through practice, circumstance and implementation.

The best course of action is to use what's been learned naturally, then refine it through practice and improve by making small changes.

The coaches' technical running guide

→ Try to land with your foot directly beneath your hips, never out in front. If the foot lands in front your forward momentum is 'stopped' slightly – in effect the leg acts as a brake. By landing underneath the body the leg allows momentum to carry on, thus letting energy from the previous stride carry efficiently into the next. Furthermore impact and stress is reduced, thus relieving the Achilles, knee, hip and back.

→ Aim to keep the heel 'unweighted' throughout the stride cycle. This can feel very unnatural, yet it's the way the world's most efficient runners run. The heel hardly touches the ground, as almost all of the weight is put through the forefoot during the weight-bearing phase of each stride cycle. As above, this reduces the shock entering the leg and the body by providing both shock absorption and energy propulsion for the next stride from the natural flexibility of the foot.

→ Aim to run with a cadence of at least 88 to 92 foot-strikes per minute. This should be the same no matter what speed you're running at. By simply running at this faster cadence vertical displacement is reduced, less fast twitch muscle fibre is used, there's less impact stress, and energy return for the next stride is greater. Put simply, a better/faster/easier run.

→ Try to propel yourself forward using movement through your hips (hip extension) rather than through your knees (knee flexion or knee extension). This will make you more efficient, with more forward (horizontal) propulsion by engaging larger muscle to do this, making the whole running process more energy-efficient.

→ Aim to accelerate the foot backward before it hits the ground. This also minimises any braking by the leg and means propulsion begins as soon as the foot becomes weight-bearing.

→ Try to keep contact time between your feet and the ground to a bare minimum. This helps minimise energy wasted in vertical movements and makes the elastic recoil in the foot more prominent.

If a little too much of that sounds like biomechanical jargon, then what follows should help make sense of the different elements mentioned and enable you to determine exactly what you need to do to improve your technique.

Cadence

In running, the word cadence refers to the number of full revolutions of the legs taken per minute (rpm): that is, the number of times both the right and left foot strike to make a full revolution or stride. Its importance is generally overlooked by non-professional runners, usually because other factors such as technique, stride length and breathing rate take precedence. However, it's something that seasoned runners need to be aware of. Top long-distance runners have a cadence of around 88–95 on average, which changes very little with speed.

Although cadence doesn't matter to most of us, if you want to get a little bit more technical or make running easier on yourself, training your cadence could help. If you've ever watched the marathon on TV, the elite runners look as if they're finding everything easy, yet they're maintaining a pace for 26 miles that most of us couldn't maintain for one! A large part of this is down to their high running cadence.

The advantages of running with a higher cadence are:

- The legs are moving quicker and therefore there's less impact, which in turn leads to fewer impact injuries. You'd think that a lower cadence means less forward momentum and so less impact, but that isn't the case: a lower cadence actually means more air time, which causes a bigger impact at each landing, hence the higher rate of injuries.
- Because slower cadence leads to more time in the air, the foot strikes the ground in front of the centre of gravity rather than directly under it. This basically acts as a break and slows you down. This is known as 'over-striding'. A quicker cadence cancels this and leads to the foot strike and push-off working together to conserve and generate momentum, meaning you run faster and it feels easier. This sounds counter-intuitive to most people, so just trust me.
- Elite runners keep to the same cadence no matter what speed they run at, but increase the length of their stride as the race speed increases. This means that the cadence they use when running at 6min/mile pace is almost identical to the cadence they use when running at 10min/mile pace.

A large stride is essentially hopping from one foot to the other in very big steps, but we can only hop so far. What this means is that if your natural cadence is 80 and you want to run a 5k race at 6min/mile, you'll find it very difficult unless you change your cadence. So increase your cadence for your slower runs, get used to the different feel of it and work up from there.

Counting and improving your cadence

To find your cadence, count how many times one foot (left or right) strikes the ground in a minute. You'll then be able to see how far you are from the 'magic' 90 strides per minute.

To improve your cadence, arguably the most important thing to ensure is that you're getting your body over your foot strike. Get someone to watch you from the side and tell you if your foot is under you or in front of you as you land. If it's in front, you need to get your hips forward so that it almost feels like you're falling into your next step. Practice keeping your feet under your body while running. It may be necessary to do this one foot at a time at first and then with both feet.

Run at a comfortable pace for a minute or two; then, staying at the same pace, try to put your feet down earlier than normal. A simple way to do this is to run directly behind another runner or very close to the front of a treadmill. This forces you to shorten your stride and hence quicken your cadence.

Reduce your 'up and down' movement. This is imperative in speeding up your cadence and making your style more energy efficient. Run on a treadmill and watch your head movement in a mirror: if your head bounces up more than an inch or two at each step, you're running with too much up and down movement. Work hard to stop this happening.

Widen your step. It will feel unnatural but forces you to run with a shorter stride. Basically, run by placing your foot to the side rather than the front and centre.

Attempt to run with shorter and faster strides. Actively force yourself to have a quicker cadence.

Once mastered, a cadence of 88–94 allows you to increase your run speed more easily and enjoy your run that little bit more.

Common gait mistakes

Speed of legs

Your leg speed should be fast (high cadence), perhaps faster than you might expect for a long 'slow' run. A higher cadence will allow you to run faster as you become fitter. Many runners make the common mistake of thinking that 'bouncing' gives them more air time, which makes them feel less tired. This may be true, but the air time actually wastes energy on upward propulsion instead of forward propulsion, meaning that your run will take you longer. The *opposite* is actually advisable: cut down the bounce, which will in turn reduce the time your feet are in contact with the ground and make you run faster. However, you may fatigue quicker. Regardless, bouncing isn't a good running technique and isn't advisable.

Feet leading the legs

The legs should be led by the knees rather than the feet. The foot landing in front of the knee is how we humans run naturally downhill, because it acts as a brake to slow us down. The same is true if the foot lands in front of the body on the flat, braking the body and thus wasting built-up forward momentum.

Knee lift

Dependent on the type of running being trained for, knee lift is very important. Sprinters require higher knee lift to increase power, so that when the leg is driven downwards into the ground it propels the body forward faster and harder. For a distance runner, however, knee lift should be low, as it's more efficient so will burn less energy, which in turn delays fatigue.

Breathing

Whether you're an Olympic athlete or a first-time runner, when you run you get out of breath. This is because as our body moves faster it requires more oxygen. With any exercise, running included, our muscles need more energy, and the body meets this need by supplying them with oxygen-rich blood, which allows oxidative glycolysis (a method of making energy) to take place.

Most of us breathe in a ratio matching our speed, and do this without conscious thought. We mostly breathe in a 2:2

rhythmic ratio, ie two steps as you inhale, and two more steps as you exhale. Breathing in a 3:3 ratio often occurs for a slow run, whereas very fast running can mean a 2:1 or even a 1:1 ratio, although a 2:2 is still much more common.

Furthermore, most runners naturally breathe through both the nose and the mouth, neither nose nor mouth being considered more 'correct'. Top coaches suggest whatever is natural to you and works best, and believe that adjusting your breathing pattern won't make you a better runner. Simply put, breathing is a natural process, and so is getting out of breath!

Exhaling as the left foot strikes is most common, and is believed to help avoid a stitch, whereas breathing out on the right foot is thought to encourage a stitch.

Tension

If any part of the body is overly tense or rigid, then precious energy is being wasted. A relaxed running style will make you faster and, more importantly, ensure you last longer. The most common mistakes are tensing the neck and jaw, especially when working hard; clenched fists or rigid knife hands are also common mistakes. Try to avoid these at all costs – relaxed hands, relaxed forearms and a relaxed jaw ensures natural breathing.

Arms

Like all running styles, what feels natural is best. Therefore swing the arms naturally like pendulums for distance running. Unless you're sprinting, when power generation is required, there's no need to force the movement. Furthermore, any arm swing, whether you're sprinting or running long-distance, should be at the side of the body and not across the chest. Swinging across the chest can restrict breathing and cause imbalance.

Hips

The hips should be straight on and should not rotate overly. In theory they should stay in line with the shoulders, but for some runners, particularly women, this can be difficult. Additionally, they should only move forward in the same plane as the run. Sideways movement (swinging of the hips) is unnecessary and will only slow you down.

Shoulders

As difficult as it may be, the shoulders must stay relaxed. This is often very difficult for bodybuilders and sportsmen. The problem is that rigid shoulders rotate the upper body in the opposite direction to the hips, which therefore slows the pace, wastes energy and can cause unsteadiness – all of which lead to a slower run.

Posture

A natural relaxed posture is one of the most important things to remember as a runner; the key is to stay upright and not to slouch. However, as the core gets tired this can be extremely challenging. The key is to train the core with specific conditioning exercises to ensure it doesn't let you down during runs (see Chapter 11).

Foot strike

→ Heel strikers

The majority of all runners (around 80%) are 'heel strikers' – meaning that the first part of the foot to strike the ground is the heel. Following this, the foot rolls on to the toes to push off into the next stride. Core strength and stability is particularly important when heel striking, as it protects the back. Therefore heel strikers should ensure the abs are tight, which keeps the torso upright, spine straight and core engaged.

→ Forefoot strikers

The other 20% of runners are forefoot strikers. This simply means that the ball of their foot is the first part of the foot to strike the ground. Due to the heel being 'missed out' of the foot strike, these runners have a slight forward lean to their style and take short, quick steps. Their cadence is therefore slightly quicker than in heel striking (which is a good thing).

So which technique is better?

We humans have been on a journey, from our ancestors' days of running barefoot – almost certainly as forefoot runners – to our recent invention of cushioned running trainers that enable us to run on our heels without huge shock waves through the legs and body. Yet recently there has been much media attention on forefoot running, as a result of barefoot running and, for the most part, Newton and Vibram FiveFinger running shoes. The question is, of course, which is better? Should we realise that our ancestors ran 'correctly' and return to our roots by forefoot running, or should we acknowledge that we've 'evolved', and accept that just as we now wear underpants and bras to stop our bits swinging around, we wear shoes to enable us to heel strike, and that this is how humans now run? I am, of course, being a little flippant; wearing underwear hasn't changed our biomechanics! However, just because we've evolved doesn't mean that forefoot running is now wrong – or does it?

Manufacturers of barefoot running shoes and owners and advocators of barefoot running clubs claim that running shoe manufacturers have 'changed the way we naturally run' through running-shoe design, and the all-important heel cushioning. They say that without these gel-, air- and cell-cushioned shoes we wouldn't have adopted the heel strike method. I can see their point, and the claim that if the shoe manufacturers admitted they were wrong it would cost them billions a year in sales

is also a fair point. However, what about our day-to-day shoes? When we walk in our normal everyday shoes we strike with our heels. Yes, there's less shock going through them when walking than when running, but it's still there. So are barefoot advocates suggesting we should change the way we walk entirely? Strangely, when talking to the head of the company that imports Vibram FiveFingers into Europe, the answer was 'Yes'. He's such a fan of the shoe and its technology that he wears them with everything, to the point where he now walks on his toes – much like a baby (as he put it).

Perhaps this 'baby walk' was the way we humans were originally designed to walk. However, I'm not sure that we were originally designed to wear neckties, sit at computers all day or drive cars; yet we've evolved to do these things, and I don't see the fashion community getting rid of neckties, let alone making all shoes suitable for walking on the toes as nature may have intended. Again I'm being flippant, but if my BSc in genetics taught me anything it's that species, including Homo Sapiens, evolve and mutate, and it's very difficult to reverse the changes. We supposedly once walked on all fours like chimps do – but we won't be going back to that any time soon.

I believe that barefoot running certainly has its place, and have no doubt that it was how we were designed to run. I also believe that it feels very liberating to do it. However, I think we've evolved too far beyond it now and that it should be reserved for running in the park or on the beach every now and again as a form of cross-training or a bit of fun. It's certainly not advisable on concrete roads and treadmills. Forefoot running, however, I'm a huge fan of. I've personally changed my running style to see the effects for myself, so I can pass on accurate experience to my clients. I've successfully used it to help a sufferer of long-term hip pain to run again.

← **Merrell Barefoot shoe**

← **Vibram shoes**

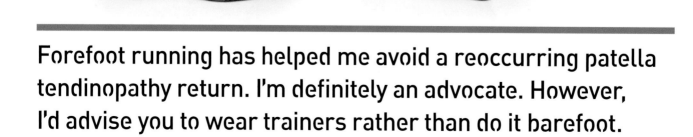

Forefoot running has helped me avoid a reoccurring patella tendinopathy return. I'm definitely an advocate. However, I'd advise you to wear trainers rather than do it barefoot.

Heel strike

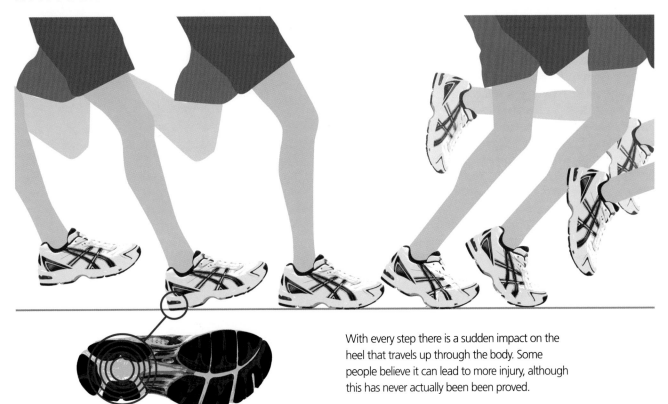

With every step there is a sudden impact on the heel that travels up through the body. Some people believe it can lead to more injury, although this has never actually been been proved.

Forefoot strike

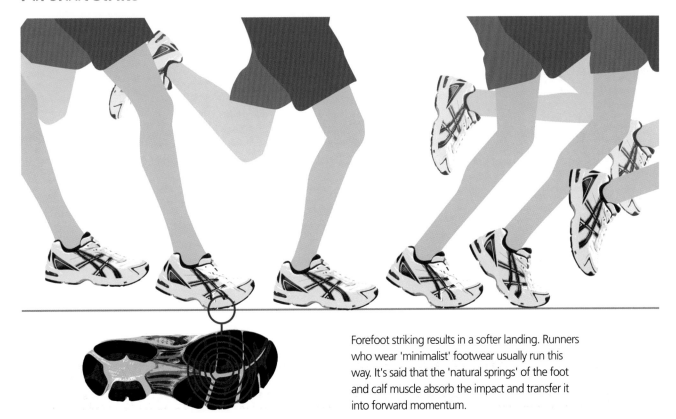

Forefoot striking results in a softer landing. Runners who wear 'minimalist' footwear usually run this way. It's said that the 'natural springs' of the foot and calf muscle absorb the impact and transfer it into forward momentum.

Attempting to run barefoot/forefoot

If you're planning or attempting to move from heel striking to barefoot running or forefoot striking there are a few pieces of advice you should heed:

Firstly, it's necessary to ask yourself a simple question: if you're pain and injury free and a successful and experienced heel striker, why change?

Secondly, to date no independent long-term study has proven that forefoot running is more efficient, faster or more economical than heel-strike running. Furthermore, the simple fact that super athlete and all-round running superstar Haile Gebrselassie (the current marathon world record holder) is a prominent heel striker suggests that heel striking doesn't hamper performance. As long as the coaching guidelines given above are stuck to and the weight of the foot contact is kept under the general centre of mass and the runner lands lightly, then the foot strike should have little to no effect when compared to VO2 max, aerobic capacity and correct mechanics.

If you're still keen to try forefoot running, then some other considerations will help:

Embrace the correct running mechanics laid out above. But be aware that these skills take time to perfect. Don't jump straight into long, fast runs just because you can complete them as a heel striker. Build up slowly. Furthermore, use conditioning and specific prehab to avoid injuries (see Chapter 11).

Barefoot running – forefoot strike and cushioned trainer – heel strike

Select the correct running shoes. Newton's, Nike Frees, Vibram FiveFingers and, of course, barefoot running itself all promote forefoot running. However, bare feet and these shoes have little or no cushion at the heel and no arch support. If a poor forefoot technique or a heel strike occurs in these shoes, it will put a large amount of impact (six times your body weight) through your entire chain of movement, from the sole of your foot to your hip. Dependent on the mechanics of your gait and mileage per week, this could have disastrous consequences. I personally tried forefoot running shoes very early on without changing to forefoot running (no one told me...), unfortunately at around the same time that I was instructed and coached in Parkour/Freerunning – and I now wear orthotics to help me with a collapsed arch problem and suffer from a recurring patella tendon injury. Whether these injuries were due to one or both of these factors I'll never know; however, I now have to live with the consequences. If the injuries were due to heel-strike running in shoes that provided no heel cushion or arch support then I learnt the hard way: learn from my mistakes rather than your own.

Slowly does it. The easiest way to pick up a running-

🏃 Handbag or Anvil

Most women worry that heavy weights will give them 'big muscles'. However, I'd put money on the fact that most women lug big handbags around all day that weigh more than the weights the majority of their boyfriends/husbands use to try to get big muscles! Keep reps above 12, but make the weights challenging. You won't get big muscles. If you do, let me know and I'll inform the bodybuilding world, as I'm sure they'd love to know your secret.

related injury is to drastically increase the amount of running you do. The key is to start with very little and not every day, and build up. My advice with forefoot and especially barefoot running would be to start with distances as short as 200–500m and certainly no more than 1km. From there, increase distances by no more than 10% per week. Although this is just a guide, it's certainly advisable.

Ensure that both prehab and conditioning sessions take place each week as well as running sessions. Too many runners, especially women, only perform running sessions. Generally this is for two reasons: running is easier and more enjoyable, so conditioning is avoided; and there's a fear that conditioning will lead to 'big muscles', and therefore slower running times and a less desirable physique. This is not the case. Running training, and specifically transition to barefoot/forefoot running, is greatly aided by conditioning, leading to better times, a stronger finish and a much better chance of avoiding injuries and recovering from little niggles. Conditioning and prehab should be part of every runner's weekly schedule, whether you're running for weight loss, fun or competition, or indeed changing your running style, and should be maintained throughout the year.

Recovery is essential when undertaking any sort of training programme, whether running, weights or swimming. Overtraining is always a risk, and rest and recovery always a requirement. This is especially true when making the transition from heel striking to forefoot/ barefoot running. DOMS (delayed onset muscle soreness) will inevitably happen due to the change in mechanics and slightly different muscles being utilised. Along with rest, the introduction of mobility and stretching exercises – both static and dynamic, before, after and on non-training days – is highly recommended.

It's important to realise and accept that it takes considerable time to make a successful transition to barefoot/forefoot striking. Realistically we're talking months rather than weeks. However, everyone is different, and as long as you go at your own pace and on your own timescale there's no reason why you can't make a successful

and injury-free transition. Furthermore, if you're currently running a lot and don't wish to cut your mileage down, then don't. Instead, supplement forefoot-striking sessions with normal running. It's possible to do this by alternating sessions or by simply doing forefoot intervals in normal runs. Over the course of several months, gradually increase the proportion of forefoot striking. As before, the 10% per week guideline is advisable in increasing the amount of forefoot running you do.

⏱ Conclusion

Running is a natural thing to do. Don't be fooled by people who think they know what they're talking about: don't bounce, don't try to stretch the foot forward as far as possible. Follow the guidelines above, and if you feel like attempting barefoot/forefoot running do so safely and slowly – choose soft surfaces, and if you get any niggles, stop, rest, and slowly start again.

CHAPTER 5
ENERGY SYSTEMS

In simple terms our bodies need energy to run. In fact we need energy for everything we do – movement, growth, repair and even keeping our heart beating. Humans, unlike some animals, have a very high capacity to expend energy for many hours doing sustained exercise, such as marathon running. Interestingly we also burn energy when our muscles are resting. The more muscle a person has, the more energy they'll expend.

It's therefore important to improve muscle tone when trying to lose weight, using weights exercises and not just relying on cardiovascular exercise such as running. The two complement each other perfectly. Despite this, the energy expenditure of exercising muscles is far greater than that of resting muscles, hence the importance of exercise in losing weight and getting fit.

There are two main reasons why you need to know about energy expenditure during running: firstly if you're using running to lose weight; and secondly if you're a seasoned runner you'll need to have the energy to make the most of your runs. Either way, some of the following should be helpful.

Energy and therefore calories are burnt during and after exercise. The amount of energy expended by the muscles at rest or during exercise varies with size, gender and age. However, it will aid with weight loss and fitness regardless. All of our energy comes from the food we ingest, as described in Chapter 6. We can get all our energy requirements from a good all-round diet containing carbohydrates, fats and proteins. Once ingested and broken down our bodies store this energy in a number of different ways until it's required.

ATP

Food produces energy, but this energy can only be used when it's in the form of the chemical compound ATP (adenosine tri-phosphate). Unfortunately, our muscles can only store small amounts of ATP at a time, so to cater for all the activities we undertake our bodies have to keep making it. If the level of activities means our muscles use up ATP faster than it can be made, then we'll get tired and have to slow down or stop what we're doing. In simple terms, if you're trying to run faster than your body can provide ATP to make your muscles work then you'll either have to slow down or stop to let the body replenish its stores.

The three energy systems

To provide our bodies with energy as we use it up, we have three different energy systems: the creatine phosphate (PCr) system, the lactic acid or anaerobic glycolysis system, and the anaerobic system. These work together to maintain the muscles' energy (in the form of ATP) at all times. For runners, these energy systems actually fit quite nicely with our differing types of running (sprint, middle-distance, long-distance):

→ **Creatine phosphate system**
For 0–30 seconds of hard/explosive work – used in sprinting: 100m, 200m and up to 400m for some of us. This system is the body's immediate supply source, providing energy far more quickly than the other systems. However, due to the way it works it can only provide energy for very short periods.

→ **Anaerobic glycolysis system**
For stamina – used in middle-distance running, 400m, 800m and 1,500m for some of us. Provides one to two minutes of hard work. This system can provide energy relatively quickly, but isn't long-lasting, so the muscles tire quickly as waste products build up in them, causing fatigue and pain.

→ **Aerobic glycolysis system**
For endurance – used in long-distance running, 5km and over. This system can provide energy indefinitely (provided sufficient fuel is available). However, it must have oxygen to work and therefore requires energy expenditure not to exceed a certain level.

The creatine phosphate system

ATP à energy + ADP + P
ADP + CP (creatine phosphate) + energy à ATP + creatine
(ADP = adenosine diphosphate, P = phosphate,
ATP = adenosine triphosphate)

This system provides immediate energy by using energy stored in our muscles. This allows for an immediate explosive response, perfect for a sprinter. Unfortunately the ATP stored in muscles only allows for 8–10 seconds of hard work, just

enough for the world's elite 100m runners. Once these initial stores are depleted more must be created to allow activity to continue, and this is where creatine phosphate (often taken as a supplement) comes into play, since this is also stored in the muscles along with the initial stores of ATP.

Simply put, creatine phosphate is a high-energy source that can be broken down to create more energy for the working muscles. The amount stored in the muscles gives us, on average, another 20 seconds of hard work before stores are depleted – just enough for most of us to complete the 200m. Only our running elite would come near to completing 400m with this energy system.

The creatine phosphate system is THE system for sprinters and they therefore train to improve it. Following a full-out sprint of 100m or 200m we must rest for several minutes to allow the body to replenish its creatine phosphate store.

The lactic acid system is incredibly important if maximum effort is needed for longer than ten seconds when the creatine phosphate system is exhausted.

Lactic acid (anaerobic glycolysis) system

ATP à energy + ADP
ADP + glycogen to ATP + pyruvic acid à lactic acid (insufficient oxygen)

This system provides short-term energy beyond that provided by the ATP and creatine phosphate stores. When we exercise for longer than around ten seconds (among very fit elite athletes this will be greater) we start to breathe heavily and deeply, simply because our muscles need more oxygen. Due to the time it takes for this oxygen to get into the bloodstream and to the muscles, any ATP or creatine phosphate stores will have been exhausted. It's then that the lactic acid system provides energy until the required amounts of oxygen arrive.

The lactic acid system uses glycogen as an energy source. Glycogen is produced from the breakdown of carbohydrates. It's then stored in the muscles and the liver. However, when glycogen is broken down to produce the demanded energy (allowing the muscles to continue working), lactic acid (lactate) is also produced as a waste product. As more and more of this waste is produced the muscles begin to feel fatigued, eventually forcing us to slow down or stop.

The lactic acid system can't be sustained for long. The length of time is dependent on the person, gender, age and, of course, fitness level. However, the 'lactic threshold' can be trained, to increase it, meaning the individual can continue for longer and longer with lactic acid building in the muscles. Top middle-distance athletes have far greater lactic thresholds than the rest of us.

Oxygen deficit

When the creatine phosphate or lactic acid systems are used, an 'oxygen deficit' is created: this means that the activity being performed requires more oxygen than it's possible to take in. When the activity is finished, it's therefore necessary to take in more oxygen to make up for and counteract this deficit. This is known as the 'oxygen debt'. By replacing this oxygen we restore the body's natural level, enabling the removal of lactic acid, the replacement of oxygen stores in the body, and the restoration of ATP and creatine phosphate stores in the muscles.

Aerobic system

ATP à energy + ADP
ADP + glycogen à ATP + pyruvic acid
Pyruvic acid + oxygen à carbon dioxide + water

Due to the fact that the aerobic system provides energy far slower than the other systems, it's the one we use for the majority of our daily activities. However, the drawback is that it provides energy far too slowly for intensive activity, hence the need for the other systems. The aerobic system's energy supplies are almost limitless, dependent on the individual, body type, length of activity and the availability of food, but in general, as far as runners needs go, they won't run out. The aerobic system is essential for runs over long periods of time, meaning long-distance, marathon and ultramarathon events.

Simply put, the system works by using oxygen in the breakdown of carbohydrate and fat to produce energy, but without any waste products that stop the process reoccurring (as in the lactic acid system). However, the aerobic system can only sustain its energy production when enough oxygen is being supplied to the muscles.

Energy systems interaction

If you're performing a marathon almost all the energy provided will be from the aerobic system, and if you're sprinting it will be the creatine phosphate system that's used. However, sometimes a 10,000m race will come down to a sprint finish, so what happens then?

Unsurprisingly, the body doesn't use the three systems completely independently and the answer is that all three systems are used in conjunction with each other. The amount each system is used will depend on the intensity of activity at that point, as well as how long that intensity needs to last:

% aerobic	Event	Primary energy sources
0	100m/200m sprint	
10	400m sprint	Creatine phosphate and lactic acid systems
20		
30		
40	800m run	
50	1,000m run	Creatine phosphate, lactic acid and aerobic systems
60	1,500m run	
70		
80	3km run	Aerobic system
90	Cross-country running	
100	Marathon running	

The 'central governor' theory

Fitness professionals, doctors and athletes have always believed that our muscles become fatigued because they reach their limit of physical ability, be that because they run out of fuel (energy) or because they're overwhelmed by toxic by-products (lactic acid), and we've never thought to question this. Why would we? It's what we were taught in school and university.

However, two top scientists – Tim Noakes and Alan St Clair Gibson – have recently questioned this belief, as they don't agree that fatigue is as simple as a car running out of petrol. So, what's their theory? Well, Noakes and Gibson believe that fatigue is an emotional response that actually begins in the brain. (A similar idea was suggested in 1924, by Archibald Hill.) They postulate that what they call a 'central governor' in the brain constantly paces our muscles to stop them reaching exhaustion. Basically, high intensity exercise could threaten the homeostasis (general standing/heart rate/temperature etc) of our bodies and thus cause damage to the heart; consequently the central governor limits the intensity

of exercise that can be performed by reducing the recruitment of muscle fibres. Less available fibres is felt as fatigue. Simply put, the output of the muscles during exercise is continuously adjusted as per calculations made by the brain in regard to a safe level of exertion for the heart and body. It's also thought that previous experience of strenuous exercise is factored in by the brain, so effectively the central governor can be trained to accept more intense exercise over a period of time.

Proof in the long run

As with any new theory, the 'central governor' concept remains controversial. But when everything is considered it does make sense. The body should always keep a reserve in case of an emergency, such as a predator or an enemy trying to kill you. To be so fatigued that you can't escape would be a big mistake in evolutionary terms, which makes the central governor theory more sensible than it might at first seem.

Paula Radcliffe – the most successful female marathon runner. Is her strength down to her governor control?

It also makes sense when you realise that fatigued muscles don't actually run out of anything critical, as despite excessive exercise the glycogen levels (energy stores) in the muscles and liver never actually reach zero. Again, it seems as if the body stops us before we hit zero to ensure that an emergency reserve is maintained. Furthermore, the central governor theory poses a huge question regarding the build-up of lactic acid as a cause of fatigue, because if this was the sole cause then athletes wouldn't become fatigued so quickly when exercising at altitude, as the slower paces that have to be taken mean that lactic acid levels remain low and we should be able to run for far longer; yet we know that altitude training still sees fatigue set in. This would be explained by the existence of a central governor, measuring the levels of blood-oxygen saturation in order to protect the heart and body and maintain homeostasis.

Lastly, the central governor also makes more sense of medical conditions such as chronic fatigue syndrome, which see individuals experiencing fatigue even at rest, something that can't be down to lack of glycogen in the muscles. Therefore psychological and motivational factors, ie the brain, must be considered the real reason for such conditions. Again, the central governor seems to make more sense in such instances.

Overriding the central governor

In a scientific sense, the central governor theory isn't that different from what was believed previously, it's just a bit 'chicken and egg'. It was thought that the muscles tell the brain when they're fatigued and hence the body stops. However, it seems to be the case that what's happening in the muscles is irrelevant. In fact the governor constantly monitors physiological factors and signals, even though they're not the direct cause of fatigue; instead they're the signals the governor takes into account to make its judgement of when to signal fatigue.

The question, then, is if the central governor is really on the case, how can the Paula Radcliffes and Moses Kiptenewis of this world carry on at the paces they do? In the past we assumed they had some genetic gift that meant their muscles didn't fatigue like the rest of us, or that years of training meant they could work longer and harder despite the influx of lactic acid. The answer could be simple: all of us might have a degree of ability to override the central governor, despite the feeling of discomfort produced by intensive exercise. This is, of course, dangerous, as continuing at the same intensity can/will cause damage to the body and heart. Consequently for most of us the override results in a natural slowing of pace; but it's thought that top athletes can override the central governor completely. But if that's possible, then how do they do it?

One possible answer is that they're blessed with incredibly strong minds, strong willpower if you will, which fits in very well with my own thoughts on the psychology developed by runners at an early age. These top athletes can literally ignore

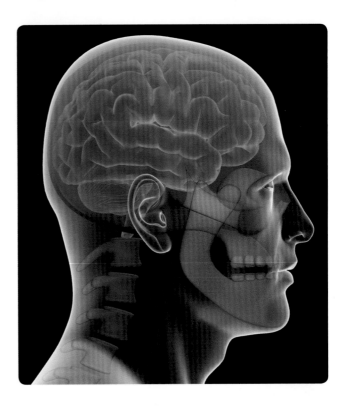

their bodies. However, this suggests the central governor is more an emotional than a physiological mechanism, which isn't quite true. However, it would help to explain why shouting, music or other distractions enable someone to keep training at a higher intensity and for longer, by occupying the mind and preventing the brain's messages from getting through to the body. A perfect example of this is our very own Miss Radcliffe. Watch her as she runs, a very strange head-and-neck thrust every step. Some Kenyans constantly tap their thumb and forefingers together. Both these traits could be learned methods of occupying the brain to override their central governor and deal with the 'pain' of doing so.

⏱ Conclusion

In reality it makes very little difference to you as a runner which energy system you're using. However, with a little knowledge you can at least understand why you're struggling or having to slow down during a specific run, or why you need a longer rest after your fifth interval. The main thing to do is to keep your body supplied with food, even if you're trying to lose weight. If you starve your body, you'll slow your metabolism and make your body store fat as opposed to metabolising it for energy. Always eat before and after training, to ensure your body has energy to burn and food to replace energy after exercise.

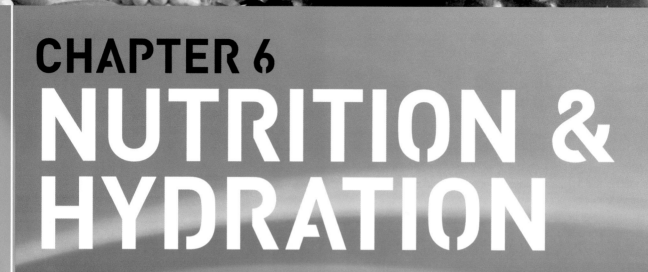

CHAPTER 6
NUTRITION &
HYDRATION

Nutrition is a very complex subject and differs considerably depending on who it's aimed at. The marathon runner who's covering up to 50 miles a week should be eating quite differently from the casual runner who's running to lose weight. Having said that, there are a number of general guidelines for nutrition that can be implemented and understood by everyone, simply to try to live more healthily.

It's therefore very important for you to understand your own fitness agenda: 'know yourself' is a maxim I like to get people to apply. What I mean by this is that you're the best one to judge where you are on the following scale:

1 Running in order to lose weight
2 Running for fun
3 Running for fitness
4 Running as part of your social life
5 Competing and training for events

Where you are in this scale is important to your calorific intake. It's worth bearing in mind, however, that you may not be in the same place in six months' time when the running bug has really taken hold! Remember, there's a huge difference between the casual runner out once or twice a week to help lose a few pounds and the semi-serious runner who takes part in such a vast amount of exercise that it's actually difficult to take enough calories on board.

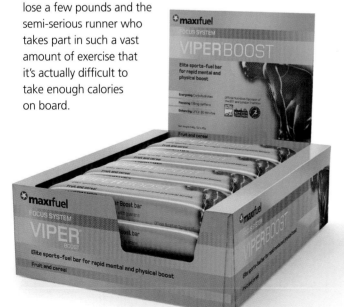

A balanced diet

Whether you're a sprinter or an endurance runner, serious or casual, it's imperative you understand the concept of a balanced diet. Most of us assume we eat a balanced diet because we don't eat exactly the same things every day. We may also try to eat our 'five a day' (five portions of fruit or vegetable), but in reality many of us don't quite manage it. Humans being habitual, we stick to food we know and like, without making an effort to be more adventurous. If this is you, try to change.

Food diary

Try writing a food diary for one week and see how adventurous or varied your diet really is. Don't cheat – write down everything you eat, even the mid-morning digestive or handful of Maltesers before bed. This honest food diary will come in handy later.

A varied diet isn't necessarily balanced; a truly balanced diet should consist of ALL of the following:

→ Carbohydrates
→ Protein
→ Fats
→ Fruit and vegetables
→ Vitamins and minerals
→ Fibre
→ Dairy
→ Fluids

Thankfully it isn't necessary to eat all of these every day, let alone at every meal. Where possible, though, an adequate quantity of the main foodstuffs should be consumed every day – that's protein, carbohydrate, fats, fruit and vegetables. Furthermore it's also important to drink plenty of fluids to help with digestion.

Carbohydrates

Humans are no different to their animal kingdom counterparts, and in terms of our energy sources we're exactly the same. Just like animals, we use carbohydrate as our main source of energy, whether it's ingested as 'simple' sugars or 'complex'

carbohydrates. 'Carbs', as they're commonly known, are a must if we're to perform well in our everyday tasks.

For runners, carbs are totally irreplaceable if a run is to be completed in a good time and good form. To attempt a run without having ingested any carbs that day will likely lead to a sluggish, slow and unresponsive body, and in turn a bad run. Furthermore, this sluggish unresponsive body won't be biomechanically sound during the run and can therefore become injured far more easily than normal. Lastly, by running without ingesting carbs the body is more likely to break down its own muscle than any excess body fat, simply due to how the human body operates when in 'starvation mode'. Breaking down your own muscles rather than eating some carbs is generally not what any runner or fitness enthusiast is aiming for. So I say again – *don't run without eating carbs that day!*

Once ingested, carbohydrate is stored in the muscles as glycogen. Running, performing exercise, in fact just being active in general, uses up glycogen. When our muscles run out of it (or run low, if you're a believer in the 'central governor' theory, discussed on page 64), we fatigue and our performance drops. It's therefore imperative to replenish carbohydrate stores first thing in the morning (breakfast), before training, throughout the day, in between training sessions and (very importantly) as soon as possible *after* training (ideally within an hour). Replenishing stores within that one-hour window allows the body to refuel that much quicker for the next training session or event.

For serious runners who undertake a large amount of training on a weekly basis, carbohydrate is the most important part of their diet. Yes, they need protein to help repair muscles damaged by the miles of road they're covering, but without a high level of carbs throughout each day they simply wouldn't be able to cover these miles in the first place. For runners at this level, even snacking on high carbohydrate foods (eg cereal bars, bread, bananas and other fruit) is necessary. They really don't have to worry about 'cutting carbs', a phrase commonly used in gyms and glossy magazines these days. Most such runners

Many people assume that not eating and then exercising will help them lose weight quicker. This isn't true. Eating some low glycaemic carbs a few hours before your run will give you energy to perform well and will aid fat-burning.

burn so many calories every day and have such high, fast metabolisms that they simply need the calories.

However, if we contrast this with someone running as part of a weight loss programme, snacking on high carbohydrate bars, fruits and breads all day wouldn't be good advice, for obvious reasons. At one end of the scale we need to replenish the body's carbohydrate stores frequently, to replace the glycogen used during exercise, but at the other end we need to manage the carbohydrate to prevent so much entering the body (especially at the wrong times) that it interferes with weight loss. The latter is much more difficult to get right than the former. However, let's not get distracted: this book is about running, not diets and weight loss.

Protein

All the muscles in our bodies are made from protein, from the facial ones that allow us to smile to the heart that circulates blood around the body. To remain healthy, to grow and to repair, our bodies need protein.

Proteins are made up of differing arrangements of amino acids. Unfortunately we humans, unlike some animals, can't synthesise all the amino acids we require to make the necessary proteins, so we have to ingest them from elsewhere. The proteins and therefore amino acids needed for normal functioning can be sourced easily by eating meat, fish, eggs or chicken. It's actually not necessary to eat protein with every meal, but it's advisable to try to do so if you're doing a large amount of running or exercise. Failing that, at least one or two meals a day should contain protein, dependent on the amount and type of running that's taking place. A sprinter will likely be working on power and muscle gain, so more protein will be needed. A marathon runner won't need as much, but long runs still require the muscles to repair, so more protein will be needed than by someone who's not running. I'm certainly not advocating taking protein powder drinks or eating protein powder every few hours. However, it's better to have slightly too much protein in the diet than too little; unless, of course, the extra protein means the carbohydrate levels of the diet are being lowered, in which case the runner might be low on energy.

→ Protein supplements

Protein supplements do have their place in specific nutrition for runners, whether you're a sprinter who requires them before and after a sprint or weights training (and even during a session), or a marathon runner who should ingest a supplement immediately following a long training session (or even at specific stages during the run). However, they aren't necessarily required if a healthy diet of protein is ingested naturally. Again, it depends on whether you're a budding Olympian, a serious runner or a casual jogger. The differences are obvious and common sense should prevail.

Personal experience...

Protein supplementation is something I've tried myself when I've found it difficult to get enough protein in my diet, for instance when I was doing so much exercise in the Marines that I was breaking down my own body for fuel, and when I was trying to build up muscle after losing a considerable amount. I've advised taking protein supplements to a wide variety of clients, big, small, male and female (no, ladies, they won't make you grow huge muscles – once again, that will be down to your 20kg handbag...).

For the record, if too much protein is ingested the excess that the body can't process ends up down the toilet and does little harm to the body. This wastage may be acceptable for budding Olympians (who are probably getting their protein supplements free from a sponsor anyway), but for most of us wasting our money just because we're trying to run sub-seven-minute miles round the local park is hardly worth the cost.

Fats

It's a common misconception that all fats are bad and should be avoided. The fact is, we actually need some fat in our diet to stay healthy. However, that doesn't give us free license to eat crisps, cream and butter with every meal. We may need some fat, but we certainly don't need large amounts, so it's important to eat a diet that's low in fat but not completely fat free. This is partly because we need some fat to stay healthy and also because foods described as fat-free are often very high in sugar, which is arguably worse than fat in the long run.

The key is to limit your intake of fried and processed foods, such as chips and burgers, where possible. These contain saturated fats, and it's best to stick to a diet that's low in these. Realistically they aren't too bad every now and then, but should certainly not be eaten multiple times a week. This may seem a little contrary to what I've said regarding the importance of protein in a diet, since burgers are a good source of protein. However, as well as protein they also have a very high fat content. A simple rule of thumb is to limit your intake of fatty meats, processed meats and meat surrounded by pastry.

Much better for you are the fats in oily fish (salmon, sardines and mackerel), nuts and seeds, which can be ingested regularly as the main protein constituent of a meal. These oils are very different from those found in meats. They're imperative to various functions of the body, specifically maintaining healthy skin and long-lasting, functioning joints (quite important to runners!), and they're therefore good for all-round health.

Fats: good and bad

Good fats are monounsaturated fats, found in olive/canola oils, peanuts, nuts, peanut butter and avocados. Monounsaturated fats lower unhealthy LDL cholesterol that accumulates in and then clogs up artery walls. They also help maintain levels of healthy HDL cholesterol, which carries cholesterol from artery walls and delivers it to the liver for disposal.

Bad fats are saturated fats, which clog the heart and are found in butter, fatty red meats and full-fat dairy products. *Very* bad fats are man-made trans fats, created when hydrogen gas reacts with oil. These are found in a large umber of packaged foods including margarine, cookies, cakes, icing, doughnuts and crisps. Trans fats are even worse for us than saturated fats, damaging blood vessels and the nervous system. They're also highly calorific.

Eat a diet rich in monosaturated fats, low in saturated fats, and if possible completely free of trans fats.

Five a day

You need to eat a variety of fresh fruit and veg each day, not just five bananas or five apples. Try to spread them through the day: breakfast cereal with banana and blueberries (that's two), mid-morning apple snack (three), half a banana before and after a lunchtime run (four), an orange after lunch (five), and broccoli and cauliflower with your evening meal – wow, seven! It's that simple.

Fruit and vegetables

There can't be anyone who doesn't appreciate the importance of fruit and vegetables to a balanced diet. We're constantly reminded by the media and supermarkets to eat our 'five a day'. Fruit and veg are said to improve our skin, help our digestive system and prolong our lives. They're good as a large constituent of any meal, and also make a perfect snack. Unfortunately, however, and despite knowing how important they are, fruit and vegetables are still the main ingredient missing from the average diet. For some reason, when most of us are peckish, instead of reaching for an apple or orange we go straight for a Mars bar, crisps or biscuits (*mmmm*, trans fats...). It therefore seems sensible to outline exactly why fruit and veg are so important.

Firstly, fruit and vegetables are superb sources of antioxidants. The thing is, although we get told about all these marvellous foods that are full of antioxidants, most of us haven't a clue what antioxidants are or what they do, which kind of makes us less inclined to source them. Well, in simple terms antioxidants help combat free radicals (oxidants), which are produced through general bodily functions, such as hard exercise (like running), or ingested from certain foods. Free radicals can cause cancer and premature ageing, so anything that helps combat them can only be of benefit. A simple yet compelling reason to eat fruit and veg.

Fruit and vegetables are also a great provider of vitamins and minerals, and most of us will have heard of them! Yet once again, we probably don't know exactly what they do. In simple terms, they perform a wide range of functions from enabling our blood to carry oxygen, to preventing us from getting common colds. Compelling reasons to source both.

In addition fruit and vegetables are a great source of fibre, which keeps the digestive system running smoothly. For runners this is very important: for a start it isn't nice to start a run without having your daily bowel movement first, and it's even worse if that bowel movement wants to take place while you're running – as often happens, as the blood is redirected to the muscles of the arms and legs and away from the muscles controlling the bowels (yes, I *am* speaking from personal experience).

Eating fibre helps reduce some forms of cancer, so start the day with cereals like muesli or porridge, with added fruit and, if necessary, some protein supplementation powder.

In a nutshell, a diet plentiful in fruit and vegetables could help enhance your running performance, reduce the chances of illness or injury, improve wound healing, improve long-term health and prevent constipation. And all you need to do to achieve all this is to eat five portions of fruit and veg a day.

Vitamins and minerals

Let's get the definition out of the way: a vitamin or mineral is a compound that can't be synthesised in the necessary amount by an organism (animal) itself (this doesn't include essential amino acids).

The majority of the essential vitamins and minerals required by the human body are provided by a healthy diet, especially if five pieces of fruit and veg a day are ingested.

Vitamin supplements are big business and sell themselves by claiming they'll prevent colds and flu, improve skin health and aid joint pains. Although all this is true, the same is true of fruit and veg. However, vitamin supplements aren't expensive, and if there's some reason why you can't eat enough fruit and veg they're advisable. Multi-vitamins ensure that the body is supplied with everything it needs to function correctly, including ensuring that the immune system works. However, *don't exceed the daily dosage*. This is set at a safe level for medical reasons: too much can mess with the body's homeostasis and lead to illness, dehydration or sickness.

Essential vitamins, their scientific names and examples of where they can be found

Vitamin A	Retinol	Cod liver oil
Vitamin B1	Thiamine	Rice bran
Vitamin B2	Riboflavin	Eggs
Vitamin B3	Niacin	Liver
Vitamin B5	Pantothenic acid	Liver
Vitamin B6	Pyridoxine	Rice bran
Vitamin B7	Biotin	Liver
Vitamin B9	Folic acid	Liver
Vitamin B12	Cyanocobalamin	Liver
Vitamin C	Ascorbic acid	Citrus fruit
Vitamin D	Calciferol	Cod liver oil
Vitamin E	Tocopherol	Wheat germ oil, liver
Vitamin K	Phylloquinone	Alfalfa

Fibre

Fibre helps with digestion, and as we already know from eating our fruit and veg, it keeps the stomach healthy and prevents constipation. Eating fibre also helps reduce some forms of cancer, which is again hugely beneficial and possibly a good enough reason on its own. Beyond fruit and vegetables, fibre is sourced from wholegrain cereals such as bran flakes, porridge and muesli, or from wholemeal bread, brown rice or wholemeal pasta. It's important to stick to wholemeal, wholegrain (brown) variants of bread, rice and pasta and to avoid the 'white' versions, as these highly processed, 'high glycaemic' versions aren't good for the body.

Dairy

The ingestion of dairy products remains controversial. Despite the fact that we've been drinking milk produced by other animals for years, we've finally begun to appreciate that many adult humans are in fact lactose intolerant, and that milk, cream and cheese doesn't do such people much good. It will give them wind at best and allergic reactions, such as blocked sinuses, at worst. If you're in any doubt, see your doctor and get tested. Failing that, cut out the dairy for a few weeks and see if you feel better.

As babies we all drink milk (or should). The advantages of breastfeeding are far too great to warrant me listing them here; yet it may not be necessary for us to continue drinking milk – especially from another species! – beyond infancy. Yes, milk has some advantages for growing children, and it may still be advisable for them to consume two to three portions of dairy food per day specifically for the calcium, which is important for healthy bones. However, humans don't have all the correct enzymes for breaking down dairy products and hence many of us are lactose intolerant, a high percentage of us without even realising it.

Nevertheless, dairy may still be beneficial for anyone taking part in extensive running, because it helps to avoid skeletal issues, particularly stress fractures, by providing the calcium to repair and improve bones. However, remember that calcium can be found in other foodstuffs, such as fish, eggs and substitutes such as soya milk (which can be used instead of regular milk and comes with added calcium). Furthermore, some bottled water manufacturers have also started adding calcium to their products.

Eventually it comes down to personal choice. There's nothing wrong with having dairy, but like anything it shouldn't be overdone, and where possible healthy variants should be chosen (skimmed or semi-skimmed instead of full fat milk); but in short, unless you think you're lactose intolerant or that dairy is doing you harm (including over-indulging in fatty cheeses) or is contrary to a weight-loss programme, a little of what you enjoy is good for you as long as it doesn't affect your goal.

Unless the day's activities have caused profuse sweating or muscular cramps are occurring, the addition of salt to food is unnecessary and should generally be avoided.

Sugar

Eating a balanced diet doesn't just mean ingesting enough of each nutrient, it also means avoiding too much of certain foodstuffs. Sugar, like saturated fats, is another prime example. Our ancestors only got their sugar from foods providing it, such as fruits and berries, but today it's a very different story, as almost every foodstuff we produce contains sugar. Not only does that mean we're ingesting too much sugar in general, but it's not even 'good' sugar from natural sources – most of it is refined and processed.

As already mentioned, things that are labelled 'fat-free' usually contain large amounts of sugar. This isn't helpful if you're running as part of a weight-loss programme and relying on a fat-free diet to help with this. Fat-free yogurt, for instance, will contain a very high level of sugar. So out of interest, start reading the labels on food and note how many things have added sugar. Also, did you know that the closer to the top of the ingredients list something is, the higher percentage of that ingredient the food contains? Sugar is often the second or third thing listed on processed foods, salt being its closest rival. (Salt helps preserve the food, but it also makes you gain weight and feel bloated as you conserve excess water.)

Sugars may not be ideal all the time, but they can be useful before or during a run. This is especially true if you're a seasoned athlete or local competition runner. If you are, it may not be a big deal to ingest quite high amounts of sugar because you'll probably burn off the energy. Nevertheless, sugars are still just empty calories – basic energy but no nutrients; there are far better foods to get energy from that will also provide nutrients and minerals. Fruits are a great example.

However, sugars can play their part and are a godsend for a struggling runner just prior to or during a run. The sugars enter the bloodstream quickly and go straight to the depleted muscles, providing a much-needed burst of energy. Remember, though, that much better sources of carbohydrate are available as part of a balanced daily diet.

Salt

Like sugar, salt seems to be added to everything we eat, especially processed foods. Despite this we all reach for the salt at mealtimes, often before we've even tasted our food. Yet our ancestors didn't put vast amounts of salt on their food – they got it naturally from their diet. Certainly some salt is required for normal homeostasis and body functioning, but most of us don't need the quantity we're getting. Having said that, running does cause us to sweat and therefore lose more salt than non-runners, so the body is consequently able to cope with a little more salt than normal. However, this isn't an excuse to eat junk like crisps and processed foods, but it might make some supermarket soups (also high in salt) less scary.

Calorie consumption

Simply put, the number of calories put into the body and the number of calories used up on an hourly, daily or weekly basis has a direct impact on any weight gained or lost. It's said that the average male needs about 2,500kcal per day, while the average female needs 2,000kcal. However, this varies hugely from person to person, depending on their size, daily activity, muscle tone and metabolism.

For example, two people who are roughly the same height, one relatively muscled and the other skinny, will require significantly different amounts of energy. This is down to their muscle tone and the subsequent metabolism changes to their calorific needs. Basically the more muscle an individual has, the more calories they need to ingest, even if they're inactive (sleeping/sitting/relaxing). This is due to the fact that toned muscles require more calories even at rest than untrained muscles. So even when inactive, one person can burn far more calories than another, just because they're fit, athletic and healthy. Now put into the picture their day's activities, a run and a conditioning session, and soon the two people's calorie consumptions and needs are very different indeed.

The fact that the trained/toned individual burns more calories at rest than the other person shows why it's so important to take part in conditioning and resistance-style weight-training, and not just the running (cardiovascular training), when trying to lose weight. Without the conditioning, running on its own isn't as efficient when it comes to losing weight and achieving general fitness.

The glycaemic index

The glycaemic index (GI) is something that's hit the news over the last couple of years, mostly as 'the GI diet'. But it shouldn't be thought of in the same way as a 'celebrity' diet, such as the Atkins diet plan or the lemonade detox. The glycaemic index is a way of categorising foods according to how fast they release sugars/carbohydrates, by classifying them as red, amber or green:

Red = fast releasing
Amber = medium releasing
Green = slow releasing

You could also interpret this to mean red = stop, don't eat; and green = OK, eat. Many supermarkets have now put these colours on their food packaging to let you know where they lie on the GI. Failing that, just look them up on the Internet or buy a pocket GI book.

The reason I'm telling you about the glycaemic index is so that you can use it to best effect when running. It's basically a measure of the effects of carbs on blood glucose levels. That is, how the carbohydrate eaten affects the level of sugar in the blood. Some carbohydrates break down quickly and release glucose into the bloodstream very rapidly. These foods are said to be high GI. Conversely, carbohydrates that break down slowly, releasing glucose gradually into the bloodstream, are said to be low GI.

To use the glycaemic index for better sports performance, it's a matter of knowing what to eat and when. Firstly, it's important to eat low GI foods throughout the day. This will keep your blood sugar levels at a constant, rather than allowing them to plummet after each meal or after snacking on high GI foods like cakes and biscuits. The high GI foods cause sugar spikes and subsequent sugar lows, which cause fatigue, loss of concentration and irritability, and in my experience are likely to lead to people skipping training sessions.

Always start the day off with a low GI breakfast; examples are porridge, muesli or perhaps wholemeal bread. It's not a problem to have something high GI with them, such as fruit, raisins or jam, but the bulk of the meal should be low GI. Protein such as bacon or eggs can be eaten as well (or even protein supplements like a protein shake), but try to avoid too much fat. Avoid high GI breakfast staples such as white bread. These will bring about a sugar low very quickly.

Any snacks throughout the day should be low GI wherever possible – oat-based cereal bars, muesli or granola bars, or wholemeal bread are again good examples. Always read the labels to check just how low GI these are. Cereal bars bound with syrup and containing sugar aren't good and will lead to a sugar low quite quickly, furthermore, they won't help a weight-loss programme. Fruit snacks are good but are generally medium to high GI so can cause a sugar spike and ensuing low. This doesn't mean fruit should be avoided (we need our five a day), but it should be eaten in conjunction with low GI foods and not overdone.

For the average exercising person who's running as part of a general health and fitness programme, and not to lose weight, any main meal should be eaten with a healthy portion of low GI carbohydrate. Examples are wholemeal brown pasta, brown rice, wholemeal bread and potatoes (boiled or baked where possible). For someone trying to lose weight, although some low GI carbohydrates are still definitely needed the portions should be a little smaller, with the vegetables and protein portions a little bigger.

High GI foods for best effect

High GI foods shouldn't be avoided altogether. On the contrary, they can be used very effectively at specific times. A glass of orange juice (full of natural fruit sugars) can be ingested first thing in the morning to kick-start the metabolism – personally, I always have a glass of water before it to help rehydrate following a night's sleep.

Furthermore, as mentioned previously there's a 'window of opportunity' following exercise in which you should refuel the glycogen stores in your muscles. The faster this occurs the better, and the more efficient your muscles will be for the next session. So if speed of refuelling is important, it makes sense to ingest carbohydrates that release sugars quickly; therefore high GI foods are perfect for replenishing these stores.

High GI foods are also useful just prior to exercise, when a quick sugar spike is necessary to give an energy boost. However, it's imperative that a low GI meal has been eaten a couple of hours prior to the exercise sessions; then sufficient energy should still be within the body for the whole session once the quick-burning high GI snack had been used up.

Simple examples of high GI foods to use prior to, during and after exercise are glasses of fruit juice, bananas, dates, fruit and sports drinks.

→ Percentage diets

The following list should help you understand how to eat your low GI carbs. The normal diet applies to anyone running for fun or weight loss, while the runners' diet is for serious runners and people training for marathons. The low carb diet should be avoided by runners, as it's unlikely to provide enough carbs to complete a run well. Bodybuilders and sports models tend to use these diets to obtain lower levels of body fat than the health profession would advise.

Normal diet: 50% carbs, 20% protein, 30% fat.
Runners' diet: 60–65% carbs, 15% protein, 20–25% fat.
Low carb diet: 40% carbs, 30% protein, 30% fat.

Supplements

Supplements are a huge business, from the cornerstone American bodybuilding corporations to the smaller British concerns recently bought out by huge pharmaceutical companies to realise the profits of this lucrative end of the market. The sports, fitness and health industries now receive massive sponsorship from supplement companies such as MaxiNutrition, PhD, Reflex, USN, SIS, Lucozade, Powerade and even Nestlé's PowerBar, to name but a few.

Protein

The main focus of most such companies is protein supplementation, due to the attractions of the aesthetic 'body beautiful' and the popularity of bodybuilding. Our media- and celebrity-craving world has made everyone believe they need to lower their body fat and up their muscle tone. In one sense this is a good thing, as it encourages fitness, but I'd rather people worried about their cardiovascular fitness and just got out and ran.

The average person (around 95% of the population) is said to need 0.8g of protein per kilogram of body weight per day, ie an average male of 80kg requires 64g of protein every day (0.8 x 80 = 64). An average female of 50kg requires 40g per day (0.8 x 50 = 40).

Having said that, 0.8g per kilo of body weight isn't suitable for someone undertaking a good running programme. As was stated earlier, due to the high intensity of running training, runners will often start to burn their own proteins during training and competitions, and therefore require additional protein. Research suggests around 1.2g per kilo of body weight per day. This can either come from food like fish, chicken and eggs, or from a protein supplement.

Carbohydrate

This leads nicely on to the other branch of supplementation that's huge business: carbohydrates. Whether we're discussing high energy sports drinks that supply sugars and help rehydrate, to powdered forms of energy like 'Go' from SIS (Sports in Science), most of these are designed to help improve performance during training or a race, by pre-fuelling before, helping stay fuelled during and refuelling after the session. Arguably these aren't necessary, and the same benefits can be gained from food as discussed already. However, despite being relatively costly they're a very easy and trouble-free way of ensuring you can perform at your very best.

 Personal experience...

When I was performing what can only be described as an Ultra running event in Wales – running with a heavy rucksack up and down the Brecon Beacons for between five and 18 hours at a time consecutively for days on end – I had to ensure my supplementation was correct. This not only ensured I had the energy to complete the event, but also that I didn't lose my body mass, which allowed me to carry the heavy rucksack. So on top of my large breakfast and dinner and what can only be described as a packed lunch, I ensured I had:

➔ A pre-start protein and carbohydrate mixed drink.
➔ Carbohydrate supplements carried in old film cases, enough for one per hour.
➔ A film case containing a post-workout carbohydrate and protein mix.

I tried and tested these ideas before the event and they worked very well, especially by ensuring I was at my best for the next day's slog.

You may be thinking this was a little excessive, especially the protein supplementation, but the sheer physical nature of the event meant I was burning so many calories each hour that I was becoming catabolic very quickly – my body was basically ready to break down my muscles and proteins to feed its energy needs. By drinking carbohydrate and protein drinks I was attempting to lower the negative effects of this.

For any sportsperson, protein supplementation can be just as important as carbohydrate supplementation, especially before and after a long run (to help reduce the catabolic effects of exercise), and also after conditioning sessions, when the muscles will have been trained and need to repair.

Hydration

Simply put, water is more important to humans than food. Two-thirds of our body weight is composed of it. Water is required for almost every single occurrence and reaction in the body, from circulation to respiration, and – even more importantly to runners – it's also necessary in the process of converting food to energy. Dehydration is the runner's enemy, but for dehydration to occur more water must be lost (sweating, respiration, urine) than is taken in. Dehydration of just 2.5% of your body weight can lead to 25% loss in efficiency, with dehydration of only 1% affecting some people who aren't used to it just as badly. Water is therefore the second most necessary essential for the human body, after oxygen.

Although we lose water all the time by simply breathing and urinating, it's sweating during exercise that causes us to dehydrate. It's said that around 75% of energy put into exercise is converted to heat and lost (which is why exercise makes us feel hot). To keep the body's temperature around its normal 37–38°C we sweat, and the lost fluid must then be replaced – otherwise the blood thickens and reduces the heart's efficiency and thus increases the heart rate, essentially slowing your speed and progress until you're forced to stop.

However, dehydration to some level is expected and deemed normal while exercising, and it's nigh impossible to drink enough while running to keep your hydration levels 'normal'. Besides, the level of dehydration that actually occurs during a run isn't dangerous and wouldn't lead to any medical problems. Besides, as soon as we finish exercising we all have an uncontrollable urge to drink – our body's way of making us ingest fluids so it can return to its normal homeostatic level of hydration.

Drinking for success

Whether racing, going for a personal best or just doing your regular training run, always begin hydrated. A good way to do this is to drink an entire half-litre bottle of water around two hours before the run. Use the toilet just prior to the run, then drink another quarter-litre just before you start. This will ensure you have enough water in your body and don't start off already dehydrated, which would inevitably lead to a lesser performance.

It's just as important to replace lost fluids immediately after a run. Wherever possible, drink another half-litre within 30 minutes of finishing. From there on, keep drinking until you no longer have dark yellow/orange urine, or until you feel better if you had a headache or felt nauseous after your run. Often water isn't the best option at this point; a sports drink such as Lucozade, SIS Go or diluted fruit juice is better at replacing fluids and sugars lost during the run.

Over-hydration

It may seem counter-intuitive, but it's possible to over-hydrate – to literally drink too much. I've personally seen this during a summer 30-miler (one of the Commando tests for Royal Marines). During this example, the individual was so scared of becoming dehydrated that he drank too much and literally flushed the electrolytes out of his system, and keeled over at mile 24.

What occurs is actually known as hyponatraemia, which means low blood sodium, as the excess water causes a massive lowering of the concentration of sodium in the blood. Hyponatraemia is generally relatively harmless,

Bear in mind what happens when you run or train in hotter climates: you'll sweat far more until acclimatised, and once acclimatised will need far less water than a few days before.

Taking painkillers such as aspirin and ibuprofen increases the risk of hyponatraemia, so you should be cautious about taking them in hot climates or while running.

causing bloating and perhaps nausea, but in serious cases brain seizure and death can occur.

Despite my personal experience while training Marine recruits, it's actually (percentage-wise) women who suffer from this more than men. This is generally because they're smaller and less muscular and as a consequence sweat less so therefore need to drink less. On average women should drink around a third less than men.

For marathon runners, or in fact anyone running for times in excess of three hours – it's advisable to avoid drinking large amounts of water and instead only drink when you're thirsty. Electrolyte-containing sports drinks that also contain sodium may be the best choice, as these help hydrate and replace lost salt. Despite all this, it's important to remember that for most runners it's dehydration rather than over-hydration that's the worry.

The urine test

Dehydration was quite common amongst recruits in the Marines, so we instructed them to carry a water bottle at all times and take sips throughout the day. This is a good tip in any walk of life, but it isn't always practical. Fortunately, the colour of your urine is a good indication of whether you need to drink more. Basically, pale yellow or clear urine indicates you're hydrated; dark yellow or orange indicates you're dehydrated and need to drink; dark orange or brown means you're seriously dehydrated and should stop exercising, get into a cool place to stop sweating, and drink until your urine is pale yellow.

We tend to require around two to three litres of liquid a day, half to two-thirds of this from fluids and the rest from food. However, as we sweat from exercise or heat the amount of fluid needed obviously goes up.

Drinking while running

It may sound simple, but surprisingly a lot of people find it difficult to drink while running. Look around your local gym next time you're there. I guarantee someone will stop running and stand on the side of the treadmill to drink, instead of drinking while running. Granted, cups and screw-top bottles don't lend themselves to drinking easily without drenching yourself, but there are a myriad bottles on the market designed for use while doing sports, all of which allow you to rehydrate on the run (see Chapter 3).

It's worth mentioning that you don't want to gulp the water down, as this can lead to a bloated, sloshing feeling, and can make you feel sick. Instead, take regular small sips. Personally, if using a treadmill I take sips every two to two-and-a-half minutes. Outside is a different story. I tend to advise one of three methods:

1 Buy and use a camelback. This is a bag of water worn like a rucksack, with a long drinking tube. These are issued in the military and are excellent for staying hydrated. However, they're only really good if you're a casual or fun runner, as they can't be used competitively, so you'll get your body used to using them (ie having lots of fluid) when training and then perhaps come unstuck on race day.

2 Buy a good-quality sports bottle that allows easy drinking and carry it in your hand as you run. Personally I don't like these unless I'm running slowly with friends. When I run on my own I find it unbalances me, and I can't relax the arm doing the carrying. However, you have to weigh the pros and cons between being dehydrated and carrying an annoying bottle. On the treadmill it's fine; outside the camelback is a better answer.

3 Over-hydrate before the run, don't drink during the run, then rehydrate after. Simple, and actually relatively effective unless you're running for long, long periods of time. For a run of 10–40 minutes this is fine, you won't dehydrate too much and can rehydrate properly on your return. However, be careful on hot days or if you go on holiday in a hot country. Run in the mornings or evenings or allow yourself to acclimatise to the heat before running properly. Furthermore I wouldn't advise this method for longer runs or marathon training – a hydration pack is far safer and will allow you to carry a phone, keys and small running jacket (in case the weather changes).

If you opt for method three you could try to simulate races where you'll have a drink stand (water bottles or cups) every kilometre or so – you could plan a run that allows you to pass your house or gym every kilometre, so you can drink and then carry on. This is a bit of a pain, but is excellent at simulating a race and getting your body used to it.

What to drink

If I'm running really hard I find I need both water and a sports drink to rehydrate and re-energise me. Having said that, water, diluted juice and sports drinks are all good at rehydrating, and generally, if your run is less than an hour, plain water is probably the best choice. However, if you're running for over an hour or feel that on previous runs you've been lacking in energy, then drinks containing sugar or maltodextrin (a slow-release carbohydrate) may be more suitable.

At race drink stations...

Never skip a drink because there's a queue. Instead, if there are drinks stations on both sides of the course go to the one on the left, as most people will go to the right because they're right-handed and tend to pick up their drink with their right hand.

If you're feeling hot and want to cool down by pouring the drink over your face and shoulders, check the content first to ensure it's just water. Pouring diluted juice or a sticky sports drink over your head is not recommended...

Sports drinks

There are a number of different types of drink that can be used when running or exercising, from diluted fruit juice and squash to sports drinks like Lucozade and Gatorade. Whatever they're made up of, these drinks are of three types:

➔ Hypotonic

These contain a greater proportion of water and a lesser proportion of carbohydrate than the human body. As the drink is less concentrated than body fluids it's claimed that they increase the speed of fluid absorption by the body, thus preventing or alleviating dehydration. Good examples are squash (not sugar-free, though) diluted at least one part squash to eight parts water, or fruit juice diluted one part juice to three parts water.

➔ Isotonic

These contain proportions of water and other nutrients similar to the human body, and are typically about 6% to 8% carbohydrate. As the drink is the same concentration as body fluids, it's absorbed at the same rate as water. Furthermore, these drinks are a perfect balance of rehydration and refuelling. Good examples are Lucozade Sport or fruit juice diluted half and half with water, or even squash (again not sugar-free) diluted one part to four with water.

➔ Hypertonic

These contain a lesser proportion of water and a greater proportion of carbohydrate than the human body. As it's more concentrated than body fluids it's absorbed more slowly, meaning the energy will be released over a long period of time. It's therefore claimed that these drinks can give an energy boost and also replace lost energy over the entire session. Good examples are sugary drinks like cola, lemonade and fresh fruit juice.

All energy drinks are a good form of energy boost and rehydration. However, they should still be used with caution. Always ensure that plain water is at hand just in case the energy drink causes dehydration or, worse, an adverse reaction. It's always worth testing an energy drink is compatible with your body prior to using it in a specific race, where an adverse reaction could have dire results.

CHAPTER 7
MOTIVATION & GOALS

The chances are you're running for some specific reason or goal, be it to get fit, to lose weight, to achieve a sub-40-minute 10km run, or to compete in a marathon. Whatever you want to achieve you'll have specific motivations, which have a huge psychological impact on you, not only when you're training but also when you're thinking about training. The beauty of these motivations is that they can be harnessed to ensure you reach your desired goal.

think everyone will agree that we're all motivated by different things and in different ways. In my last book, about Royal Marine fitness, I frequently spoke of the importance of 'knowing yourself'. What I mean by this is be honest with yourself, get to know what makes you tick, what motivates you, what annoys you, and even what makes you stop training. The more self-aware you are the easier it will be to see your weaknesses and strengths, to avoid or work with the former and harness the latter. The important thing is to know what your motivation is, and to keep it in your mind, especially when times get hard. The classic example for runners is that early morning alarm when you can hear the rain and wind against the window; your immediate thought will be 'maybe I'll give it a miss today'. At that point use your motivation, fix it in your mind and accept that you have to work towards it, then and there, or it will slip a little bit further away.

 Runner's psychology

Certain sports that we take part in as children and pursue into later life develop and change our psychology and mental strength when it comes to physical and sporting potential, either because of some link to our ability to overcome our central governor (see page 64) or because they create a different understanding of the work ethic required in sport. I was a cross-country runner at school as well as a track runner. I believe the hours of running training and races, especially in the depths of winter, helped me develop a mental strength that has enabled me to approach difficult and challenging events with a relative sense of ease, in the knowledge that I have the mental capability to complete whatever I start.

I also played a lot of football when I was young, to a relatively high level, but I don't feel that I developed the same 'runner's psychology' from it. It can, of course, all be coach/mentor-specific and depend on how hard you were pushed.

I believe I learned more than just a work ethic; I learned how to push myself, how to suppress my central governor, how to cope with pressure and the ability to 'carry on regardless'.

So if you didn't develop this 'sportsperson's psychology' at a young age, from running, rugby, swimming, ice skating, gymnastics, rowing or the many other sports I've omitted, then try to understand and develop it now, in line with your motivation and chosen goals. That strength of mind could be the key to achieving the success you want.

SMART training

The acronym SMART is a good way of putting your goals into effect. It ensures they're not only thought out and fully considered, but are realistic and achievable as well. Hence SMART stands for:

S Specific
M Measurable
A Achievable
R Realistic
T Timed

Specific

'Specific' means that your goal (or goals) must be specific and not general. What I mean by this is not just saying 'I want to be able to run for a long time' or 'I want to lose weight'. These aren't specific enough, so you'll lose track of them quickly or will get halfway to your goal and then think 'That'll do'. But as we've already established, 'That'll do will never do'.

The key is to state how far or for how long you wish to run for, how much weight you wish to lose, what dress size you want to get into. Then you have a real, specific goal, a tangible bullseye to aim for, one that, with hard work and dedication, you WILL reach, and will be proud of yourself for doing so.

Measurable

This goes hand in hand with specific. By being specific regarding the number of miles you want to run, the time you want to achieve or the amount of weight to lose, these goals become measurable. For example, saying your goal is 'to be fitter by a certain date' isn't measurable, whereas saying you want to be able to run 5km in under 25 minutes by July is measurable. So set measurable goals, aim for them, and if you don't quite make them within the parameters you set, believe me, you'll have made far more progress than if you didn't set any parameters in the first place.

Achievable

Simple really: when setting a goal it must be achievable. For example, if I suddenly decide my goal is to beat Usain Bolt's record for 100m and be the fastest man in the world, I think everyone will agree I'm kidding myself. Equally, if you're new to running and your goal is to run a marathon in three weeks' time, that's unachievable for most people. So be sensible; be honest with yourself, but equally, don't set the bar too low. There's a big difference between making life easy for yourself and setting achievable goals.

Realistic

Setting realistic goals brings us back to the Usain Bolt example above. Not only was that unachievable, it was also unrealistic. Simply put, there's no point having a goal if it's unrealistic. For example, not many of us could run a marathon in under 2½ hours, so this wouldn't be a realistic aim. Nor would learning to fly by flapping your arms. You'd simply be wasting your time. So keep it realistic – it makes the process so much more enjoyable, especially when you finally reach your goal!

Timed

Timing your goals is very important, but the timing must be realistic. Setting realistic time scales will ensure you reach them, firstly because you'll have something to aim for (without any pressure to improve you might let other things come between you and your goals), and secondly because you won't get disheartened by not attaining your goal, despite training as hard as you could. Set timed goals as realistically as possible, then even if the times have to be modified at least you've had something to work towards.

Always set yourself goals and aims. That way your training won't become stale and pointless. If you get bored, find a new goal, speak to friends, find out their interests and challenge yourself. Live life, don't let it pass you by.

Motivation

Not everyone is motivated by the same things. Some people are competitive, and if they know someone who's running the local 10km they have to try to beat them. Other people are motivated by an event, such as a bride wanting to lose weight for her wedding day. So know yourself and what your motivations are. Focus on them and use them for encouragement whenever you can't be bothered. If you're not sure what motivates you, the following list may help:

→ Goal orientated
This is motivation from the desire to achieve or even surpass a goal. This may be a certain length run, the marathon, a dress size, or even just beating your friend who always wins a summer barbecue sprint session! Whatever your goal, it's the goal itself that's the motivation to train.

→ Group orientated
Group motivation revolves around our nature as social animals. Humans don't like to feel left out, we want to be accepted as part of 'the group'. This desire to be part of and achieve within a group is great motivation. Within athletics or running clubs, the group members feed off each other's positive energy and motivation. This doesn't mean all your training needs to be done within the group, far from it. For many members, training will purposely happen outside the group, to try to improve fitness and become more highly regarded within the group.

→ People orientated
This relates to the desire to have an impact on those around you. This may mean your fitness must improve to allow you to take the kids out to the park on Sunday and kick a football around. It could be that your new partner is an avid runner and you wish to join in that part of their life. Conversely, it could be the vanity side of training, needing recognition for the goals you've achieved and physical stature attained. Although such vanity can be frowned upon, it's still motivation to be fit and healthy and better than being lazy and unhealthy.

→ Habit orientated
This is motivation provided by the need to feed a running/exercise habit. Some would argue that this is an addiction – to the endorphins released when running, to the feeling of burning calories and excess fat, or perhaps to the never ending goal of personal improvement. The 'habit' usually develops during formative years, from being part of a sports team or training culture at school/college/university, which has made training become part of a lifestyle. The dangerous side of this motivation is when it becomes THE focus of your life. It can also lead to a very controlled lifestyle and eating habits, and in some people eating disorders.

🏃 Milestones

If your goal is particularly big, or a considerable way off, it can be worthwhile setting a number of smaller 'milestones' (little goals) along the way. Imagine your goal is to run the London marathon, but you've done little more than run for the bus in the last five years. Your motivation is obviously the marathon itself (which you've hopefully given yourself at least a year to build up to), but it's a long way off in both time and fitness terms; so it would be sensible to add at least one achievable milestone – for example, it might be a local half-marathon in eight months' time. A half-marathon is far more achievable, but will still require significant training.

Personally I'd add a series of smaller milestones leading up to the half-marathon. These could be a few runs of specific length or in specific times – for example, four miles, six miles and eight miles etc, or 20-, 30- or 40-minute runs. As these milestones are reached it may be necessary to reassess at what point your main goal will be achievable (you may be ahead of or behind schedule), and change your training accordingly.

Motivation by others

Most people find that when they train with a partner or have a personal trainer the motivation to do well is somehow increased. This seems to be true whether the partner or trainer actively gives encouragement or not. The beauty of this is that the level of achievement is far greater than can usually be attained when working individually.

Although it's very important to have the ability to self-motivate, generally by the goal-focussed methods discussed in this chapter, it still helps if others encourage or coerce you to deliver more to attain the goal you've set yourself. Let's take Olympians as an example. Although they're very self-motivated and disciplined when it comes to maintaining focus, everyone has a low point or a bad day, and this is when their team-mates, coaches, partners etc really prove their worth by motivating, encouraging and inspiring them to achieve the best they're capable of.

Using others

Once you've identified your motivation, it's important to ensure you don't forget it. So tell people about it; tell your spouse, your friends, your room-mate. If you're going to run the marathon, get sponsorship and let people know – believe me, not wanting to let others down is a huge motivation in itself. You never want to be the one to let the side down, to disappoint your team-mates. By telling people you're going to beat 40 minutes in your next 10km or you're going to lose two kilos by summer, you start to add a little healthy pressure, which in itself becomes a motivator. Furthermore, your real friends will ask you how it's going, are you on track, and those reminders will help you on your way. Lastly, you may well become an inspiration for them and they'll join you on your fitness quest. So tell people, not only for your own inspiration, but to spread the word.

Habit and addiction

For many people, myself included, running and training isn't a chore; it's not something to find time for, it's part of the daily routine. For us, a day without some sort of physical training (unless it's a specific rest day) is an uncomfortable feeling, and the necessity to ensure that a session takes place the following day is heightened all the more. The fact that training is habitual means it's not dreaded but looked forward to, and is therefore self-motivational and something to be enjoyed. If you can get to this point by enjoying your running, be it for the thrill, the competition or the social side, then you'll always lead a fit and healthy lifestyle.

For some people, however, giving training such a high priority can be taken a little too far, especially when the day's events are scheduled around the exercise session, and slowly the exercise regime starts to control their life. It's at this point that the person is probably addicted. A running or training addiction in itself is not too severe a problem, unless their health, social life and personal relationships start to suffer. At the point when two or even three sessions a day are ruling one's life, rest days are never taken and the body starts to suffer and decline, the addiction has become more than a habit or motivation – it's become a problem. So know yourself, be honest with yourself, discuss your training with friends and professionals and you'll keep on the right side of a healthy addiction to being fit and healthy.

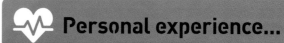 **Personal experience...**

After my right wrist had complete ligament rupture I was in a cast for eight weeks and rehabbing for nearly a year. Yet I have no issues with my right hand these days – weights, fight training, climbing and pull-ups are all as good as before.

Lack of motivation

A lack of motivation and the following slump in training can affect us all, whether we're Olympic athletes or local gym-goers. We all have good days and bad days, and we can all lose motivation. But what about those of us who don't have coaches, team-mates or training partners to revive our enthusiasm? What happens when slumps occur and we have to deal with them ourselves? It's not an easy problem to overcome. It's the point when you have to focus on your goal even more. The trouble is, even the hardest special forces soldier or Olympic Champion still has demons of doubt sometimes, and no matter how much we concentrate on our goal that doubt and lack of motivation remains.

What's the answer then? Well, to really understand how to get over a lack of motivation, and how to use the various methods I describe further on, it's worth understanding what causes these slumps in the first place. Again, knowing yourself means you can correct yourself.

→ Fatigue

This is the major cause of lack of motivation; if you've trained hard for days and then wake up early to go for a run with your body stiff and achy, it's very difficult to get motivated. If your body is very stiff and achy then it's probably already fatigued and you're possibly on the verge of overtraining. Although it might seem difficult to do, rest is the key. Fatigue has probably occurred due to lack of rest, perhaps the beginning of an illness or simply from training too hard, which is probably due to a slight addiction to the training, running or the goal itself. If intense sessions continue without rest the fatigue will continue and your goal will slip into the distance.

→ Overtiredness

Some people (yes, guilty!) try to stick to their training programme even if they've had a very long day at work or, worse still, have been out for a night, come back in the early hours and woken up with a hangover. Believe it or not this isn't a good for your body or long-term training goals. The problem with a hangover is that the body's full of toxins and needs rest to recuperate; by forcing it to work when it's in dire need of fuel and rest doesn't help fitness gains, it just puts pressure on the heart, causes the body to become catabolic (ie it breaks down its own muscles) and can lead to injury.

Lack of sleep is very similar. It usually means you feel laboured when exercising and can't perform at your best. Being awake for more hours than normal means the body requires more fuel, but by exercising you're probably doing the opposite, so will again become catabolic and reverse all those days of training. Know yourself, listen to your body and react accordingly.

→ Overtraining

Overtraining is a real problem if people set impractical goals but see them as achievable. They start training more often and more intensely for sustained periods of time. They also start ignoring rest days, and eventually overtraining-related fatigue sets in. When this occurs the body and mind will demand rest, often by causing injury or illness. A serious consequence of overtraining is the lowering of the immune system, meaning the body will eventually succumb to flu or something worse. The body then becomes susceptible to injuries such as torn muscles, and overuse injuries such as patella tendinitis.

→ Repetitive training

By repeating the same race-paced session or interval session again and again in the hope of seeing vast improvements, the body is never allowed to rest adequately and repair. The heart becomes stressed, and the pulse rate increases at rest. Effectively, repetitive training causes overtraining-type issues within those muscle groups (in a runner's case the heart) consistently exercised, which can ultimately lead to injury and illness. Vary the training, vary intense days, rest days and easy days. If something works well, give it a day or two, then repeat it and better it. Don't attempt it on successive days, as you'll never improve.

→ Illness

Illness or injury result in lack of motivation, simple. You've worked so hard to get where you are and being ill or pulling a muscle has stopped you progressing. Even worse it's making you lose ground. You're getting more unfit and further from your goal by the minute! So what do you do? You try to train while you're ill. *But don't be tempted to do this.* It's not wise to train when you're ill, the body is busy fighting off infection, and by training you put it under further stress which is bad for the heart. Rest until you're better – don't try to come back too early or the illness may also come back. First session back, be careful and take it easy. Don't stress about losing fitness when you're ill, it takes a lot longer than you think. However, try to figure out why you became ill. Is it because your body is run down from overtraining, or because training has taken place when you were overtired? Sometimes illness and injury are signs that things need to change.

→ Injury

Injury is slightly different, but that's dependent on the injury, of course. For example, a pulled muscle in the hamstring will mean no lower limb activity, but an upper body session could take place. Just be careful and take it easy. Use the PRICE programme (see Chapter 15) to look after the injury and ensure you take it easy for the first few sessions back, to avoid a relapse. Again, not that much fitness is lost from a minor injury. Full fitness can be regained even after severe injuries.

➜ Environment

It's something we never consider, but a drastic change in climate or environment has an adverse effect on motivation and training. This is because certain environments affect the body drastically until acclimatisation occurs, and thus can severely decrease performance; this is true of very hot and very cold climates. Rather than letting the heat or cold demotivate you, take a few days prior to any hard training to do very easy runs, preferably in the mornings or evenings when the climate won't affect you as badly. This will help with acclimatisation and keep your motivation high.

➜ Cold months

People often lose motivation during the winter, when it's cold and raining. It's not easy to drag yourself outside before or after work, especially in the dark, wet and wind. Of course, the opposite is true in the summer when the good weather is often inspirational and makes you want to get out and run in the sun. In winter, try to focus on your goal and motivate yourself beyond that day's training; think of that 10km time, finishing that marathon, or the extra calories you'll burn off during the run as your body tries to stay warm. Furthermore, the exercise-induced elation that follows a session in really adverse conditions is something to be experienced. As with really hard interval or hill sessions, the exhilaration from knowing that you've trained really hard is incredible – even if it's only because the session is over for another day!

➜ Diet

Diet, energy, calories or just fuel is SO important. Think about your body as a car. A car can't go anywhere if it has no petrol in the tank, and your body is the same – it will also come to a halt without fuel. If you're struggling for motivation ensure you've eaten well and aren't lacking energy. Training when energy levels are low is bad for both the heart and the body and can lead to injury. Certain environments, especially the very hot, suppress the appetite, so it may be necessary to work really hard on getting the calories in. There are lots of ways of achieving the right calorie intake, from low glycaemic loading to isotonic energy drinks. Remember, food is fuel, and unless you're running for weight-loss purposes it should be seen as that.

➜ Reaching a plateau

At some point most runners reach a point where no more improvements can be made. They can't seem to add another interval at the same speed, they can't quite beat that 5km time or add another mile at the same speed. If your goal(s) have been reached this isn't a problem, and you can be content just running to stay at this level of fitness. However, if your goal is still some way off motivation will drop dramatically. If nothing obvious is causing this plateau – ie overtraining, diet or illness – then the best method of overcoming it is to change your regime and vary the sessions. Changing the path to a specific goal isn't a problem as long as it still leads to success.

➜ Psychological factors

I'm not a psychiatrist or psychologist. I'm sure loads of papers have been written to explain why motivation may drop or a plateau continues despite adopting different approaches to get through it; but at the end of the day it may be a psychological problem that's to blame. My philosophy is again down to the importance of knowing yourself – the importance of being self-critical, of being able to see that you're cutting the calories to try to lose more weight and hence can't perform and have lost motivation; to see that there's something in your life taking your focus away from your training, such as family problems or a love interest, leading to a lack of focus and drive. Whatever it is, reassess your life, refocus and continue.

However, it's important to consider what the true goal of your training is. It may be that the family or love interest should be put above fitness, priority-wise. It may be that you're running to lose weight to help you find a love interest, yet if it's a new love interest that's causing your lack of motivation then surely that isn't actually a bad thing?

Lack of progress

Sometimes, for reasons we can't necessarily pinpoint, and despite seemingly doing everything else correctly, we fail to improve or progress. This can be very disheartening and a real setback. However, all is not lost. There are a few techniques that can help you to get over these little mountains.

→ Visualisation
Visualisation is a method adopted by top sportsmen all over the world. It was also used extensively by Bruce Lee when he was trying to master a new skill or better a previous one. Visualisation is simply going through the sequence of events in the mind and 'seeing' yourself perform them successfully. It can be used to overcome constant failure at something (like a personal best for high jump) or to perfect a technique (like a golf swing). For runners, visualisation might be seeing yourself cross the finish line in first place, or simply running with perfect technique and cadence.

→ Self-study
This involves recording yourself performing a technique and then watching and analysing the performance. Not only does this allow you to review your technique and note where improvements can be made, it also allows you to reinforce the technique by watching it. 'Mirror neurones' exist within our brains that fire up the correct pathways when we watch others perform activities; so watching yourself provides the same stimulus and allows analysis to take place. It can be very helpful to record yourself running and then see where you could improve, be it serious faults like pronation or simple improvements like cadence.

→ Rest
This has already been mentioned, but is so important that I'm mentioning it again. If your body needs rest, listen to it. Don't overtrain or you'll become injured or ill. Be sensible and live to fight (run) another day.

→ New angle
Often when a goal is out of reach we get so fixated on it that we can't see the other options. A varied running programme is always better for the body and general fitness, but when a goal becomes so specific that the training is too focussed on it all-round fitness can get neglected. If rest has been tried and no other option seems viable, then take a few weeks or even a month off and try another type of training that improves the same area of fitness but in another way (see Chapter 10). For example, swimming, cycling or even rowing will all maintain heart and CV fitness while allowing the legs and body to recover.

 Personal experience...

Before I became a Royal Marine PTI, a PTI friend of mine could see I was struggling to reach a personal goal. I wanted to be able to run a certain number of miles in an hour, and although I could run at the required speed, with the correct cadence, I would always overheat and have to slow down about 30–40 minutes in. I was consistently attempting the run, trying to add a mile each time to eventually reach the goal, pushing my body harder and harder and tipping water over my head to cool down, but I just couldn't do it. He advised me to buy a heart-rate monitor and only look at my heart rate – not speeds or distances – and just run for set time periods at set heart rates. He said I'd find it slow and boring, but it would work. He was right, it was slow and boring, but within a couple of months of 'heart-rate training' I was rested, stronger and fitter, and managed to complete my goal, not once, but on numerous occasions. This new angle really worked for me, so I advocate not only trying new angles but also the use of heart-rate monitors (see Chapter 9).

 Conclusion

Set goals for your training and running. In fact, set goals for your life. Just make sure they're SMART goals. If you struggle to complete your goal, set milestones to help you, or else by *knowing yourself* correct any problems and reach out for that goal again. Of course, goals may not be to everyone's taste, especially those content with where they are in life and lacking any real desires. Personally I think everyone can improve some part of their life, even if it's beneficial to their spouse or family rather than themselves. But for most of us it's human nature to want to improve, so set yourself a goal or a challenge, give yourself a time-frame, and make it happen.

CHAPTER 8
WARM-UP, COOL-DOWN

The warm-up is something we are all aware of, yet all too often conveniently forgotten about prior to training. This is more the case prior to running than conditioning or weights sessions. A simple, short, sharp warm-up not only prepares the body and aids injury avoidance, it clears the mind and also prepares it for the training to come. In the Marines we were taught 'fail to prepare, prepare to fail' and 'if you haven't got time to warm-up, you haven't got time to train'.

Skipping the warm-up and cool-down prior to and following a run are the most common mistakes made by runners. We all do it when we're short of time. However, a mantra I learnt in the Royal Marines is 'If you haven't got time to warm up, then you haven't got time to train.' Take it from me, ignoring the warm-up is the single most common way to get injured as a runner. A simple planned and constructive warm-up prior to exercise is worth its weight in gold. Furthermore, once it's learned it can be repeated every

time. In fact for many runners it becomes part of the pre-race ritual. Equally as important is the cool-down, or, most important, the stretch routine at the end of a session. This again aids injury prevention and promotes recovery by giving the body time to return to normal.

There are a number of specific benefits to taking the time to perform a 10- to 15-minute warm-up, especially as the impact from running – particularly for unconditioned runners – causes a great amount of stress to the body and connective tissues.

Why warm up?

→ It prepares the body for the demands of a run
Warming up helps with performance over the first part of a run, and can be the difference between success and failure. This is because as the cardiovascular system begins to work the blood vessels open more fully, allowing more blood to flow around the body and thus warming and supplying the major muscles and organs with an adequate supply. The increase of blood causes an increase in the rate of oxygen exchange from blood to muscle and tissue, which in turn allows the body to exercise to a higher aerobic level before the reduction of energy stores and rapid fatigue.

→ It warms the muscles, ligaments and tendons thoroughly
Running is particularly stressful to the joints and soft tissues, especially when performed on hard surfaces. A thorough warm-up ensures the muscle fibres, ligaments and tendons become more elastic, basically because they're taken through their full range of movements. This increases flexibility and thus reduces potential injury. Furthermore, there's an increase in the release of the joint lubricator, synovial fluid, which only occurs with increased activity and again reduces injury risk.

→ It increases the core temperature
When running there's a natural increase in energy production, which causes an increase in heat. This allows the joints and muscles to become more flexible, helping to avoid injury. However, it also allows the body to start all the processes necessary in thermoregulation prior to the real run beginning, meaning the body will be more efficient when it starts.

→ It increases mental focus and prepares the mind for physical stress
A warm-up allows the mind to start focussing on the run ahead. It allows all the problems of the day to be forgotten and enables the brain to concentrate on the physical act of running.

→ It rehearses neuromuscular channels and their function
The warm-up rehearses the body for the specific movements necessary during running by sending messages from the brain that will also aid coordination. A running-specific warm-up can be learnt and repeated, almost like a ritual. This prepares the body and mind for the run ahead like nothing else can.

→ It allows adaption to an extreme environment
If the run is to be performed in radical heat or cold the warm-up allows the body and CV system to gradually adapt to the climate. Forgetting the warm-up and heading straight into the run is more likely to lead to issues with the body's regulatory systems.

Psychological warm-up
It's sometimes necessary to prepare psychologically as well as physically. For obvious reasons this is more important when the warm-up precedes a competition or a particularly hard run.

The psychological warm-up can form part of the overall warm-up or can be something done while travelling to the session. For me, a piece of inspirational music is key to my psychological prep. You should also think about your motivational goal, be it weight loss, a personal best time or completing a marathon. A method used by athletes, especially to calm themselves and focus, is to visualise themselves performing or competing effectively and efficiently.

The phases of the warm-up

1 Passive warm-up
Increases the body temperature using external means such as clothing, direct heat and massage. However, does little to motivate the body.

2 Psychological warm-up
Primarily used by professional sportspeople prior to hard runs, races and personal bests. For the most part it requires bringing out a certain amount of physical aggression, which can be achieved by visualising the high of achieving one's goal or by means of inspirational songs.

3 General warm-up, mobilisation and initial pulse raiser
The main bulk of the warm-up, which should be executed in a very controlled manner. Start slowly, ensuring all initial movements are neither dynamic nor ballistic; then gently increase the pace through joint mobilisation into the pulse raiser, to get the heart and breathing rates up and induce sweating.

4 Stretching, ideally dynamic
Dynamic stretching is simply stretching the muscle via active exercises in the range of normal movement.

5 Second pulse raiser
Like the first pulse raiser, but finishing at race/run pace or slightly quicker.

6 Run/activity specific
For a sprint race, a few bursts from the blocks. For a steeplechase, a few specific hurdles/stretches. Always be specific to the activity ahead.

Factors affecting the warm-up and cool-down

Performing a warm-up is not always that simple. Temperature, high or low, can be a major concern, and a number of other factors should also be considered.

→ **Environment and climate** – It's often necessary to increase or modify the warm-up and cool-down periods when running in specific environments. For example, if a run outdoors has been hampered by wind and rain, performing a cool-down in the same conditions will have little benefit to the body other than opening it up to illness – seeking shelter and cooling down in the warm would be far more beneficial.

→ **Warm-up duration** – People often ask 'How long should I warm-up for?' However, there's no set time – like a run, its length varies depending on your aim. It depends on the exercise ahead, the time of day, the activity prior to the warm-up, and how you're feeling; you may need a long warm-up to get in the right frame of mind, or you might be raring to go. Personally, I've conducted two-minute warm-ups prior to a gentle run in relatively warm conditions, as the run itself will warm me as I gently progress my pace. Conversely, I've performed a 30-minute warm-up prior to an important race.

→ **Session type and intensity** – The type of session will directly affect the type and length of warm-up – a particularly intensive and ballistic session like sprints or plyometrics will always leave the muscle more susceptible to pulls and tears than a slow run. These sessions must therefore be preceded by a more comprehensive warm-up.

→ **Session duration** – A good proportion of your time should be allocated to a warm-up and cool-down. It's not wise to curtail the warm-up or skip the cool-down because time is short, as they're known to prevent injuries. However, you must avoid being unrealistic! If you only have an hour for a run, a five to ten-minute warm-up would suffice, followed by a hard 40–45 minute session and a five to ten-minute cool-down.

→ **Session aim** – It's sometimes worth focussing initially on the warm-up and not the content of the session. For example, a slow long run doesn't need a very extensive or vigorous warm-up (unless in a very cold environment perhaps); therefore start the run nice and slow before building up the pace – that way the first part of the run itself raises the heart rate and core temperature and is in effect the warm-up. Conversely, a sprint session should have something to raise the core temperature but also a series of dynamic stretches to lengthen the muscle and negate any pulls or injuries.

→ **Ability level** – If you haven't run for a long time, especially following long periods of inactivity or injury, a more prolonged warm-up should be performed. This not only protects against further injury, but often gives you confidence in the recovered injury prior to the session. Furthermore, if you haven't exercised for a long time and are using running as a method of getting fit, the warm-up itself may feel like a hard session. It's important, however, to continue with it, as the warm-up and more importantly the cool-down will help reduce the muscle soreness you'll inevitably have following a period of inactivity.

→ **Training first thing in the morning or following a very static period** – If you've been up and walking around all day, then in effect you've been partaking in a low level warm-up all day. Your joints are somewhat mobilised and the muscles somewhat warm. However, if you've been in bed all night the opposite is true and it's necessary to complete a slightly longer warm-up.

→ **Attempting a new exercise or significantly harder session** – The muscular soreness that can result from adding another few miles to a run can be incredible. In these instances it's a good idea to prepare the body and mind with a longer warm-up.

→ **Training on successive days** – Despite not generally being advised (as it can lead to overtraining and overuse injuries), there are times when this is necessary, or it may just be part of the programme. For example, some events require you to run every day, so when preparing for these it makes sense to train on successive days. Similarly, running a marathon or half-marathon requires training on consecutive days in order to cover the requisite miles. When doing these types of session it's necessary to spend extra time warming up before training so as to avoid injuries like muscle pulls or tears.

→ **When tired or fatigued** – Training when fatigued or overtired isn't a good idea. However, it's not always avoidable. To decrease the chance of injury a lengthy warm-up is advisable.

Dynamic stretching

Simple examples of a pre-running dynamic stretch are five slow squats to stretch the adductors and glutes (groin and backside), five lunges on each leg to stretch the quadriceps (front of the thigh) and five 'Russian walks' on each leg (scraping the bottom of the shoe down an imaginary wall from as high as possible) to stretch the hamstrings (back of upper leg). Leg swings can also be used, basically swinging the leg from the hip through its natural movement.

Dynamic stretching

1 Squats, run a few steps, then repeat.

2 Walking lunges, run a few steps then repeat.

3 Hamstring stretch (Russian) walk, run a few steps then repeat.

4 Calf stretch walk.

Second pulse raiser

Following the dynamic stretch it's imperative to raise the pulse again and develop the warm-up. The dynamic stretch allows more ballistic exercises to be performed such as sprints, strides, hops and jumps. These should be performed for 2–5 minutes to ensure the onset of sweating and that the neuromuscular pathways are firing.

Where possible perform the most suitable exercises for the session ahead – for example, for a sprinting or plyometric session some hops and jumps, but for a marathon some plain running, pushing the pace to slightly faster than that which will be used for the event, with perhaps a few short sprints.

Ideally your pulse rate at the end of the warm-up should be around the same as that expected during the actual event. When warming up for a hard run or a race the warm-up should finish by running at a speed equal to (for a sprint) or quicker than (for a longer run) during the event itself, but for a maximum 20–30 seconds. Not only does this ensure the body is warm, but it also ensures you feel psychologically and physiologically comfortable at that speed prior to attempting it competitively.

Dynamic stretches and warm-up routine can be performed on a treadmill or outside prior to run

Example of a general warm-up

1 Run slowly between two points (even if only 5m apart). While running mobilise the upper body's joints. Although running appears to use only the legs the upper body must still be mobilised, as the arms drive the body when running. This is especially important during sprint events.

2 Mobilise the upper limbs for one to two minutes by moving the arms through a series of planes of movement. Examples are punching to the front, floor, sky, left and right, performing bench press, shoulder press, biceps curls, upright rows and lat pull-downs in the air, and lastly swimming strokes – front crawl, back stroke, breast stroke and reverse breast stroke – also in the air.

3 Stop running between the two points at one end and mobilise the neck by looking up, down, left and right. Following this, continue to run backwards and forwards between the two points. It's now necessary to mobilise the lower limbs further by:

→ Gently flicking the toes out to the front while running forwards and backwards.

→ Gently bringing the knees halfway up to the waist while running forwards and backwards. Ensure the arms move the thumb from hip to lip.

→ Gently flicking the heels halfway up to the rear, again while running forwards and backwards. Each should be done two or three times.

4 To raise the heart rate (thereby ensuring the body temperature is raised to gain all the benefits of the warm-up), increase your running pace between the two points and repeat some of the exercises above – toe flicking, knees to waist and heel flicks, but this time all the way through the full range of motion. Perhaps perform the exercise slightly easier the first time, but increase the pace the second and third time. The heart rate should now be raised considerably and hopefully sweating should have started. If a further pulse raiser is needed, run back and forth between the two points to get the heart rate up and induce sweating.

The cool-down

Like the warm-up, the cool-down is often neglected. At some point I've heard nearly everyone I've trained say they'll skip the cool-down and 'stretch in the shower'. I've done the same myself! However, the cool-down shouldn't be skipped. Not only will it help avoid injury, it will promote recovery from the session and allow development of the muscles' flexibility, which will pay dividends in the long run.

A five to 30-minute cool-down helps return the body to its 'normal' state gradually, promoting recovery, providing time to review the training that's just occurred and preparing the body for the next training session. A cool-down can be especially important if a subsequent session is going to be performed within 24 hours.

Cooling down also prevents blood pooling. This is where the muscles aid the heart and cardiovascular system moving blood around the body; basically, as the muscles contract they help squeeze the veins and push blood back to the heart. If you sit or stand still following a hard session the blood pools in the lower extremities, as the muscles are no longer contracting to help it return. The result is a lack of blood and therefore oxygen to the head, which can result in losing consciousness as the body renders itself horizontal to ensure that blood is recirculated.

The cool-down should focus on deliberate controlled movements. There should be no need for any ballistic or dynamic movement – 'bouncing' when stretching is a dangerous practice and should be avoided. The phases of a cool-down should include:

Reducing

Following a run, continue to jog or at least walk. Reducing rather than stopping exercise does the following:

→ Ensures skeletal muscles remain active, which ensures blood is pumped around the body and doesn't pool in the legs (which causes fainting).

Don't skip the cool-down. Not only does it help avoid injury, it promotes recovery from the session and allows development of the muscles' flexibility.

→ Lowers the pulse rate slowly and steadily, which ensures blood is still pumped actively round the body, removing waste products from the muscles.
→ Allows sweating to continue, which enables the body to control its temperature properly.
→ Ensures the mind has something to concentrate on and stops the sick feeling that often accompanies a hard run.
→ Keeps the blood flowing to deliver nutrients to the muscles, which are essential for recovery.
→ Oxygen continues to be delivered to the muscles to ensure lactic acid is cleared and the body is moved closer to normal levels.

Re-dress

It's easy to get cold very quickly after exercise, especially when training outside or in a cold gym. This means the warm muscles that are about to be stretched get cold and aren't as supple as you thought, and so injuries occur. By simply replacing some layers the temperature is maintained and the muscles kept warm in preparation for the stretch.

Recover

Walk about, maintaining good posture and keeping your head up. Bending over or sitting down reduces the amount of oxygen the lungs can take in, while walking around and staying upright allows deep breaths to be taken. It's important to walk or even jog lightly to allow the pulse to lower slowly under control. Keep your mind focussed on the session, don't allow it to wander. Think about the run, what went well and what could be improved. A period of reflection after each run is highly rewarding.

Relaxation

Stop walking around but continue to take deep breaths. Lie down on your back – this will aid in lowering the pulse further, as blood-pooling can't occur if the body is horizontal. Concentrate on relaxing – think of being somewhere else, on a beach, in bed, whatever relaxes you most. Soon the heart and breathing rates will return to almost normal. This is an almost meditative state – in fact if you can't escape thoughts of work try meditating techniques such as concentrating on your breathing or slowly moving an imaginary ball of light from vertebra to vertebra until you reach your head.

Stretch

There are two types of stretches: maintenance and developmental. At first it's best to stick with maintenance stretches, which should be held for 8–10 seconds. These ensure the muscles stay flexible and help improve flexibility to some extent. In time it's worth moving on to developmental stretches, which should be held for 30 seconds per stretch (done two or three times each).

Eat

It's important to eat something after exercise. As explained in Chapter 6, there's a small window of opportunity to replace the glycogen stores within your muscles. In fact, research suggests that those who ingest carbohydrates and protein within an hour of exercise will recover quicker and exhibit faster muscle repair than those who don't. If eating following a run is difficult then have a specialised supplement drink or eat/drink something highly glycaemic – pure fruit juice and bananas are great examples and will take advantage of the fact that the body can digest, process and store nutrients much faster than normal following a good run.

We all skip the cool-down at some point. It's not until we start the next session and feel the muscle aches that we regret it!

Treat

If any little niggles or muscle pulls have occurred, use an ice pack to start immediate recovery. Believe me, it will pay dividends! A number of times when I've tweaked a hamstring or even inverted an ankle, using an ice pack on the area for ten minutes every hour or so has taken days off the recovery time and even seen me running the next day. Obviously recovery depends on the severity of the injury, but either way an ice pack will certainly aid the healing process. (See Chapter 15 for correct icing technique.)

Stretching routine

The following stretches should be performed during the cool-down process. All can be performed as a maintenance stretch (8–10 seconds) or developmental stretch (30 seconds). For a maintenance stretch take a deep breath and then breathe out as you go into the stretch; count or time five seconds, take another deep breath, breathe out and increase the stretch as you do so. Hold for a further five seconds. At first these stretches will feel uncomfortable, but not painful. Be strong-willed and stick with them. However, stop if you feel any pain. Ideally perform each stretch two or three times.

Developmental stretches work in entirely the same way; they're just held for longer. Take a deep breath, put the stretch on as you breathe out and then hold for around ten seconds; breathe in deeply again, breathe out and increase the stretch, hold it for ten, then repeat one more time and hold for 30 seconds. Again, try to repeat each 30-second stretch three times. However, once or twice is sufficient at first or if time is short.

 ## Groin (adductor) stretch

→ Sit up with your legs bent as if you're going to cross them. Put the soles of your feet together and pull your heels in towards your groin. Take hold of your ankles and place your elbows on the inside of your knees. While keeping the soles together, heels in, hands on ankles, use your elbows to push down through the knees, flattening the legs out and stretching the groin. You should feel a stretch on the inside of both legs.

 ## Single-leg hamstring stretch

→ Remain seated following the groin stretch. Keep the left foot tucked into the groin, but extend the right leg so it's straight and the left sole nestles into the inside of the right thigh. Reach forward as far as possible and take hold of part of your right leg (the bottom of the foot is the final aim, but at first the ankle or shin is fine). Try to bend from the lower back as you stretch, and don't round the upper back too much. Keep the leg straight. The back of the knee should be on the floor. Repeat for the left leg. You should feel the stretch on the upper back of the outstretched leg.

③ Quadriceps stretch

Roll on to your left side, ensuring your left leg is straight. Bend your right leg and take hold of your right foot and pull it up towards your backside. Try to keep your knees level with each other, and your shoulders, hips and knees in line. This will avoid structural injuries. To increase the stretch, pull the foot further into your backside and ease the hips in a forward direction. Repeat lying on the opposite side for the other leg. You should feel the stretch at the front of the bent leg.

④ Glutes (backside) stretch

Sit on the floor with your left leg outstretched and right leg bent up. Staying seated with your left leg outstretched, place your right foot over the left leg and allow it to nestle into the outside of the left thigh parallel to it. The right leg should now be up across your chest. Keeping the right foot on the floor, hug the right leg into the chest with the arms. Repeat with the opposite leg. You should feel the stretch in the buttock of the bent leg.

⑤ Double-leg hamstring stretch

Similar to the single-leg hamstring stretch, the double-leg involves sitting with both legs outstretched and then reaching as far down them as possible (taking hold of the shins, ankles or bottoms of the feet). Try to bend from the lower back, not the upper back. Stretch should be felt in the backs of both legs.

> **Relax**
> When stretching, remember to remain relaxed and to breathe!

⑥ ITB stretch (best performed with a foam roller)

➜ A form of iliotibial band stretch can be achieved by performing the quadriceps stretch described above and then raising the foot of the lower leg and hooking it over the knee of the upper leg. Repeat for the opposite leg. Stretch should be felt down the outside of the leg closest to the floor

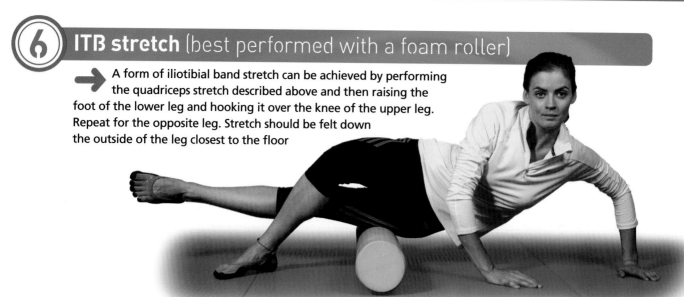

⑦ Abdominal stretch

➜ Lie flat on your front and place hands under the shoulders as if you're going to do press-ups. Push down through the hands as if performing a press-up but don't allow the hips and legs to rise off the floor, ie rotate through the lower back. Try to straighten the arms as far as possible without raising your hips off the floor. Stretch should be felt through the abdominals at the front of the lower torso.

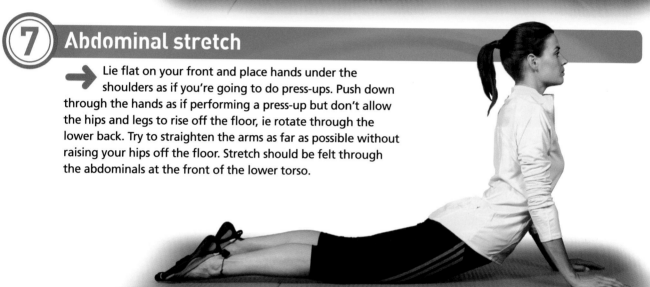

⑧ Back stretch

➜ Lie flat on your back, arms outstretched to your sides as if on an imaginary crucifix. Take one leg across the body (for example the right leg) and try to get the foot of that leg as far up towards the opposite hand as possible. To increase the stretch, allow the left hand to touch the right shoulder. Repeat on the opposite side. Stretch should be felt around the middle of the spine.

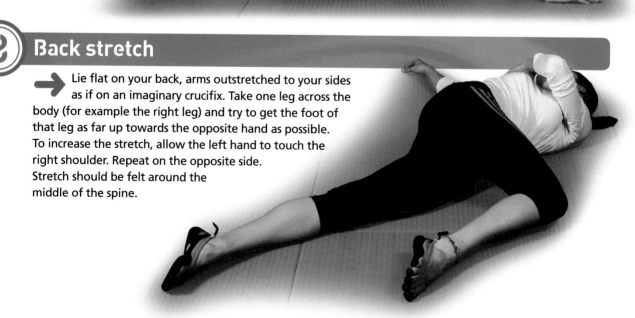

⑨ Calf stretch

→ Pushing with straight arms against a wall or partner, place one foot in front of the other about shoulder-width apart. The rear leg should be straight, front leg bent. Your body should be at an angle of about 45°. Force the heel of the rear leg into the floor. To increase the stretch, move the rear leg further away from the body without bending it. Repeat stretch for opposite leg. Stretch should be felt at back of rear lower leg.

⑩ Hip flexor stretch

→ Kneel on the floor, then step forward with the right foot into a lunge-like position with the left knee rested on the floor. Place your hands on your hips and gently push the hips forward. Repeat stretch for opposite leg. Stretch should be felt at the top of the thigh, in the hip of the forward leg.

⑪ Standing groin stretch

→ Stand with feet 1½ times shoulder-width apart. Take hold of your ankles and place your elbows on the insides of your knees. While keeping the back straight, feet on floor and hands on ankles, use the elbows to push through the knees, flattening the legs out and stretching the groin. You should feel a stretch on the inside of both legs.

🏃 Separate stretch sessions

To really make the most of developmental stretching, it's worth planning-in some specific stretching sessions. Yoga classes are often a good way of increasing flexibility, especially if you're not good at motivating yourself for stretching sessions. Otherwise 20–30 minutes' sat on the floor in front of the TV performing a number of maintenance stretches is an easy alternative.

12 Standing hamstring stretch

➡ Step forward with the right leg so that the front of the left foot is 10–20cm away from the back of the right foot and they're parallel to each other. Keep the right leg straight and left leg bent and 'sit' back to initiate the stretch in the back of the right leg. Repeat for left leg. You should feel the stretch on the upper back of the forward leg.

13 Standing back stretch

➡ In a standing position, with your legs just under shoulder-width apart, drop the chin on to the chest and allow the upper body to fold, lean forward and hang down. Don't bend the legs – ensure they're as straight as possible. When coming up from the stretch ensure you do so slowly and safely. Stretch should be felt in the backs of both upper legs and for some people in the lower back.

14 Standing glutes stretch

➡ While standing, place the right leg across the knee of the left leg so that the right ankle nestles across left knee. Now squat/sit back. The right leg should be horizontal, parallel with the floor. Repeat with the opposite leg. You should feel the stretch in the buttock of the leg not on the floor.

13 Standing quadriceps stretch

➡ Stand up straight. Bend your right leg and take hold of your right foot and pull it up towards your backside. Try to keep your knees level with each other, and your shoulders, hips and knees in line. This will avoid structural injuries. To increase the stretch pull the foot further into your backside and ease the hips in a forward direction. Repeat for other leg. You should feel the stretch at the front of the bent leg.

PNF or contract-relax stretch

Proprioceptive neuromuscular facilitation (PNF) is a technique that 'cheats' the muscles and allows a stretch to be increased, sometimes drastically. The technique combines alternating contraction and relaxation of the muscle; this causes responses in the nerve that usually inhibits the contraction of the muscle. This results in a decrease in resistance and increased range of movement when stretching the muscle. Although PNF stretching usually requires a partner, this isn't always necessary. PNF stretching is supposedly far superior in improving flexibility. The technique utilises the fact that the golgi tendon organs relax a muscle after a sustained contraction has been applied to it for longer than six seconds, thus an increased stretch can be seen.

The four stages in PNF stretching are easy/maintenance stretch; six to ten-second contraction; one to three-second relaxation; and developmental stretch:

→ Easy/maintenance stretch
During this stage the muscle stretches slightly but not to its maximum, ie the 'stretch' in the muscle just starts to be felt.

→ Six to ten-second contraction
During this stage the muscle is contracted as hard as possible, to build end of range strength, which is vital in developing flexibility. The breath may be held to increase the contraction and also assist in the contrast to the next stage.

→ One to three-second relaxation
Breathe out and relax the muscle for a few seconds.

→ Developmental stretch
Increase the stretch as far as possible; this should be beyond the range achieved previously. Ideally the process should be repeated until no further increase in stretch can be seen.

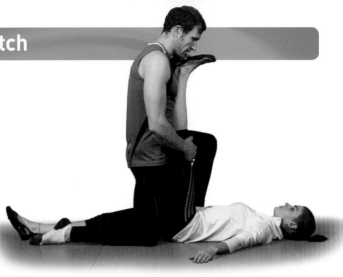

Performing PNF
Start by stretching as normal at the limit of stretch for 10 seconds. Immediately following this, without getting up or moving, contract the muscle against a resistance (your own hand, a partner or a wall) for 10 seconds. Following the resistance, relax for a few seconds and then stretch again for 10–15 seconds. There should be a noticeable difference in flexibility. The first few times you perform such stretches it's advisable to do so in the company of others.

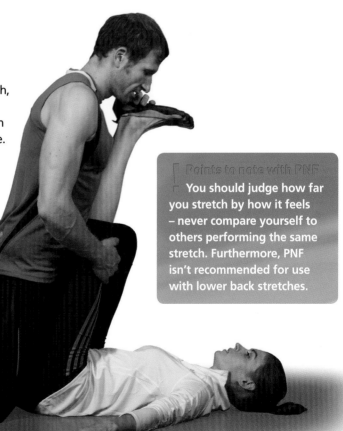

> **Points to note with PNF**
> You should judge how far you stretch by how it feels – never compare yourself to others performing the same stretch. Furthermore, PNF isn't recommended for use with lower back stretches.

CHAPTER 9
TRAINING PROGRAMME

Training programmes for specific running events aren't hard to find; pretty much every fitness magazine from *Zest* to *Men's Running* print them at specific times of year. As marathon build-up season approaches most magazines put forward their version of the must-have, no-fail marathon training programme. The same is true for 10km, 5km and half-marathon training programmes. I've attempted to compare as many of these as I can and put together a simple programme for each.

One for all and all for one

As I've already said, we're all different, and what works for you may not work for the next person. I've therefore included a cross-section of training types, from easy runs to continuous runs, interval sessions, hill sessions and where necessary swimming, bike and conditioning sessions. If they don't suit you, simply adapt them as necessary.

→ Adaption and implementation

The programmes are designed around training four or five times a week. However, this may be impossible and you can only train three times a week. If that's the case, then adapt the programme to suit you and implement it as best you can. What do I mean by this? Well, for example, I've made Sunday the long-run/long-training day for most of the programmes, with Monday as a day off (in the most part). This is perfect for the majority of us who work a five-day week, giving us Saturday to unwind and relax and Sunday for our longest run. However, people who work a four days on, two days off shift pattern or work at weekends will need to modify the programme to coincide with the appropriate days of their week.

Six-week beginners' plan

Week	Monday	Tuesday	Wednesday	Thursday	Friday	Saturday	Sunday
1	Run 1min, walk 3min, repeat x 4	Rest	Run 1min, walk 3min, repeat x 5	Rest	Run 1min, walk 3min, repeat x 6	Rest	20min brisk walk
2	Run 2min, walk 3min, repeat x 4	Rest	Run 2min, walk 3min, repeat x 5	Rest	Run 2min, walk 3min, repeat x 5	Rest	25min brisk walk
3	Run 3min, walk 3min, repeat x 3	Rest	Run 3min, walk 2min, repeat x 3	Rest	Run 4min, walk 2min, repeat x 2	Rest	30min brisk walk
4	Run 5min, walk 2min, repeat x 2	Rest	Run 5min, walk 2min, repeat x 3	Rest	Run 6min, walk 2min, repeat x 2	Rest	35min brisk walk
5	Run 8min, walk 2min, repeat x 2	Rest	Run 10min, walk 2min, repeat x 2	Rest	Run 8min, walk 1min, repeat x 2	Rest	40min brisk walk
6	Rest	Run 12min, walk 1min, repeat x 1	Rest	Run 15min, walk 2min, repeat x 2	Rest	Rest	5km run without walking or stopping

5km plan

Week	Monday	Tuesday	Wednesday	Thursday	Friday	Saturday	Sunday
1	Rest	Easy 15min, Fartlek 15min	Rest	Easy 10min, 4 x 3min 100%, 2min recovery, easy 10min	Rest	Easy 30min	Easy 10min, 5km race pace 10min, easy 10min
2	Rest	Easy 30min	Rest	Easy 10min, a touch faster than 5km race pace 10min, easy 10min	Rest	Easy 35min	Easy 10min, 5 x 3min 100%, recovery 2min, easy 10min
3	Rest	Easy 35min	Rest	Easy 12min, a touch faster than 5km race pace 10min, easy 12min	Rest	Easy 40min	Easy 5min, 5km race pace 20min, easy 5min
4	Rest	Easy 40min	Rest	Easy 15min, Fartlek 15min, easy 10min	Rest	Easy 45min	Easy 10min, 6 x 3min 100%, recovery 2min, easy 10min
5	Rest	Easy 40min	Rest	Easy 10min, a touch faster than 5km race pace 15min, easy 10min	Rest	Easy 35min	5km race pace 30min
6	Rest	Easy 30min	Rest	Easy 15min, Fartlek 20min, easy 10min	Rest	Very easy 20min	5km race pace (and personal best!)

Ten-week 10km plan

Week	Monday	Tuesday	Wednesday	Thursday	Friday	Saturday	Sunday
1	Rest	Easy 20min	Conditioning 40min	Easy 10min, 3 x 2min 80%, recovery 2min, easy 10min	Easy 10min, 3 x 2min 80%, recovery 2min, easy 10min	Rest	60min easy non-running CV (swim, bike, row, cross-train)
2	Conditioning 30min	Rest	Easy 10min, conditioning 30min, easy 10min	Hill run 20min	Rest	Easy 30min	Easy 30min
3	Rest	Conditioning 30min	Easy 10min, 4 x 3min 80%, recovery 2min	Rest	Conditioning 40min	Hill sprints 30min	Easy 40min
4	Rest	Easy 10min, 4 x 3min 80%, recovery 1½min	Easy 10min, conditioning 10min, repeat x 2, easy 10min	Easy 35min	Rest	Easy 30min	Rest or Swim/bike 30min
5	Rest	Easy 10min, conditioning 10min, repeat x 2, easy 10min	Easy 10min, 2 x 6min 80%, recovery 3min	Rest	Easy 10min, 6 x 1min 100%, recovery 1min, easy 15min	Rest	Easy 60min
6	Rest	Conditioning 30min	Easy 20min, 10min at 10km race pace	Rest	Easy 10min, 6 x 3min 80%, recovery 1½min	Bike, swim, cross-train 60min	Easy 30min
7	Rest	Easy 10min, conditioning 10min, repeat x 3, easy 5min	Easy 10min, 2 x 8min 80%, recovery 4min, easy 16min	Rest	Easy 10min, 5 x 4min 80%, recovery 1½min	Easy 10min, conditioning 10min, repeat x 3, easy 5min	Easy 70min
8	Rest	Easy 10min, conditioning 10min, repeat x 2, easy 5min	Rest	Easy 10min, 2 x10 min 80%, recovery 3min	Rest	10km race pace 30min	Easy 75min
9	Rest	Easy 10min, conditioning 10min, repeat x 3, easy 5min	Easy 15min, 80% 15min, easy 15min	Easy 10min, 8 x 1min 100%, recovery 1min, easy 8min	Rest	Rest	Easy 30min, 10km race pace 15min
10	Rest	Easy 40min	Easy 10min, 3 x 5min 80%, recovery 2min, easy 10min	Rest	Rest	Easy run 10min	10km race pace (and personal best!)

10km road to 10 miles cross-country

Week	Monday	Tuesday	Wednesday	Thursday	Friday	Saturday	Sunday
1	Easy 20min	Rest	Easy 20min	Rest	Easy 20min	Rest	Easy 45min
2	Easy 30min	Rest	Easy 10min, conditioning 10min, repeat x 2, easy 5min	Rest	Easy 20min	Rest	Easy 50min
3	Rest	Easy 20min	Easy 40min	Rest	Easy 30min	Rest	Easy 50min
4	Rest	Easy 60min	Rest	Easy 50min	Rest	Easy 50min	Easy 30min
5	Rest	Rest	Easy 55min	Easy 10min, 6 x 1min 100%, recovery 1min, easy 10min	Easy 55min	Rest	Easy 80min
6	Rest	Easy 30min	Easy 60min	Easy 10min, 3 x 5min 80%, recovery 3min, easy 5min	Rest	10km race pace 35min	Easy 90min
7	Rest	10km race pace 30min	Easy 70 min	Easy 10min, 8 x 1min 100%, 1min recovery, easy 5min	Rest	10km race pace 35min	Easy 100min
8	Rest	Easy 35min	Easy 70min	Easy 10min, 3 x 10min 80% recovery 3min, easy 5min	Rest	10km race pace 35min	Easy 110min
9	Rest	10km race pace 35min	Easy 80min	Easy 10min, 4 x 5min 80%, recovery 3min, easy 5min	Rest	10km race pace 40min	Easy 120min
10	Rest	Easy 40min	Easy 80min	Easy 10min, 5 x 5min 80%, recovery 3min, easy 5min	Rest	10km race pace 40min	Half-marathon
11	Rest	10km race pace 40min	Easy 90min	Easy 10min, 5 x 5min 80%, recovery 3min, easy 5min	Rest	10km race pace 40min	Easy 100min
12	Rest	Easy 40min	Easy 90min	Easy 10min, 5 x 5min 80%, recovery 3min, easy 5min	Rest	10km race pace 40min	Race pace 80min
13	Rest	Easy 40min	Rest	Easy 30min	Rest	Rest	10miler (and personal best!)

12-week half-marathon programme

Week	Monday	Tuesday	Wednesday	Thursday	Friday	Saturday	Sunday
1	Rest	Easy 10min, 2 x 8min 5km race pace, recovery 2min, easy 5min	Easy 30min	Rest	Easy 10min, 2 x 5min hills, recovery 2min, easy 10min	Rest	Easy 60min
2	Rest	Easy 10min, 5km race pace 10min, repeat x 2, easy 5min	Easy 30min	Rest	Easy 10min, 2 x 7min hills, recovery 2min, easy 10min	Rest	Easy 70min
3	Rest	Easy 7min, 5km race pace 7min, repeat x 3, easy 5min	Easy 35min	Rest	Easy 10min, 3 x 5min hills, recovery 2min, easy 10min	Rest	Easy 75min
4	Rest	Easy 3min, 5km race pace 3min, repeat x 6, easy 5min	Easy 35min	Rest	Easy 40min, to include as many hills as possible	Rest	Easy 60min
5	Rest	10km at 10km race pace	Easy 40min	Rest	Easy 10min, 2 x 10min hills, recovery 2min, easy 10min	Rest	Easy 80min
6	Rest	Easy 5min, half-marathon race pace 12min, repeat x 2, easy 5min	Rest	Rest	Easy 10min, 3 x 7min hills, recovery 2min, easy 10min	Rest	Easy 60min, half-marathon pace 20min
7	Rest	Easy 15min, half-marathon race pace 30min	Easy 40min	Rest	Easy 40min, to include as many hills as possible	Rest	Easy 60min
8	Rest	Easy 5min, half-marathon race pace 10min, repeat x 3, easy 5min	Easy 40min	Rest	Easy 10min, 3 x 8min hills, recovery 2min, easy 10min	Rest	Easy 70min, half-marathon pace 20min
9	Rest	Easy 10min, half-marathon race pace 25min, easy 10min	Easy 45min	Rest	Easy 10min, 4 x 5min hills, recovery 2min, easy 10min	Rest	Easy 100min
10	Rest	Easy 3min, half-marathon race pace 5min, repeat x 5, easy 5min	Easy 50min	Rest	Easy 10min, 4 x 6min hills, recovery 2min, easy 10min	Rest	Easy 75min
11	Rest	Easy 3min, 10km race pace 3min, repeat x 8, easy 5min	Easy 60min	Rest	Easy 15min, 10km race pace 3min, repeat x 5, easy 2min, easy 15min	Rest	Easy 60min
12	Rest	Easy 5min, 10km race pace 5min, repeat x 3, easy 5min	Rest	Rest	Easy 20min	Rest	Half-marathon (and personal best!)

16-week marathon programme

Week	Monday	Tuesday	Wednesday	Thursday	Friday	Saturday	Sunday
1	Rest	Easy 4 miles	Hills 4 miles	Rest	10km race pace 4 miles	Easy 4 miles	Easy 9 miles
2	Rest	Easy 4 miles	Yasso 800s: 2 x 800m, 800m recovery	Rest	Half-marathon race pace 5 miles	Easy 5 miles	Easy 9 miles
3	Rest	Easy 3 miles	Hills 5 miles	Rest	10km race pace 5 miles	Easy 5 miles	Easy 12 miles
4	Rest	Easy 4 miles	Yasso 800s: 4 x 800m, 800m recovery	Rest	10km race pace 4 miles	Easy 4 miles	Easy 10 miles
5	Rest	Easy 4 miles	Hills 6 miles	Rest	Easy 2 miles, 5km race pace 2 miles	Easy 4 miles	Easy 13 miles
6	Rest	Easy 5 miles	Yasso 800s: 6 x 800m, 800m recovery	Rest	Easy 2 miles, 5km race pace 2 miles	Easy 6 miles	Easy 15 miles
7	Rest	Easy 6 miles	Hills 7 miles	Rest	Easy 2 miles, 5km race pace 3 miles	Easy 5 miles	Easy 16 miles
8	Rest	Easy 5 miles	Yasso 800s: 6 x 800m, 800m recovery	Rest	Easy 2 miles, 10km race pace 4 miles	Easy 4 miles	Easy 14 miles
9	Rest	Easy 3 miles	Hills 8 miles	Rest	Easy 2 miles, half-marathon race pace 7 miles	Easy 3 miles	Easy 18 miles
10	Rest	Easy 4 miles	Yasso 800s: 8 x 800m, 800m recovery	Rest	Easy 2 miles, half-marathon race pace 8 miles	Rest	Easy 20 miles
11	Rest	Easy 4 miles	Easy 7 miles	Rest	Easy 2miles, half-marathon race pace 8 miles	Easy 4 miles	Easy 20 miles
12	Rest	Easy 7 miles	Yasso 800s: 8 x 800m, 800m recovery	Rest	5km race pace 5 miles	Easy 8 miles	Easy 15 miles
13	Rest	Easy 5 miles	Easy 4 miles, 10km race pace 4 miles	Rest	Easy 6 miles	10km race pace 5 miles	Easy 22 mile
14	Rest	Easy 8 miles	Yasso 800s: 10 x 800m, 800m recovery	Rest	Easy 7 miles	10km race pace 7 miles	Easy 15 miles
15	Rest	Easy 5 miles	Easy 2 miles, 5km race pace 3 miles	Rest	Easy 5 miles	10km race pace 5 miles	Easy 12 miles
16	Rest	Easy 2 miles, 5km race pace 3 miles	Rest	Rest	Rest	Easy 3 miles	Marathon (and personal best!)

Designing your own programme

If you're not aiming at a specific event or race and just want to get fit, lose weight or challenge yourself, you may want to design your own programme. There are no hard and fast rules for this, though there are a few things you should keep in mind:

● The seven components of fitness (see below).
● Variation (don't perform the same sessions repeatedly, and gradually make things more challenging to ensure progression).
● Overtraining (see Chapter 15).

The seven components of fitness

Although Usain Bolt and Paula Radcliffe are both incredibly fit, are they fit in exactly the same way? The answer is probably not. It's unlikely that Usain would have been as successful as a marathon runner, and Paula would be the first to admit she wouldn't be among the top female sprinters (although her 3,000m times are very impressive). Some of this is down to genetics, but more significantly both athletes train for their own specific events.

I've always believed that to have all-round fitness someone must be fit across all seven components – flexibility, endurance, stamina, skill, strength, speed and power. Yes, someone can be fit without actually being fit across the board, but to avoid injury and be at the top of their game it's important to at least train in each component to some degree. One component may be more important than another for a specific sport, but ignoring one or more because they don't seem relevant could potentially leave you open to injury and a lack of overall fitness. Whether you're training for health, fitness or weight loss, design a programme that covers all seven components to ensure you're really fit.

→ Flexibility

Flexibility entails having the maximum range of movement around a joint allowed by the muscles, tendons and ligaments.

As we've seen, every training session should involve a comprehensive warm-up including mobility work and dynamic stretches, and end with a comprehensive cool-down and static stretch session. This will have a marked improvement on recovery time and help produce strong, healthy muscles. Separate stretching sessions are also very beneficial, either in the evening after a hard session or on a rest/rainy day. Sitting on the floor in front of the TV in the evening is a perfect time to perform a stretch session, but always remember to warm the muscles first.

The following points are worth knowing:

● The type of joint – ie hinge (knee/elbow) or ball and socket (shoulder/hip) – determines joint mobility.
● A lack of flexibility can injure muscles and tendons. Inflexibility can affect the curve of the spine, which in turn can have dramatic effects on posture. Inflexibility can also have a dramatic effect on the safe and correct performance of exercises, which can injure or fatigue muscles, ligaments and tendons.
● Over-flexible joints can also be problematic, as they can become unstable and damage muscles, ligaments and tendons. Injury and the resultant swelling or scar tissue can affect flexibility by causing too much range of movement or too little.
● Flexibility training becomes more important in later life to offset the effects of ageing.

Flexibility training is particularly important in reducing the risk of injury and promoting recovery after exercise or following injury. It should be incorporated into every fitness regime but is often neglected.

→ Endurance

Endurance is the body's ability to resist fatigue whilst performing relatively prolonged exercise of low to moderate intensity.

Runners (except sprinters) require a high level of endurance fitness. In fact it's probably the most important component, as having a good level of endurance ensures you can run for a long time. The easiest way to train endurance is to go on long, slow to medium-paced runs. This is a gradual process, and either time or distance should be used as a marker and built on. For example, running 20 minutes one session, then 25 the next, and so on, or 2 miles, then 2½, and so on. This progression is seen in the programmes above. You could also use a heart-rate monitor (see further on).

Though it's not necessary it's beneficial to see if improvements are being made, so measure the rough distance covered if running to time, or the time if running to distance. In terms of your training, long runs are obviously necessary to any runner's overall fitness programme, even that of a sprinter, so any basic fitness regime should involve at least one long endurance run a week (unless injury prevents, in which case a swim/bike/row could take its place).

Lastly, remember that the efficiency of the heart in pumping oxygen may limit your ability to endure and perform during endurance activities. The heart is a muscle, and just like any other muscle must be trained for it to strengthen and grow. My advice to anyone wanting to get into fitness would be that the heart is the most important muscle to train, so train it well and you should live a longer, more healthy life.

→ Skill

A skill is the ability to know when and where to use a specific technique that's required to complete an activity, and to be able to use it successfully.

It might at first seem that developing skills isn't very important in running, but as the previous chapter has shown there are actually a number of techniques that need to be mastered in order to run economically, quickly and without injury. A competitive runner has to know when and where to use their 'kick' to win a race. Have no doubts, a runner's game plan is a skill, as is knowing when to utilise it.

Everyone reading this book has probably heard the phrase 'practice makes perfect', so it'll probably surprise you when I say it doesn't! What practice does do, is make permanent – ie if something's practised (repeated) over and over it's committed to muscle memory and becomes the way your body performs it. The problem is, if a bad technique is practised over and over then that too can become permanent. So when thinking about developing your running ability a far better phrase to use is 'perfect practice makes permanent', ie by repeating a technique correctly and perfectly, over and over, it will become permanent. It's always worth practising when you're fresh to ensure the correct technique is performed, since it's easier to slip into bad habits when you're fatigued.

→ Stamina

Stamina is the ability of the body to resist fatigue whilst performing repetitive high intensity work.

This type of training is important to middle-distance runners, sprinters, and of course sports players like footballers. However, it also has a place in long-distance running.

The best way to train stamina is to perform repetitive sprints/intervals a set number of times. Training stamina is essential for all-round fitness and is an excellent way to lose weight, since sprints and intervals raise the metabolism and burn a lot of calories. An individual's speed is also increased by performing this sort of training, which is highly beneficial to anyone wanting to make running their hobby or chosen sport. In addition some types of stamina training can be beneficial to lean muscle formation and gain, if that's your goal.

→ Strength

Strength is said to be the maximum force that specific muscles can generate against resistance.

Strength training is often neglected by runners, who see bodybuilders 'pumping iron' and lose interest in favour of the road, track or treadmill. However, Usain Bolt and Michael Johnson didn't get world records without strength training. Even marathon runners require strong muscles, ligaments and tendons, as well as strong minds, though it's important to achieve this without gaining too much weight. Good overall strength ensures you can cope with whatever a run throws at you without risk of injury, and aids overall fitness.

As mentioned, strength training and in particular resistance training strengthens tendons, ligaments and supporting muscles and helps limit injury. This is especially important for runners, as every time the foot strikes the ground the muscles are put under huge amounts of stress. Furthermore, strength training improves core strength, which is important in avoiding injuries and in running success.

→ Speed

Speed is said to be how fast the muscles can move given a set objective.

We all initially think of this as our sprint speed, but it could equally be our reaction time in ball sports. To train speed you need to do repetitive drills when not overly fatigued. Doing so when fatigued will lead to bad technique, and even injury. Speed training is quite similar to the sprint drills laid out for stamina work, but concentrating on technique and training over shorter distances so that it doesn't become interval training. Speed isn't just important to sprinters – any runner who's been caught in a sprint finish to the line will know what I mean. Sometimes a marathon is won over the last ten metres – if you lose you'll curse the times you missed your speed training in favour of another eight-miler!

→ Power

Power is the functional relationship between strength and speed. It's a key component in athletic performance, and especially in sprinting. However, endurance running is also greatly enhanced by increased power.

By improving power the efficiency and quickness of muscle movements is maximised, which in turn creates further efficiency and a greater VO_2 max for endurance. So whether you're a sprinter, middle-distance or marathon runner, your personal best times will benefit from increasing your power.

To train for power properly you require some muscular strength beforehand. This means that the prehab and conditioning for running you've (hopefully) been doing is even more beneficial, by increasing your strength levels with resistance exercises and strengthening tendons, ligaments and support muscles to limit injury. Furthermore, for power training it's very important to have a strong core, so ensure you do the abdominal-associated exercises to stabilise those muscles.

Lastly, it's important to take up power exercises slowly, as they can easily cause injury if done incorrectly; therefore progress slowly, remember that genetics rather than power training can dictate your speed, and be realistic.

⏱ Conclusion

It's important to design a training programme that encompasses all-round fitness and doesn't concentrate too much on a specific event. Obviously, to complete a marathon running training has to take place, but strength work, flexibility, skill and stamina sessions are all important too. Although it's not necessary to train all seven components every day, or to train them evenly, it's important that all get some attention to ensure all-round fitness and injury avoidance. For most fun runners a training programme that includes all seven components in some form or other is ideal. Obviously if your end goal is to complete a marathon then power training may not be at the top of your list but it should still be included every now and then. If your end goal is to lose weight, then sessions covering all areas will be worthwhile.

It's worth adding that not all the components need to be trained in one session. They can be mixed from one training session to the next. However, one type of training may interfere with another type, so the following order should be kept to if performing on the same day:

1 Warm-up
2 Skill
3 Power/speed
4 Strength
5 Stamina
6 Endurance
7 Flexibility

Heart-rate training

The heart rate can be used as a guide to exercise intensity. Every individual has different abilities or fitness levels and therefore corresponding working heart rates (WHR). The traditional method of working out someone's heart rate zones can be inaccurate by plus or minus ten beats per minute or more.

Heart-rate training zones

Research has shown that with arm work alone, such as arms-only swimming, the same VO_2 max cannot be obtained as is reached when running, even though the heart rate may reach its maximum in both cases. Therefore to gain maximum benefits a swimmer will achieve a greater training effect by running, as it uses a greater muscle mass and creates a greater load on the CV system than arms-only swimming at the same heart rate.

→ Training zone adjustment for different activities

Research has also shown that compared to running, the heart rate will be a little lower when performing cross-training and using other activities such as swimming and cycling. In fact for accurate heart rate usage the following should be noted:

Cycling	Subtract 10 beats per minute
Swimming	Subtract 10–15 beats per minute

Methods of measuring the pulse rate

→ Manual pulse measuring

The heart rate can be measured by feeling the pulse in the wrist or neck while timing using a watch. To minimise inaccuracies the count is taken over ten seconds and then multiplied by six.

→ Heart rate monitor (HRM)

I'd advocate everyone owning a heat-rate monitor. The main advantage is the immediate feedback when training in different activities, conditions and terrain.

→ Percentage of the maximum heart rate

Estimated using the working heart rate (WHR) equation below. Our maximum heart rate decreases with age, so we need this crude equation to estimate our maximum and therefore working heart rates. It gives us our 'estimated maximum heart rate' (EMHR), which is then multiplied by the required percentage to estimate the working heart rate – for example, if I wanted a long slow run that would exercise my heart, improve my cardiovascular system and not stress my body too much, I'd use 60%; conversely, if I wanted to work hard and push myself I'd use 80%; furthermore, if I wanted to go for a race pace or even a personal best I might use 90–95%, but this is really only necessary for competitive athletes and runners. (*NB* This method is not individualistic so isn't very accurate.)

Males	220 minus age (in years) x % = WHR
Females	226 minus age (in years) x % = WHR

The heart can be very misleading in its actual indication of exercise intensity, since it can be affected by the weather, climate, psychological state, hydration state, sleep patterns and other factors.

Monitoring the resting pulse rate can be a good indication of recovery from previous training sessions, thus can help prevent overtraining.

→ Karvonen working heart rate equation

This alternative is far more accurate, as it uses either a measured (MMHR) or estimated (EMHR) maximum heart rate. To use this equation, a measured maximal heart rate (MMHR) is first required, which can be obtained from an exercise stress test. To perform this test, after warming up thoroughly a best effort one-mile run is performed. The last half to quarter of a mile should be at absolutely maximum effort. The time and heart rate should be noted during the last ten seconds and at the finish.

Next, the measured resting heart rate (MRHR) is needed. Immediately on waking from a good night's sleep, the pulse should be taken. This should be done on three consecutive mornings and an average taken. (Some people find a full bladder leads to a higher heart rate, so it may be necessary to empty the bladder and then return to bed for a few minutes before taking the pulse.)

Finally it's necessary to establish the heart rate reserve (HRR). To find this deduct the measured resting heart rate from the measured maximum heart rate, ie MMHR – MRHR = HRR. However, it's also possible to find it by deducting the measured resting heart rate from the estimated maximum heart rate, ie EMHR – MRHR = HRR.

Once the HRR has been calculated it's possible to work out very accurate working heart rates. To do this, multiply the HRR by the percentage wanted and then add the MRHR. This will give the working heart rate, ie (HRR x %) + MRHR = WHR.

Example: A 40-year-old male starts an endurance programme, working at 60% maximum heart rate –

Estimated maximum heart rate (EMHR)	220 minus 40	180bpm
Measured maximum heart rate (MRHR)		70bpm
Heart rate reserve (HRR)	180 minus 70	110bpm
Working heart rate (WHR)	(110 x 0.6) = 66 + 70	136bpm

Where possible use this equation to get the accuracy you need for training.

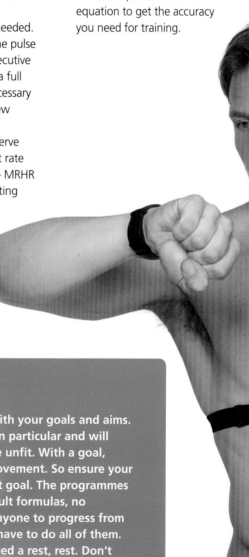

⏱ Conclusion

A training programme goes hand in hand with your goals and aims. Without a goal you're training for nothing in particular and will soon skip sessions, lose interest and become unfit. With a goal, however, you'll be focussed and crave improvement. So ensure your training programme will help you reach that goal. The programmes above are simple and easy to use – no difficult formulas, no complicated sessions. They should enable anyone to progress from novice to local marathon runner. You don't have to do all of them. Take your time and know yourself: if you need a rest, rest. Don't overtrain just because the programme says you must train.

Running can be used as training for another sport or activity, or another sport or activity can supplement your running training. Either way, this is known as cross-training. Boxers, footballers and many other sportsmen/women have used running to improve their overall fitness for their sport. Equally, many runners find swimming once a week greatly improves their lung capacity and general fitness for running.

Running to improve your sport

If you're a footballer, rugby player, tennis player, martial artist ... or to be honest any other sportsperson, then running should be part of your programme, as cross-training is important to competing well at any sport. Obviously you need to drill your sport, practice specific techniques so that they become skills, and master your game, but fitness is often the key in every sport, and sometimes the difference between winning and losing. For example, you can be the best tennis player in the world, but if you only have the fitness for a 15-minute match, when those 15 minutes are up you'll fail to get to the ball, miss shots and eventually lose. The same is true for rugby, football, gymnastics etc. You name it, fitness is key.

Performing long, slow continuous runs, interval training and speed work will increase your endurance, stamina and speed (respectively) no end, making you a better competitor. Never underestimate the importance of cross-training and using running to improve your fitness. Buy a heart-rate monitor and use it to plan and execute your running training to support your sports-specific training.

 Personal experience...

When I was playing a lot of football or preparing for a new season I'd run on a treadmill while watching whatever game was playing on TV. Today I use this technique with clients using running as cross-training for their football and football-loving clients who want to lose weight or get fit. I get them to run on the treadmill while watching their favourite team, instead of going to the pub. Run for 45 minutes first half, have a 15-minute stretch at half-time, then run for another 45 minutes – just like the players.

Cross-training for runners

Choosing the right form of cross-training can have an excellent effect on your running ability. This is because some people who find really pushing themselves when running a hard task are able to boost their cardiovascular system by exercising at a much higher intensity when training for another sport. For instance, though I've always been a runner I hit a bit of a plateau at one point, but was also training for a specific swimming test. I'd always disliked swimming as I never felt like I could get enough oxygen, but when I'd worked at it to a point where I could swim non-stop, relatively quickly for very long periods, I found that it had also improved my running! My heart rate was actually slightly lower at my higher speeds and I could maintain them for longer – my cardiovascular system had improved.

Training the upper body

Some cross-training activities can be used to focus efforts on the upper body rather than the legs. Rowing, canoeing, surfing and kayaking all provide great strengthening sessions for the upper body.

Muscle imbalance

Long-distance runners often get muscle imbalance due to their long runs and neglect of the rest of the body. Performing upper body cross-training can make a big difference and should therefore be included at least once every couple of weeks.

Injury

Cross-training is a great way to cope with the stress of injury. I personally found cycling and swimming a godsend when I tore my patella tendon.

Cross-training examples

→ Swimming

A great all-over body conditioner that has more effect on the upper body, which is just what runners need. Perfect for improving the CV system due to the hypoxic effects of holding your breath as the stroke is performed. Due to its non-impact and non-weight-bearing nature it's great for rest sessions, easy sessions and injury rehab.

→ Cycling

A great CV builder and workout that's non-impact, so can be great as a precursor to running after injury or as a low-impact alternative once a week. Builds the muscles of the legs, which can be detrimental to runners if performed too often. Spin classes at gyms, road biking and mountain biking all offer their own unique challenges.

→ Rowing

If you've never done a 500m sprint on an ergo in the gym, give it a go. If you consider yourself fit, try ten with two minutes rest between each and then see how you feel. Rowing really is an all-over body workout. It's possibly the best in terms of building a strong CV base. Furthermore it's non-impact, so can be good for the injured. It builds the upper body, the core and the lower back – great for runners.

→ Skiing

Like rowing this can be a complete body workout, and you may find your heart rate is a bit higher due to the risk factor and the consequent adrenaline boost. With this, though, comes an injury factor – it's very easy to cause leg injuries that could prevent you from being able to run ever again. You have been warned.

→ Kayaking or canoeing

Very similar to rowing as arm and back builders, which is great for runners and good for the injured. Both also have the adrenaline factor of skiing if done in the sea or on fast-flowing rivers. Conversely they can be enjoyed with friends and family along a quiet river on a rest day. Personally I recommend both.

If a client asks me which piece of kit they should buy for their home — treadmill, ergo or bike — I generally say ergo. The ergo works the whole body, and is an awesome piece of kit for weight loss and fitness gains.

→ Ice or roller skating

Skating can be great if you're good at it, but an injury waiting to happen if you're not. Best strap the wrists and be cautious. Beyond that, skating tends to works exactly the same muscles as running, so is a good cross-training tool for strengthening the running gait and improving speed, and superb for strengthening the lateral rotator muscles and stretching the ITB from the biomechanical mechanism of pushing off. However, it's not recommended as part of a rehab session.

→ Surfing

Ideal as part of a running programme, as it exercises the arms and shoulders when paddling out, plus the core and proprioception of the ankles, knees and legs when standing up. Another great one for the family on rest days.

→ Climbing

An excellent sport for improving strength, flexibility, core strength and personal awareness, but if performed without adequate supervision can also be incredibly dangerous. Go to a local climbing wall, or hire a qualified instructor (ask to see their certificate and insurance). If you like the sport, then learn, become competent and climb for yourself. Adhere to the mantra 'start slow and stay low' – especially when bouldering (climbing low, without ropes, but moving laterally) – and you'll be fine.

→ Trampolining, gymnastics, Parkour

All of these are incredible for increasing spatial awareness and generating a powerful body, from legs, to core, to shoulders. They're also a lot of fun, and a real break from running. However, as with many cross-training activities, injuries can happen easily, so go to a club with a safe training environment and qualified instructors and learn at your pace.

→ Martial arts

I've been a keen martial artist since I started karate at the age of seven. True martial arts forms encourage a lot of stretching, which is great for any runner, as is the absolute power their techniques encourage in the body. The downside is that injuries can occur, especially from the mixed martial arts that are popular today. If your main goal is running, then avoid sparring; if martial arts are your main goal, then running is a great supplement for CV fitness.

→ Yoga

Yoga has all the benefits of flexibility, joint mobilisation and lengthening of the spine. It's also very good at relaxing you, especially at times of stress, like injury. Some of the positions need holding for significant lengths of time, and therefore encourage upper body strength that isn't provided by running.

→ Pilates

Very similar to yoga in its uses to a runner, providing relaxation, strength, mobility and flexibility. It's also amazing at sorting out any little imbalances and injuries, especially in the back and core. An excellent addition for injury-prone or core-weak runners.

→ Circuits

For general, non-specific fitness, circuit training is probably the best one-off method of developing endurance, stamina and strength. However, although it's a superb fitness tool it's just that – a tool. It shouldn't be used in isolation, but only as a supplement to other types of training. Only one or two circuit-training sessions should be undertaken per week, and should be combined with running-specific sessions.

→ Circuit exercises

Fatigue will build up during any circuit, and that exercise technique may consequently suffer. Therefore it's best to avoid complex exercises that require specific techniques. Any exercises that are relatively dangerous if done badly, or need a 'flat-back' – eg weighted squat or weighted bent-over row – should be executed with caution. For best results, circuit training should combine bodyweight exercises with resistance exercises (free weight and/or machine). Torso exercises should cover both abdominals and lower back. Basic core stability is another worthwhile inclusion and often a good rest station. Some very good circuit-training applications by High Definition Fitness are available for iPhone, iPad, iPad and Android.

⏱ Sensible choice

You may have noticed that I haven't included any of the normal 'sports' we tend to do as hobbies, such as rugby, basketball, football, netball or hockey. The reason for this is simple: these are contact or semi-contact sports and therefore injuries and knocks are inevitable and unavoidable. I've personally trained hard for a specific running event only to seriously injure myself playing rugby the week before! My advice is, if running is your passion choose cross-training programmes that support this and doesn't jeopardise it, as two months off running because of a stupid kick-about with the lads from the pub will leave you with big regrets and a real slump in motivation.

CHAPTER 11
CONDITIONING & TRAINING

To improve as a runner, running training itself isn't enough. It's also necessary to strengthen certain muscles, not only to ensure they're strong enough to propel you at the speeds you want, but also to ensure you don't fall fowl of the injuries that tend to plague runners. Many people are guilty of making running their entire fitness regime. Although this may aid them to lose weight, it is not sufficient on its own for general fitness and wellbeing.

However, the big pitfall in performing weights exercises for distances longer than sprint is performing too few repetitions, which tends to build muscle mass. Muscle mass causes bulk, which slows an individual over the distance. Instead you should work on muscular endurance, and therefore 15-plus repetitions. What this does is strengthen the cells on an individual level, meaning less cells/muscle fibres are needed for each stride, which in turn means less oxygen and less energy is needed per stride. All this means the runner is more efficient and so can run further and longer at a given speed.

Weight-training sessions should be performed one to three times per week, usually on non-running days, but sometimes within a running session (see the programmes in Chapter 9).

Bilateral training

Many runners are actually unbalanced in terms of their muscular strength. This is largely because we're all right- or left-handed and therefore right- or left-footed. If there's a step, we always step up on it with our favoured foot, thus strengthening it more than the unfavoured leg. Another possibility is that an old injury wasn't rehabbed properly, and has been run on despite being weaker for some time. This can have knock-on effects up the body, through the hips and into the core.

One way to avoid this is to ensure individual conditioning takes place for the legs and muscles. A perfect example of this is the Bulgarian split squat. As each leg is exercised separately the quadriceps and hamstrings of both legs are trained, but they're forced to work independently, ensuring that over time they're as strong as each other, therefore ensuring that the body is more equal left to right when running.

When starting a training programme you may notice that one leg is far stronger than the other (this is especially true when returning from injury). However, it's important not to increase the weight on the good leg but not the other – both must be increased at the rate of the weaker leg, thus giving it a chance to catch up with the stronger leg so that they can be exercised equally.

Exercise descriptions

For all of these exercises, select a weight that's comfortable but testing. Generally speaking, for strength gains perform 2–6 repetitions, for muscle growth perform 8–12 repetitions and for muscular endurance gains perform 15+ repetitions. Personally I'd advise mixing between all three dependent on your individual strengths, weaknesses and goals. For example, a marathon runner may need to gain some muscle growth due to wastage from long, draining runs, while a 5km runner may need to work on muscular endurance for that last 500m kick. Whatever your goal, conditioning and training is a must. Rest between sets should be kept to a minimum when performing endurance sessions and a little longer for muscular growth and strength. For endurance sessions I'd recommend anything between 30 seconds and a minute; for growth and strength two- to five-minute rests are advisable.

Leg exercises

A runner's legs are arguably their most important tool along with their heart and lungs. Without well-trained, hardened legs with great stamina and good endurance, running can become a very difficult hobby. As a runner, if no other conditioning/training is undertaken, leg training should at least be touched upon. The following exercises introduce a few ways to strengthen, tone and build the muscles of the legs to support running.

Step-ups

This exercise can also be done with or without weight. The basic premise is to have a step (around a foot high) in front of you. You step up with the right foot, then the left foot, down with the right foot and down with the left foot. This can be repeated a certain number of times or over and over for a set period. Always ensure the whole foot, not just half, is placed on the step. It's important to change the lead foot so they share the initial (harder) step-up equally – eg perform ten right foot first, then ten left foot, then back to right etc.

Works the quads, hamstrings and glutes.

Progressions

→ **Barbell**
As for squats/lunges. The exercise is performed with a bar across the shoulders.

→ **Dumbbells**
As for squats/lunges. The exercise is performed with dumbbells in the hands.

→ **Side step-ups**
The same exercise, but standing side-on. The lead foot must step on far enough to allow the other foot on as well. Remember to change sides. Any weighted variations could be used. The adductors (insides of the legs) are also worked during this exercise.

Squats

➡️ Squats can be performed as a bodyweight only exercise, or with weight added. The technique for both is basically the same.

Stand with the feet parallel, pointing forward, shoulder-width apart. Ensure the arms are out of the way so they don't start pushing on the tops of the thighs if the exercise becomes difficult.

To perform the squat, bend at the knee until the upper leg is parallel with the ground, ie the knee is at a 90° angle. While squatting it's imperative to keep the back straight and upright and not to bend forward. Furthermore it's important that as the knees bend they go forward over the big and second toes, and that the heels remain on the floor at all times. On the way up the back should remain tight and upright, the heels flat and the backside (glutes) squeezed. Once completely upright, repeat.

Works the quads, hamstrings, glutes and calf muscles.

Progressions

➡️ Barbell weight

The basic exercise is the same, but a barbell is placed across the back of the shoulders behind the neck, the hands gripping the bar either side of the head. Once you've mastered it the weight should nestle on the traps and won't cause discomfort, though a lot of people use padding at first or find they bruise slightly. It's even more important when using weight to ensure the back is kept upright, as if any forward leaning is allowed the balance can be lost. Again, ensure the heels remain on the ground.

➡️ Dumbbell squat

Similar to the barbell squat but with weights in the hands. More emphasis is placed on the quads. Keep the head up and looking forward. Squat as normal so the knee is about 90° before returning to the start position.

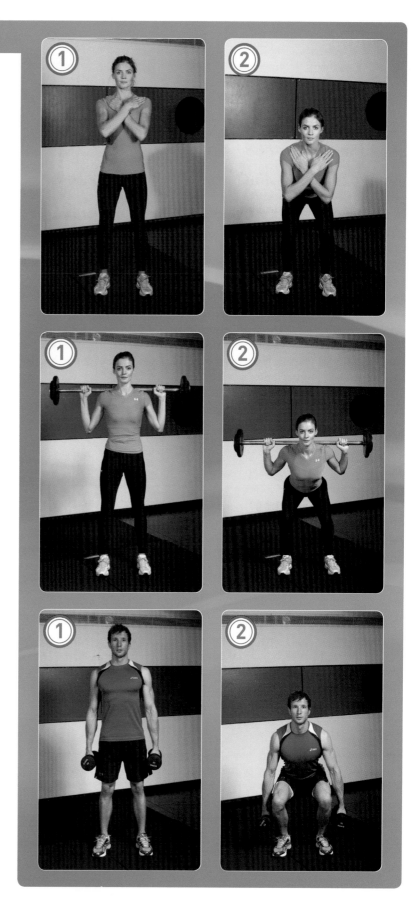

Lunges

➡️ Like the squat, the lunge can be performed with or without weight. Again, it's basically the same in either case.

Stand with feet parallel and pointing forwards just under shoulder-width apart. As with the squat it's important to keep the hands from supporting the legs, so the arms are crossed in front of the body. With one foot, say the right, take a large step forward, around shoulder-width and a half. Ensure both feet remain pointing forward as if on train tracks. With the right foot planted the right leg should be bent until its upper part is parallel with the ground and the left knee is just under an inch off the floor. The right knee shouldn't go further forward than the right foot; if it does then a longer step must be taken next time. It's important to keep the back straight and upright; don't lean forward. The right leg then powers the body upright by pushing off the floor and the right foot is retuned to its starting point next to the left. Repeat for the left leg.

Works the quads, hamstrings and glutes.

Progressions

➡️ **Barbell lunges**
With the barbell in the same position as for squats, the same exercise is performed, paying particular attention to staying upright and taking a long enough stride forward each time.

➡️ **Dumbbell lunges**
As per normal lunges but with dumbbells of equal weight in each hand, allowed to hang naturally at the sides of the body. It's important to stop the dumbbells swinging wildly. This exercise has some effect on the grip (forearms) and shoulders.

➡️ **Walking lunges**
These can be performed with or without a barbell or dumbbells. Start the exercise as normal, but instead of powering back to the start position off the right foot, the left foot steps forward to meet the right foot. The exercise is then performed on the left leg. In this manner a set amount of ground can be covered by 'walking lunges'.

Leg press

➡ A simple weights machine that mimics the squat action. Although it's effective it's not as good as the real squat exercise. Useful in a general muscular programme and especially good for building strength following an injury or long period of inactivity, as it requires less stabilising muscles than the squat.

Sit in the machine, ensure the knees are around 90°, select a sensible weight and press it through the heels. Control the weight and never just 'drop' it.

Leg extension

➡ An isolation exercise for the quads using a specific machine. Especially good following injury or to correct a muscle imbalance. Sit in the machine. Ensure the cushioned supports are correctly placed for your body. The padding you push against should be in the ankle/lower shin area not the foot, as this would cause injuries to the ankle ligaments.

Leg curl

➡ An isolation exercise for the hamstrings using a specific machine. Especially good following injury or to correct a muscle imbalance, which many people have in their hamstrings when compared to their quads. Lie in the machine, ensuring the supports are correctly placed for your body. The padding you push against should be at the bottom of the calf. A common mistake is to lift too much weight, so be careful, the hamstrings are easily pulled. Ensure a thorough warm-up prior to this exercise.

Leg curl with partner

→ A simple exercise that isolates the hamstring. The exerciser lies on the floor, face down. The partner kneels over the exerciser's lower legs, putting weight through the exerciser's calf muscles thus pinning them to the ground. The exerciser then contracts the hamstrings to pivot through the knees to lift the whole body upright. Beware – some people find this exercise very tough.

Standing calf raise

→ The calf raise involves going up on tiptoe from a position with the feet pointing forward just under shoulder-width apart. A momentary pause at the top is followed by a slow return to the start point. Some balance is required for this exercise.

Progressions

→ **Barbell calf raise**
As above but performed with a barbell on the shoulders as for the squat. Control must be maintained to ensure the weight doesn't cause the body to 'fall' forward.

Seated calf raise

→ While sat on the edge of a bench, a dumbbell is placed on the fleshy part of the end of the quad/knee of the leg to be exercised and the weight is 'lifted' by going on to tiptoe with the other foot. Pause at the top before slowly returning to the start point. Ensure both legs are exercised equally.

Bulgarian split squat

➡ Performed in a similar fashion to the lunge, but with the rear foot raised on a step/bench. Stand with feet parallel and pointing forwards just under shoulder-width apart. The arms are crossed in front of the body or down by the sides. Place one foot, say the left, on a bench, step or block behind you. Toes should be an inch from the edge nearest the body but no more. With the right foot planted the right leg should be bent until its upper part is parallel with the ground and the left knee is lowered to an inch off the floor. The right knee should not go further forward than the right foot; if it does, then a longer step must be taken next time. It's important to keep the back straight and upright; don't lean forward. The right leg then powers the body upright by pushing off the floor through the heel. Do a set number of reps and then repeat for the left leg.

Works the quads, hamstrings and glutes along with the core.

Progressions

→ **Barbell/dumbbell**
The barbell or dumbbell alternatives described above could be used.

Deadlift

➡️ A compound exercise that works the lower back, the glutes, adductors, hamstrings, quads, lats, traps and grip strength.

To perform a deadlift, place a barbell (light to start with) on the ground in front of you with the bar touching your shins. Take hold of it in both hands a little wider than shoulder-width apart, ensuring your hands/arms are placed outside your legs. Many people prefer a 'split grip' (ie one hand overgrasp, one hand undergrasp), but it's personal preference. Ensure thumbs are around the bar. Arms should be straight, head up, and chest up and out. It's important to look straight ahead with shoulders back to keep the back straight. Take a big breath and hold it to make the body/core/back solid and tight. Exhale as you complete the lift: the bar should be lifted in a slow, controlled manner. Pulling is done by extending legs and hips and pushing feet into the floor. Arms and back remain straight and the bar is kept close to body. At the top there should be a slight pause before holding your breath again and returning the bar to the floor under control, pushing the hips back.

NB Ensure the back is kept straight at all times! Always return the weight to a 'stop' on the floor before repeating. Do not bounce the weight.

Side hurdle steps

➡️ This exercise works the hip flexors above all else, which are the first muscles that tire for a sprinter; the knees drop and speed is lost. Hurdle steps improve the endurance of hip flexors and quads to ensure the knees can stay high for the entire race. To perform the exercise you require either a running hurdle or a piece of rope tied between two points at just below hip height. Stand side-on to the obstacle and step over sideways, ensuring the body doesn't twist and the knee remains high. Ensure both feet are on floor before returning over hurdle. Perform a set number of reps, ensuring form is kept.

Step-overs

➡️ Using a bench or sturdy box, one foot (say right) is stepped up on to the box as in step-ups. The other foot (left) is then stepped over, without touching the box, and on to the ground on the other side. Step the right foot to join it. Turn around and repeat, left foot first. Always step over in a controlled manner and don't just flop down as if you're tired. The step down is so controlled it's almost an eccentric lower. Works the quads, glutes and hamstrings.

Hamstring bridge

➡️ A hamstring and glute-specific exercise that requires no weights. Also helps work the core. To perform the exercise, lie on your back with feet flat on the floor and knees bent. Raise one leg into the air pointing the toe towards the ceiling. Drive the heel of the foot still in contact with the ground into the air, raising the hips until they're level with the knee and shoulder; pause slightly before returning the backside to the floor and repeating. Perform on one side then the other.

Fitball hamstring curl

➡️ The core, hamstring and knee and hip stabilisers all have to work during this exercise. Lie on your back and place the heel of one foot on a fitball/Swiss ball. Now lift the hips off the floor with the arms to stabilise the body, in a similar way to the hamstring bridge exercise. Use the raised foot to roll the ball in towards the backside. Hold for a split second, then roll the ball back out, ensuring the hips remain up and in line with the shoulders and knees. The shoulders and neck should remain relaxed.

Lower back exercises

The lower back is one of the most important and yet overly neglected areas to train, not only for runners, but in general. A strong lower back supports the strength in the legs and hamstrings and allows that strength to be transferred through the body. A weak lower back leads to a prematurely tired body when running, and more worrying, lower back pain after running, when at work or even when trying to sleep. Use these exercises to help strengthen your back for running and general day-to-day fitness.

Good morning

→ This involves placing a bar/barbell across the shoulders behind the neck. Stand with feet shoulder-width apart. Ensure legs are kept straight and back is straight and not rounded. While keeping the head facing forward, bend forward until upper body is parallel to the ground. Hold for a split second, then return to start position.

Progressions

→ **Dumbbells**
The same exercise but holding dumbbells instead of a barbell across the shoulders. Dumbbells have to be held, not rested. This is a harder exercise as the shoulders/arms must also work.

Dorsal raise

➡ Lie face down on the floor with fingertips on temples and shoulders relaxed. Lift the chest off the floor while keeping the lower body on it. Hold briefly, then gently lower to the floor, breathing out. Trains the muscles of the erector spinae of the lower back.

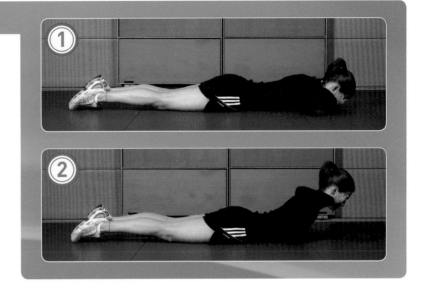

Superman dorsals

➡ Lie on your front with the legs straight and arms extended above the head. Lift one arm and the opposite leg a few inches and hold for a few seconds. Once complete, slowly lower back to the floor. Repeat for the opposite arm and leg.

Pelvic lifts/bridging

➡ Lie on your back with your knees bent and arms at your sides. Raise the pelvis towards the ceiling so the shoulders, hips and knees are in line. Hold the position for a few seconds, ensuring the glutes are squeezed while holding. Release the position and lower back to the floor. This exercises the lower back, abdominals, glutes and hamstrings. To progress the exercise try with arms across chest.

Torso/Abdominal exercises

Along with lower back exercises, torso or 'abs' exercises help stabilise the body and allow strength in the legs to be harnessed throughout the body. A strong 'core' helps support runners as although their legs are propelling them, their 'core' is keeping them upright and helping them breathe proficiently. Furthermore, the abs help protect the internal organs, aid posture and prevent against lower back injuries. Here are just a few suitable exercises.

The sit-up

→ While lying on your back with legs bent, feet together, knees together and fingertips on temples, sit up under control to a near vertical position so that the elbows can touch the tops of the knees. Ideally the feet should remain flat on the floor and the fingertips in touch with the temples. Don't be tempted to put the hands behind the head and pull up through the arms – this will injure the neck. Once vertical, open the arms to open the chest at the top position. Then lie back under control so that the head, shoulders and elbows are back in contact with the ground. Repeat the exercise, ensuring your form is correct.

The half-sit

→ If you find the regular sit-up difficult, try putting your hands on top of your thighs and sliding them up to touch the tops of your knees. This should gently lift the torso off the floor and start exercising the correct muscles to improve regular sit-ups. However, don't allow the body to 'flop' back down to the ground – this will injure the back. Lower under control, eccentrically.

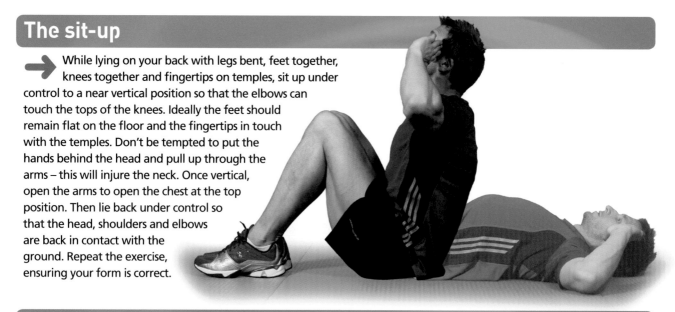

Sit-up progressions

→ **Weight across chest**
As for regular sit-up, but instead of placing fingers on the temples hold a weight placed on the chest under crossed arms. The abs have to work harder when sitting up.

→ **Weight outstretched**
As above but instead of holding the weight across the chest it's held in the air directly above the head. As the sit-up is performed the weight stays above the head, on the way up and the way down. It's important to keep it directly above the head and not allow it to come forward over the chest (which makes the exercise easier). This exercise has some effect on the shoulders depending on the weight held.

→ **On fitball**
As for normal sit-up, but instead of being done on the floor it's performed lying with the back on a fitball. Due to the instability of the ball the general core muscles and abs have to work harder to exercise and remain balanced.

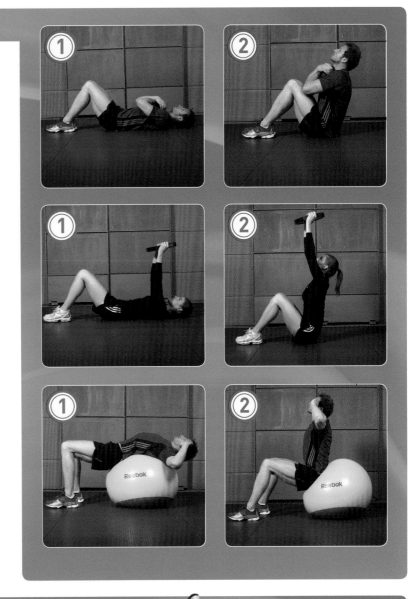

Reverse crunch

→ Lie on your back with hands flat on the floor, either by your side or just under your backside, to flatten the lower back. Keeping upper and mid back on the floor, bring the legs in towards the chest, sucking the abs in as you do so. The knees should be rocked towards the face, ensuring the hips/lower back are curled off the floor.

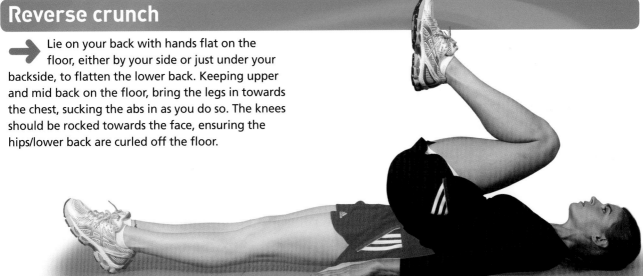

Straight leg hip extension

➡️ Lie on your back with your legs straight up at 90° to your body. Place the hands next to the body or just under the buttocks to flatten the lower back. Push up from the abdominals with your legs pointing straight up. Aim to force the toes as high as possible. Control down (don't flop) and repeat.

Flutter kicks

➡️ Lie on your back with your hands on the ground by your side or just under your buttocks to flatten the lower back. Raise your legs about 6in off the ground and perform 'flutter' kicks in the air as if you were lying on your back in water trying to propel yourself along (kick from the hip, not the knee). Keep the legs as straight as possible at all times and point the toes.

Fit ball rollouts

➡️ Place the forearms on to a fitball, with the body in a plank-like position. Tuck the pelvis under by contracting the abs (imagine sucking the bellybutton in towards the spine). Now roll the arms away from the body on the ball. This should make the abs, especially the lower ones, really work to support the body. To regress this movement, perform the exercise on the knees.

Sit-up feet fixed

→ As for the regular sit-up, but instead of trying to keep the feet on the floor they're trapped under a bar (can be purchased from sports shops to attach to door frames), under furniture or held by a friend or training partner. This makes the exercise much easier by recruiting the hip flexors (made up of 13 different muscles). Not so good for exercising the abdominals but excellent for improving the hip flexors, an important group of muscles for running.

Progressions

→ **Weight across chest**
Same exercise as above but with a weight held across the chest.

→ **Weight outstretched**
Same exercise but with a weight held above the head throughout.

Heel push

→ Instead of fixing the feet as above, the heels are used to pull against something put between them and the buttocks under bent legs. A small rucksack, a 20kg disc weight or even a football could be used. By using the heels to pull in against the object, the hamstring muscles are contracted. This means that the hip flexors must relax. By relaxing these the exercise becomes very abdominal-specific and is thus surprisingly difficult at first.

The plank

➡️ One of the most underused and underrated core exercises around, but so simple and with so many variations that a whole workout can be designed around it.

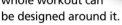

Despite its apparent simplicity it's actually relatively hard and commonly performed badly. Lie face down, keeping the feet and legs together, and raise the upper body by leaning on the forearms and elbows. The head should be kept up and not allowed to hang. Shoulders, hips, knees and ankles should be in line at all times; the waist/lower back particularly should not be allowed to sag or be raised into the air. Once the correct position has been achieved it should be maintained for a set period. Try 30 second to begin with, then increase a minute at a time. A five-minute plank is particularly impressive.

Progressions

➜ On hands
Instead of resting the weight on the elbows, the hands are used. Basically the fully extended press-up position is held.

➜ Feet raised
The normal plank is held, but a box/bench is used to raise the feet. Again the straight body position is imperative.

➜ One arm
The normal plank exercise but with only one forearm, elbow or hand in contact with the ground. The other arm should be placed behind the back.

➜ Arm lift
The normal plank is performed, but once the position is achieved the legs are raised alternately, completely straight, rotating from the hips. This works the glutes but also unbalances the plank and causes the core to work harder to readjust. This can be performed for a set time or a certain number of leg raises.

➜ On hands
As above, but instead of raising the legs the arms are raised. The feet are kept together on the floor. Again, raising the arms unbalances you and makes the core work harder.

➜ On fitball
Performing the plank with the feet or arms on a fitball greatly increases its difficulty. The instability of the ball means the core has to work really hard to maintain the plank position.

➜ Side plank
The body is turned to face one side or the other and the plank is performed on the forearm in contact with the ground, directly under the shoulder. It's important to keep shoulder, hip and knee in line and not allow the hips to sink to the floor.

Side bends

→ An oblique-specific exercise that involves standing up straight with feet shoulder-width apart, holding a dumbbell or other form of weight in one hand. Imagine the body is between two panes of glass so can't bend forwards or backwards. Bend sideways to lower the hand holding the weight until it's in line with your knee, then lean all the way over to the other side to touch opposite knee with your free hand. Repeat a certain number of times. Ensure you perform the same number on the other side.

Progressions

→ **Double weight side bends**
The same exercise as above, but with a dumbbell or equivalent in both hands.

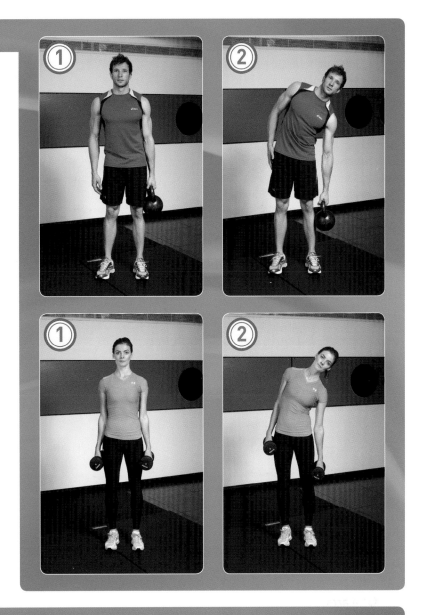

Saxon side bends

→ Still imagining yourself between two panes of glass, a weight is held above the head with straight arms. A bit like a tree swaying in the wind the body pivots at the waist to the side, then back to the centre, then to the other side and centre. A small weight is best to start with, as this is quite a challenge.

Tyre/object drag

➡ Perhaps more for sprinters, but would develop extra power for whatever distance you run. Using a climbing harness, chest harness or simply by tying a piece of rope round the waist, attach an object like a tyre to the other end. Select a certain distance or certain time and pull the object for that time/distance as quickly as possible. This exercise is best performed on grass or sand but can be performed on concrete if necessary.

Skipping

➡ Normal skipping with a skipping rope for a set time or number of jumps. If you've never skipped before you may find it difficult to skip without mistakes at first, but with a bit of perseverance it will soon become natural. The great thing about skipping is a skipping rope doesn't take up much room, and skipping can be done almost anywhere.

Dumbbell swing

➡ Place the weight between the legs with handle parallel to the shoulders. Squat down and take hold of the handle, keeping the back straight and head up. Perform a powerful squat, paying particular attention to driving the hips forward (a hipthrust) and squeezing the glutes together. In doing this momentum allows the weight to come up to around eye level by rotating through the shoulders. As the weight starts to drop through gravity bend the legs into the squat position again, and as it comes between the legs drive up again and thrust the hips forward. Do a certain number of reps or for a set time.

Box jumps

➜ Great for developing power. With a box one to two feet high in front of you, stand facing it with your feet shoulder-width apart. From a standing start jump up on the box. Step/jump down carefully and repeat a set number of times as quickly but controlled as possible.

Wood chops

➜ Usually performed holding a light weight, though it can be done without. Holding the weight/arms out in front at about eye/chest level, bend the legs and rotate the torso to one side and lower the weight to the floor at the outside of the foot on that side. In an explosive movement, rotate the torso back and bring the weight back to the centre and beyond, up to the highest point of the opposite side (as if diagonal from the floor/foot on the other side). Once the weight/arms are at the high point, repeat the exercise as quickly as possible, but still controlled. Ensure both sides are exercised equally.

Cable wood chops

➜ Using a cable machine, select a relatively light weight. Take the cable handle in the hand closest to the machine and step out, taking up the tension. Allow your opposite arm to come across the body and take hold over the top of the other hand. Keeping your arms at arms' length, take them across the body to the far side without turning the hips at all: they should remain forward at all times. Hold for a split second, then return to start. Repeat for desired reps and change sides.

Running backwards

Running backwards has gained momentum in recent years, not only as a rehab tool for certain injuries (jumper's knee) but as a form of fitness and in particular a form of conditioning for the leg muscles. Backwards running is classed as a 'retro movement', which means the reverse of any normal movement.

Running backwards initially feels very unnatural, but with practice a decent speed can be achieved. It's worth starting out with backward walking, and then move into very slow backward jogging. It's also worth doing only a short stint initially, say 3–5 minutes, then 8 or 10 minutes and before long 20 minutes, 30 minutes and beyond. Personally I'd advise running backwards only on treadmills until you achieve a degree of proficiency, then perhaps on grass. Running up and down hills backwards definitely adds difficulty, but is also relatively dangerous.

Downhill

Running backwards downhill is dangerous, full stop. Before doing it make sure you're very confident at running backwards on a treadmill or on grass. It's very easy to pick up speed when running backwards downhill, but don't be tempted to do so quicker than you're ready to. If you do fall, try to absorb any impact with your arms and your backside so that your head is less likely to hit. Proficient backwards runners also advise learning to roll out using a backwards roll.

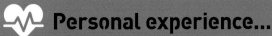

Personal experience...

I first encountered running backwards while in the Marines, when I suffered from quite a bad tear to my patella tendon. As I'd put up with the injury for around nine months it was going to take the same sort of time to heal. Part of my rehab, before I could run forwards again, was running backwards, the theory being that there's far less impact than running forwards, added to which backward running is almost an eccentric movement, which is what's necessary to help heal a tendinopathy (be it patella, Achilles or biceps).

Uphill

Compared to running backwards downhill, running uphill isn't very dangerous. It's difficult to run quickly when running backwards and doing so uphill makes it even more so, meaning it will always be at a lower speed. Again, if you do fall try to stop your head hitting the ground using your arms and backside.

Physical benefits

Research suggests that running backwards helps balance out some of the stresses and strains that can occur during normal running. It's thought to work the tissues oppositely. In backwards running the heel is used to push off rather than the ball of the foot. Pushing off in this way works the tibialis anterior muscle (which gets little work in normal running) as well as the ball of the foot, which is good for prehabbing for barefoot running.

The main benefit of backwards running is that the muscles are used in the opposite way to how they are in forward running, ie an eccentric version of a concentric movement is performed instead of a concentric version of an eccentric movement (hence my being asked to run backwards when rehabbing my patella tendinitis, usually rehabbed using eccentric lowering). Whether for rehab or for general fitness training, both concentric and eccentric movements have advantages, hence backwards running could be included.

Other advantages include gains in balance, and enjoyment from doing something different and challenging. Lastly, due to the constant need to look behind more neck mobility is learned than in forward running. Although this can initially stress the neck muscles, in the long term it can lead to adaptations in them and a less rigid style when running forwards.

Prehab

The term prehab refers to an exercise programme performed to prevent injury, whereas rehab or rehabilitation is performed following injury to ensure full recovery and a swift return to fitness. In general a prehab programme will have one or both of two elements:

→ Sports-specific focussed exercises and activities for your running needs, to specifically avoid injuries that tend to plague runners.

→ Personal exercises to either prevent the return of an old injury, or prevent you from suffering an injury you're likely to be prone to from your current running gait (overpronation, for example).

The philosophy of prehab is simply to prevent injuries, but its success depends on people performing the exercises. The major obstacle to this is that compared to a good run, prehab can be boring and uninspiring.

The sports therapy world suggests that you include a prehab programme in your training, and the more advanced you become as a runner the more necessary it becomes. The thought process behind this is that as we undertake our daily training regimes we can cause negative effects within our bodies, such as tight muscles and strength imbalances. Imbalances can occur naturally with any activity but can be reinforced with each workout, and it's such imbalances that are usually to blame for injuries.

Prehab programme

A good prehab running programme should aid total body balance and provide sports-specific exercises to strengthen areas needed for running. Balances should include range of motion, strength, coordination and stabilisation. For runners, much of the focus of prehab exercises will be on coordination and stabilisation of the legs, knees, hips and core. Core instability is common in runners but is mainly due to a lack of education and understanding. Simply performing upper and lower body weights and running routines leaves the core without a direct focus or training routine, and can predispose us to injuries from a weak core.

When to prehab

Prehab can be done one of two ways: as part of a workout or as an independent session.

If performed as part of a workout, simply perform a few prehab exercises as part of the warm-up or cool-down. Personally I prefer doing so in the warm-up, especially if the session is going to be hard, as afterwards fatigue may prevent good quality exercises. If doing prehab as a separate session it's usually relatively low tempo, so can be used as rest days.

Basic running prehab programme

A full runners' prehab programme will be between 8 and 12 exercises and 2–3 sets of each as a circuit, the idea being to work the entire body and also keep the heart rate relatively high. Aim for 12–15 reps of each exercise to work on muscular endurance rather than strength. A good prehab circuit should only last around 30 minutes.

 ## Side lunges

➡ Performed to provide some lateral movement, as running only involves forward movement.

 ## Dumbbell run

➡ It's important to include full body exercises to encourage the body's left and right sides and upper and lower parts to work together rather than independently.

3 Lunge with arm drive

Once again to improve full body movement and coordination.

4 Bulgarian split squat

A great exercise for ankle stabilisation and to improve balance while working the major muscles of the leg.

5 One-leg squat with toe touch

Another great stabiliser and balance exercise, but even better for the hip and ankle stabilising muscles.

Squat jumps

Including plyometrics exercises develops power, and jumping exercises are perfect for this.

 Oblique twists

Performed to provide some rotational movement as this too is often lacking in running, yet a strong core is paramount.

 Conclusion

Prehab and general conditioning for running or weight loss are unfortunately what most people neglect when they start exercising, their thought process being the more running you do the better runner you'll be or the more weight you'll lose. Sadly this is wrong. Weight training and conditioning helps avoid injury, builds a strong healthy body and tones muscles to burn more calories when sleeping, working and resting. Simple.

Core stability exercises

→ With all core exercises you need to obtain neutral spine first. To do this, make sure the pelvis is level with the floor (ie the front isn't raised too high and the back isn't dropped too low), then suck the abs in 100%, trying to bring the belly button in to the spine. Squeeze the backside 100% as well. Now release both to around 50%. This should feel like you could protect yourself from a punch in the stomach. You should adopt this neutral position for all abs/core and, in some schools of thought, any conditioning at all.

→ **Basic core exercises work the hips, abs and lower back**

With all these exercises, imagine you have a plank of wood coming out of the hips that's parallel with the floor. On the ends of this plank are cups of water full to the brim: you can't spill a drop, so as you perform the exercises keep the core tight and don't let the hips wobble.

1 Sat on fitball foot raise

2 Sat on fitball leg raise

3 Lie on fitball leg raise

4 Fitball kneeling

5 Fitball standing

6 Fitball rollouts

Even if you follow all these exercises three times a week, you may still get an injury from running, but they'll certainly help you avoid injury and may well lead to quicker recovery, as the muscles will already be conditioned.

CHAPTER 12
RUNNING A MARATHON

It seems strange that the epitome of athletics is the 100m sprint, and yet the epitome of recreational running is the marathon — the two couldn't be further apart. For a large percentage of recreational runners, whatever their reason for starting, the marathon ends up being their goal, despite the fact that only around 10% of them will complete one. Just look at the 20,000 plus people who finish the London marathon each year of the 30,000 places on offer.

The basics

A marathon is a 26.2-mile run (official distance 42.195km or 26 miles and 385 yards). It got its name from the legend of Pheidippides, a Greek messenger said to have been sent to Athens from the battlefield of Marathon to announce the Greek victory over the Persians. This event apparently took place in September 490 BC. The story goes that he made the run without stopping once, before shouting 'We have won!' as he arrived and collapsing dead from his efforts. There are some different accounts of the legend, particularly that Pheidippides actually ran from Sparta to Athens, but none of them make any difference – the fact is that thanks to his extraordinary achievement we now have 26.2-mile runs all over the world.

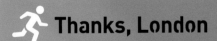 **Thanks, London**

It's thanks to the London marathon of 1908 that we have the distance as it now stands. The race was planned to be 26 miles exactly, starting in Windsor Castle and finishing at White City Stadium. King Edward VII was due to start the race, but due to falling ill was advised not to leave the courtyard of Windsor Castle, and the start was moved accordingly. This added 385 yards to the race, meaning it was run over 26.218 miles. In 1909 another marathon was run in London and used the same course, and despite not being an Olympic event it soon became an annual celebration. When in 1924 the IAAF (International Association of Athletics Federation) settled upon this distance as the standard for marathons it was rounded up to 26.22 miles.

→ Marathon distances

These days marathons are huge events and big business. There are over 500 marathons contested throughout the world each year, many of which have as many competitors as the London one. Although each of them is 26.2 miles, originally – as far back as 1896 and the original Olympic games – the exact length of the event varied depending on the route established for each venue, so the marathons of the first few Olympic Games weren't of a set length. Most were around 40km (25 miles), roughly the distance from Marathon to Athens by the longer, flatter route. Between 1896–1924 the marathon changed, with the longest (in 1920) being 42.75km. However, in 1924 the distance still used today was set.

The wall

U nlike 5km or 10km runs, where there's no 'wall' to be hit, in longer endurance events such as half-marathons, marathons and beyond there certainly is. The term 'the wall' is synonymous with the marathon, and for a very good reason: because so many runners (around 60%, it's thought) experience such fatigue around the 20-mile mark that it's like running into one. Simply put, your body has no energy, your glycogen stores are depleted and your muscles are failing to move your legs.

For most people glycogen stores last around 20 miles, but at that point, instead of using glycogen for 75% of its fuel and fat for the rest, the body is left with only fat to use, and fat's not an efficient fuel compared to glycogen. For a start more oxygen is required to burn it (great, its not like you're running a marathon or anything), and it also burns far less easily, so energy isn't released as fast; and as if that's not enough, burning fat requires a little glycogen as a catalyst, and without it the fat just can't burn – hence the wall.

Avoiding the wall

The best ways to avoid the wall are to improve your glycogen storing capacity, so that hopefully you won't hit the wall at mile 20 (it would happen around mile 28, when you've finished); or take on carbohydrate in the early miles to ensure you've replenished your glycogen stores on the way round.

Both of these are simply achievable. To increase glycogen storage capacity, perform long runs as part of your marathon training programme. It really is true that putting in the miles beforehand makes the whole process a lot easier. Runs of 14 miles plus will help increase your glycogen storage threshold if performed over three to six months before the big run.

To increase the amount of glycogen in your muscles on the day, a careful plan of eating and drinking should be followed. Basically, carb-loading the day/night before and ensuring you take on sugars during the run will make a huge difference. Many veteran marathon runners also run the first few miles a little slower than the rest of the event. They do this to conserve glycogen stores for around the 20-mile mark, when they'll be needed to avoid the wall. It's far better to run slow for the first few miles then increase to your normal pace than to run too fast and drop back to your normal pace. Don't be caught up in the hype of the day; run at your practised pace.

 Personal experience...

I hit the wall on a particular military course. I'd been running up and down the Brecon Beacons for 13 hours non-stop and had four to five hours to go. I'd just descended and ascended a stretch of steep terrain and on arriving at the top I felt drained. I ate two Snickers bars and a flapjack bar but was still failing to become energised enough to go on. Once the fuel kicked in, however, the body started working again. But it's a funny feeling when your body just can't seem to move you.

Depleting glycogen stores can be dangerous, as eventually it will affect the blood glucose that's usually only for the brain. When this happens dizziness and passing out are common. Keep fuelled and you'll avoid this.

Carbohydrate loading is accompanied by excess water retention, so you'll feel bloated. This is natural and will come in useful during your sweaty Marathon.

Carb loading

Developed in the 1960s by Swedish sports physiologist Gunvar Ahlborg, carb loading has been the talk of endurance athletes for decades. Everyone seems to have a different way of doing it, and this is partly because things have changed from what Gunvar originally thought. He suggested that a long run (an hour or so) is undertaken a week ahead of the big day: this depletes glycogen stores. Over the subsequent three days you eat 60% carbs and exercise lightly, and the next three days, leading up to the race, you eat 75% carbs, with reduced fat and proteins to ensure overall calories are equal. Cease all training and rest for the big day. However, it's now thought that the same loading can be achieved without the depletion, though many runners still follow the depletion regime as it fits with their training programme.

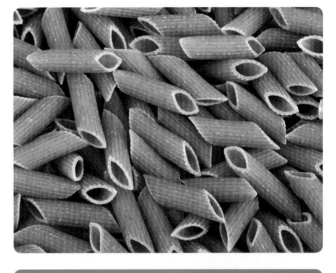

♥ Personal experience...

On military cross-country courses I'd put old camera film cases in my rucksack filled with SIS Go, a simple carb and electrolyte-rich energy drink. I'd add these to water and drink them every hour or so. This not only gave me the extra fuel I needed, I believe it kept cramp at bay too.

I don't expect everyone to carry a rucksack with sports drinks and powders, but don't be afraid to eat and drink during your run. In the big marathons spectators often have chocolates, sweets and, if you're lucky, bananas to give out. After the first hour or so, start taking these. Try to eat every 30 minutes and drink at least every 15 (dehydration alone can bring on the wall, as thicker blood requires more energy to move it around the body). I guarantee it'll make your life a lot more pleasant a few hours later.

Running overseas

Running abroad is slightly different to running at home and you should be aware of a few specifics and tips. Firstly, if the climate is going to be vastly different arrive as early as possible and acclimatise beforehand. If this is impossible, then spend some time in the sauna/steam room and perform a few training runs in extra layers to get your body more used to the heat.

While taking part in a Navy Aquathlon in South Korea I was lucky enough to learn a valuable lesson from an American competitor whose luggage had gone missing: always pack your essential race gear in your carry-on luggage. Your trainers and perhaps your heart rate monitor and watch are the main ones. Socks, shorts and T-shirts can usually be replaced. Apparently a sports bra *should* be carried if possible as they aren't necessarily easy to replace.

If flying to your race, ensure you drink plenty of water on the flight and try to avoid alcohol – it won't help you on race day. Equally, try to sleep on the plane, and when you arrive try to get used to the local time difference ASAP. If you don't have time to do that, try to get used to that time zone before you travel.

If eating in the local area, be careful: food poisoning would not be a good thing before the big race. My advice is to eat in places the race organisers have recommended (many do in race literature) or hit a supermarket and sort for yourself. Speaking of the local area, walk or jog around it to get an idea of your surroundings: a sports shop may be handy, as well as a sports masseuse. Equally, practice the route to the race so that you know how to get there and how long it takes – then give yourself longer on the day. Having said all that, ensure you don't tire yourself out before the race. Take it easy and rest up. Leave the tourist sites until after the little 26-mile jog you've got planned.

Training

There's a marathon training programme in Chapter 9. However, the following may also be of help.

Working out your pace

To get a rough idea of your pace ability for the marathon, divide your –

5km minutes per km pace by 0.85

or

10km minutes per km pace by 0.88

or

half-marathon minutes per km pace by 0.95

– then multiply the answer by 42.2 and divide the result by 26.2. This gives you a rough idea of your pace. (To convert miles to kilometres multiply by 1.609.)

⏱ Conclusion

A Marathon is a big undertaking. It isn't easy and isn't suited to everyone. Having said that, barring medical problems or injury it's achievable by anyone. My biggest piece of advice is do the training, and start it early – it will make the whole process easier. Lastly, be careful. Once you've done a marathon you'll be one of two kinds of people: those who'll never do it again and those who want to do every major marathon in the world. You have been warned!

🏃 A few top tips

1 If you're not an experienced runner or someone who's been involved in fitness for many years, going straight into a marathon training programme isn't a good idea. Instead, get a few 10km races and half-marathons under your belt first – that's why half-marathons are there. If you're running half-marathons you could be up to marathon standard in three months, otherwise allow yourself six months.

2 Not all marathons are the same – heat, climate, elevation, terrain and weather all make a difference. Chicago and London have the world record-breaker statistics, so stick to them first!

3 As Marathon training increases, the long hours and many miles start to take their toll on the body's joints. To protect the ankles, knees and hips when the muscles really start to tire, ensure you have the best shock-absorbing trainers and replace them regularly.

4 On race day, don't be tempted to try to get the first few miles done quickly so they're in the bag. By pushing on too quickly at the start you'll deplete glycogen stores early and cause issues like the wall later. Run at the pace you trained at.

CHAPTER 13
SPRINTING

Due to the fact that sprinting is so different from other forms of running, it seemed sensible to devote a whole chapter to it rather than inserting bits and pieces throughout the book. This does not mean you cannot perform long distance/middle distance running and sprint training at the same time. Many competitive runners will tell you what a difference a quick finish/strong sprint finish makes.

Basic sprint technique

The following should be learned, trained and mastered for a good basic sprint technique:

- Eyes focused at the end of the lane.
- Head in line with the spine and held high.
- Face relaxed, no tension, mouth relaxed.
- Chin down but not jutted out.
- Shoulders down and relaxed.
- Back straight (not hunched).
- Abdominals tense but not sucked in like neutral spine.
- Arms move in a smooth forward and backward action up and down, but not across the body. The hands should move from hip to lip.
- Elbows held at 90° at all times (angle between upper arm and lower arm).
- Hands relaxed with fingers loosely curled and thumb upwards.

Perfect technique in phases

For a professional sprinter, the actual race is broken down into five phases. We'll use the 100m as the example sprint:

1 The start – approx 15m.
2 Acceleration phase – approx 15–20m.
3 Transition phase – approx 20–40m.
4 Maximum velocity – approx 40–80m.
5 Speed maintenance – 80–100m.

A professional runner will work on each of these phases very specifically, and if this is something you're interested in there are lots of books out there on sprint coaching. However, for this book we're going to split the sprint into three phases.

Phase 1
The start

1 The bodyweight is evenly distributed over the four points of contact in the start position (hands and knees).
2 Front knee angle is around 90°, rear knee angle is around 100–130°.
3 Both legs drive away explosively.
4 The front leg extends, driving into the ground but remaining in contact with the ground.
5 Rear leg swings forward as the now extended front leg and body form a straight line.
6 Arms swing opposite to legs, with elbows at 90° and hands swinging from hip to lip.

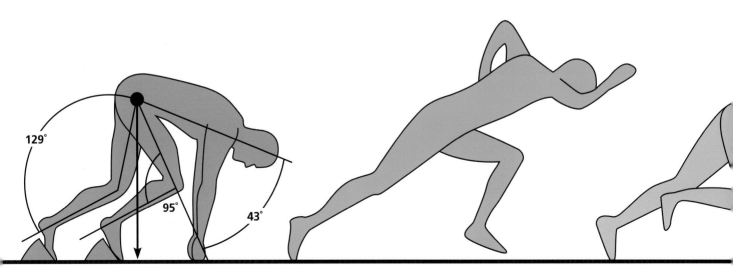

Phase 2
Acceleration

1   After the first two strides, the foot touches down in front of centre of gravity.
2   The forward body slant/lean from the start position decreases until normal sprinting position is reached after about 20m distance.
3   Head is relaxed, with eyes focused straight ahead.

Phase 3
Race speed

1   The body is almost straight, just a 5° forward lean for momentum.
2   The leg striking the ground folds quickly and tightly into the glutes in a relaxed heels to backside motion.

3   The front leg powers forward and upward at maximum speed. When the front thigh reaches maximum knee lift, the lower leg swings forward in a relaxed movement.
4   The foot meets ground directly under the body's centre of gravity with slight plantar flexion (ankle extension).
5   Only the ball of the foot touches the ground (as in forefoot running).
6   Shoulders remain relaxed and torso does not twist.
7   Elbows are still at 90° and kept close to the body.
8   Hands continue to swing hip to lip with an explosive and aggressive hammering action.
9   Head is in line with the body and shoulders and facial/neck muscles remain relaxed by keeping the mouth slightly open.
10 Do not slow down at the finish line – burst through it as if the race finished 10m beyond.

Sprint technique drills

The following drills are designed to make a sprinter a better runner in terms of technique and stimulate the correct muscles to work in the most efficient way. Combined, this should make him/her faster. The drills can be used as part of stand-alone sessions or incorporated into the warm-up to stimulate the appropriate neuromuscular action for the range of movement and correct posture of the race ahead. Unless stated otherwise, sprint drills should be conducted wearing trainers, not spikes.

High knee raises

10m – jog – 10m – rest

➡ Sprint 10m concentrating on raising knees up to your waistband and arms hip to lip. Jog for 10m, repeat drill for 10m and then rest.

Fast knee pickups

10m – jog – 10m – rest

➡ Run on the spot with high knee-raise to waist height. Hip to lip with the arms and concentrate on the power generation from this. Now continue the action but move forward 10m, concentrating on the number of ground contacts with the feet rather than how fast you cover the distance. Try to get as many ground contacts as possible.

Skipping

20m medium pace — jog

— 20m fast pace — rest

➡ Skip as you did as a child for 20m at a steady pace, jog for 10m, then skip again as fast as possible.

Bounds

3 x 20m

➡ In a similar manner to skipping, but trying to gain as much elevation as possible, bound from one foot to the other. After 20m turn around and walk back to recover fully between attempts.

Elbow drive

On the spot

➡ Stand on the spot and concentrate on driving your elbow in a straight line. Keep your elbows flexed at 90° while keeping your arms relaxed. If necessary have someone stand behind you with their palms as targets and swing your elbows back to hit them. Again, hands go from hip to lip.

General sprint conditioning drills

The following pages show a few drills used by sprinters to mobilise the legs, joints and muscles prior to, after or on non-training days. The drills are not particularly challenging in terms of fitness, so are therefore a very good addition to a sprint warm-up. As sprinting is so dynamic, it is often very easy to pull or tear a muscle. This is even more likely when training outside in the colder months so it's important to use these as part of a warm-up.

Walking on toes

Two repetitions over 20m

→ Develops balance and strengthens lower leg muscles (reduce shin splints). Walk on the balls of the feet – free leg to be lifted so that thigh is parallel with the ground, lower leg vertical and the toes dorsiflexed (pulled up to the shin). Holding the end position for a second or two develops balance and makes drill more challenging.

Walking on heels

Two repetitions over 20m

→ Develops balance and strengthens the lower leg muscles (reduce shin splints). Walk on the heels of the feet – free leg to be lifted so that thigh is parallel with the ground, lower leg vertical and the toes dorsiflexed (pulled up to the shin). Holding the end position for a second or two develops balance and makes drill more challenging.

Leg drives

20 seconds each leg

➡ Develops hip flexor strength and speed. Stand facing a wall or a partner with your hands at chest height. Position your feet so that the body is straight and at 45° to the wall. Ensure neck stays in line with spine. Bring one leg up so thigh is parallel with the ground, lower leg vertical and toes dorsiflexed, then drive the foot down towards the ground. As the toes make contact, quickly pull the foot up and return the leg to its starting position, repeat for set time.

Leg cycling

20 seconds on, 10 seconds off, for 4 minutes

➡ Develops the correct leg sprint action and strengthens the hamstring muscles. Stand next to a wall, rail or partner and hold to maintain balance. Stand tall, tense the abdominals. Lift the thigh of the other leg so it's parallel with the ground, the lower leg vertical and toes dorsiflexed. Sweep the leg down and under your body, pull the heel up into the buttocks, cycle the leg though to the front, pull toes up, bring upper thigh through to be parallel with the ground, extend the lower leg and straight into the next cycle. This is also a great warm-up exercise.

Plyometric drills

Plyometrics is a technique that uses the stored elastic energy of a muscle to make the contraction more powerful. Using running as an example, the strong muscles in the upper leg are slightly stretched prior to contracting to drive the body forward. As the muscles are stretched, elastic energy is stored within them. When the muscles contract this elastic energy is released, which makes the contraction that much more powerful.

Surprisingly, this extra power doesn't take up much extra energy; in fact it provides more power without any extra effort, and this principle is the same whenever a muscle is stretched prior to a contraction. Any training method that applies this principle is known as plyometrics.

The key feature of plyometric training is the combined training of the nervous and muscular systems to allow faster and more powerful changes of direction. With training it's possible to reduce the time needed to make these changes in direction, which in turn means speed and power are increased. It's because of this ability to improve speed and power that this type of training is so beneficial for sprinters.

Plyometric training uses a series of exercises, repeated one after another, to increase this speed and power. Exercise examples are bounds, hops, jumps, leaps and skips. The downside of plyometrics is the incredible strain that's put on the muscles and joints. A good warm-up is therefore imperative. Furthermore, for beginners it's worth starting slowly rather than jumping straight into the more advanced exercises. Additionally, starting on grass or using gym mats is a good idea until the muscles, joints, tendons and ligaments have had time to make initial adaptations.

Jump to higher level

1 Find a higher level or sturdy box about one foot to one metre high.
2 Stand in front of the box or higher level and jump up two-footed.
3 Land softly on both feet.
4 Step back down (don't jump) and repeat.

Progressions

→ **Lateral jump to higher level**
Same as above but stand sideways on to the box or higher level (not facing it). Jump up and to the side on to box. Step down and repeat. Ensure you train both sides equally.

Initially pick three or maybe four different plyometric exercises and do three sets of six repetitions of each, increase this to three sets of eight repetitions, then three sets of ten repetitions. Then up the repetitions to twelve, or add another set of ten or another exercise.

Two-footed low hurdle jumps

➡️ Set out some low hurdles, cones or even six to eight jumpers in a row with about a foot between each. Jump two-footed over each hurdle. Repeat.

Progressions

➡ **One-legged same leg bounds**
As above but one-footed.

One-legged alternate leg bounds

➡️ As above, but switch legs between each hurdle. So take off right, land left, take of the left, land right, etc.

Lateral two-footed hurdle bounds

➡️ As above, but stand side on. Bound sideways over hurdle on both feet, and repeat. Try not to pause between hurdles.

Drop/depth jumping

1 Stand on a higher level, eg a sturdy box.
2 Start off at 1ft height and increase over time.
3 Drop (don't jump) off the higher level. Absorb the impact but jump up in the air as soon as you hit the ground.
4 Land safely on the floor.
5 Step back on to the box and repeat.

Drop jumps, jump over

➡ As above but instead of jumping into the air after landing, jump over a hurdle or second box.

Two-footed tuck jumps

1 Jump straight up in the air as high as possible, bringing knees up to chest.
2 Land on balls of feet and repeat immediately.
3 Try to reduce ground contact time by landing softly and springing back up straight away.

Lunge jumps

1 Stand with one leg around 2ft further back than the other, standing on the ball of back foot.
2 Keep head up and back straight.
3 Perform a further lunge into the movement by bending at right hip and knee until thigh is parallel to floor, then immediately explode vertically into the air.
4 Switch feet in the air so that the back foot lands forward and front foot lands further back in mirror image of start position. Land softly.
5 Exercise both legs equally.

Lateral push-ups

1 Start sideways on to a box or higher level with nearer hand on top of the box and your further hand on the floor.
2 Using both hands on the box to drive upwards, move vertically as high as possible.
3 Land on the opposite side on the box, with opposite hand on top of box and other hand on the floor.
4 Repeat to come back to original position.
5 Exercise both sides equally.
6 This can also be done with the legs. One foot on the box and one foot on the floor.

Chest pass

1 Stand approximately 2m from a wall, facing it. Hold a light medicine ball (2–5kg) between your hands.
2 With back straight and knees relaxed, brace abdominals and push ball powerfully away against the wall.
3 Meet the rebound with bent arms and hands ready to immediately push the ball back (don't catch then push back).
4 Perform for set reps or time (20–30seconds).

Weights for sprinters

The kind of weights performed by sprinters need to be quite different from the conditioning and prehab for middle- and long-distance runners. Where muscular endurance was key there, here we need power and strength. Hence a lot of Olympic-style lifts are used, concentrating on proper technique, absolute quickness and power. Generally three to five sets of three to eight reps.

Bench press

Laying face upwards on a bench, a weighted barbell is taken from straight arms (above the chest) to bent arms, just touching the chest, before being returned to the start position. A compound exercise that also involves the triceps and the front deltoids, and recruits the upper back muscles and traps. It's important not to 'bounce' the weight off the chest. Breathe out hard on pushing up and try to be explosive.

Dumbbell chest press

Very similar to bench press, but instead of a barbell two dumbbells are used. The exercise is performed in the same way, but due to the instability of two dumbbells it's good for the supporting muscles of the shoulders. Breathe out hard on pushing up and try to be explosive.

Shoulder press

➡️ Can be performed seated or standing using a barbell or two dumbbells. The weight is held above the head and lowered to just above the shoulders, then raised again. A compound exercise that also involves the trapezius and the triceps. Breathe out hard on pushing up and try to be explosive.

Push press

➡️ Similar to shoulder press but with a larger weight that's too heavy for the shoulders to lift on their own. Therefore a small squat is performed first and exploded upwards, giving momentum to the shoulders.

Biceps curl

➡️ An isolation exercise for the biceps. Simply hold a barbell in two hands or a dumbbell in each hand and curl up to the shoulder using the biceps. Hold for a split second and lower under control.

Triceps extensions

➡ An isolation exercise for the triceps. Using a cable machine, pull the rope at shoulder height down to waist height using the triceps. Hold for a split second and control up.

Shrugs

➡ Hold a barbell with your palms facing inwards, about shoulder-width apart, with your feet also about shoulder-width apart. Ensure arms are fully extended. It's easy to injure the back if this exercise is performed badly, so ensure the core and lower back are controlled. Shrug shoulders as high as possible towards the ears, thus lifting the weight up. Pause briefly, then lower bar back into starting position. This exercises the traps, deltoids and upper back.

Bent-over row

➡ This exercise is performed while leaning over, holding a barbell in both hands. The bar is pulled up into the lower chest/abdomen. It's a compound exercise that also involves the biceps, forearms, traps and rear deltoids. It's very important to fix the back and keep the core tight. The back should be straight, not curved. Some people find this position difficult to maintain so you should be very careful, as it's easy to injure your back if you have bad posture. For this reason some heavy lifters wear lifting belts to help support the lower back.

Additional exercises

Whole body
- Snatch
- Power clean

Both these exercises are very technical and not something to learn from a book or the Internet. Consequently I'm not going to describe them here. If you wish to learn them, go to a gym or athletics club and get qualified coaching.

Legs
- Squat
- Lunges (see Chapter 11)
- Leg curls (see Chapter 11)
- Seated calf raise (see Chapter 11)

Core
- Ab exercises varied
- Straight-legged dead lift (see Chapter 11)
- Good mornings (see Chapter 11)

○ Conclusion

A whirlwind tour of the world of sprinting. If only Usain Bolt's records were that easy! Most sprinters train three times a day when they train – all for around ten seconds' work on race day. There are numerous books on sprinting that cover the subject in detail, but hopefully this chapter has provided a sound starting point if this is where your interest lies.

CHAPTER 14
WOMEN & RUNNING

Competitive women's running is actually a relatively new addition to the Olympics (less than 50 years) and the fitness world in general. However, with running being so easy to take up it's become one of the fastest growing hobbies for women in their 20s and 30s. Added to which, unlike many other sporting hobbies, running is something couples can share, whether as a long continuous heart-rate run in tandem or interval sessions with one resting while the other works.

Women are a little different!

Research has shown that female athletes (not just runners, but from many sports) are twice as likely to suffer from lateral knee damage and kneecap damage, and that female runners are three times more likely to suffer injury to their glutes and, astonishingly, around ten times more likely to report lower back injuries than men. It's believed to be their very different body shapes and leg and feet structures, leading to sometimes very different running patterns, that have caused these higher injury rates.

→ Biomechanical differences

All women have a wider pelvis than their male counterparts and, in general, shorter upper legs. Added together these mean that a typical woman's running gait has hips and thighs turned inwards and the legs taking on a kind of 'X' shape (see picture on right). This bending sideways at the knee causes strains and impact on the hip, knee joints and lower back, which can lead to injuries.

Shoe and clothing manufacturers have tried to combat this with trainers and leggings than can slightly alter the angle of the feet and the way the muscles act on the joints (supposedly). This technology can apparently help stop the 'X' shape and thus protect the joints and prevent the associated injuries. Whether this is true or not is debateable, but if you've suffered and recovered from this type of injury and are looking to run again any preventative measure is worth trying.

On top of the biomechanical differences, there are obvious differences to the equipment needed by women, like sports bras. There are also woman-specific versions of nearly every item of runners' equipment, from lycra leggings to heart-rate monitors. These take into account a women's physique, body shape and other differences, to

ensure the runner is more comfortable than if using the male equivalent. There are other things to consider as well, from running at 'that' time of the month to security when running alone, and let's not forget pregnancy and how to cope with running during and after it.

Women's clothing and trainers

It's not imperative to buy the best and most expensive kit on the market. However, it's also not the best plan to run in your old pyjama bottoms just because they look like tracksuit trousers. Treat yourself to some new kit that makes you feel good, that's flattering and comfortable. Not only will this lessen any feelings of self-consciousness when pounding the pavements, it will also support and aid your running ability, and the cost will be an added incentive to go and run, to get some use out of your purchases.

Trainers are a different story. Don't make do with your flatmate's cast-offs or the trainers you used at uni. Go to a sports shop and have your gait analysed. Listen to the sales person's advice and be honest with them. If you're new to running, tell them. If you're planning to take up cross-country and trail-running, tell them. And remember, you don't have to buy from them – don't feel obliged just because they've given you great advice. Go home, research on the Internet, and if you can find the shoes you settled on in the shop but cheaper, call the shop and see if they can match the price. However, be prepared to

pay a decent amount for good shoes. The more 'technology' is in the shoes, the more protection they'll provide for your joints (supposedly), the longer they'll last – and the more they'll cost.

→ Should you buy women-specific trainers?
Simply put, yes! Not only are there differences in the structure of feet between men and women, but there are also major differences in sizing standards and designs.

In general, men have longer and wider feet, and the arch, first toe, lateral side of the foot, ball of the foot, ankle and overall foot shape are all significantly different. Running shoe manufacturers know this and have factored it in when designing their women's ranges. Most importantly, women tend to have a narrower heel and forefoot and a lower instep than men, so if a women runs in a man's shoes the likelihood is her heels will slip up and down, causing blisters from friction. In short, injuries can occur, so when choosing a shoe, make sure it's a women's shoe – the colours will be nicer anyway.

Before trying on new trainers always walk round town for a good 30 minutes to an hour, so that your feet swell up as they would when running.

Make-up

There are two trains of thought regarding make-up when running: wear it, don't wear it. If you choose to wear make-up when running it will run, smear and end up looking worse than wearing none. Furthermore your clothing will get smeared, as the sweat produced by exercise causes make-up to run. It's better to take all the make-up off.

Yes, I'm a man, and don't understand this side of women's lives. However, I wrote this chapter in conjunction with a female who's run three or four times a week since her late teens. She assures me that even waterproof mascara isn't worth the effort, as when you sweat and attempt to wipe your eyes you'll inevitably smear the product. Again, simply put it away for the duration of the run.

If you're considering taking up running for weight loss or health and fitness you may be thinking that you don't really sweat when you run so can therefore wear make-up. But if you're not sweating when you're running then you aren't running at the right intensity for your desired goal. Whether you're just starting a running programme having never run before, or are the next Paula Radcliffe, you should be sweating when you run.

My best advice is to accept that when you go for a run you're not going to look your best, and remember that running is a step towards achieving the body, lifestyle and fitness that you want, which will make you look and feel your best. So for that brief percentage of the day take the make-up off, tie the hair back, run your heart out, and if you're anything like me you'll look red, blotchy and a bit dazed for 10–15 minutes afterwards but feel great for the rest of the day.

Tying back your hair

If you've ever been in a rush on a hot summer's day when your hair hasn't been tied back, you'll know what a pain sweaty strands of hair stuck to your neck and face can be. None of us look our best when exercising, but that doesn't mean we need to look unattractive. Tying back your hair gets it out of the way, keeps you cooler, and makes you feel more comfortable. My girlfriend described to me a time when she forgot her hairband while at the gym. She still tried to run on the treadmill, but the constant need to wipe her hair from her face distracted her so much she felt unfit while running at her normal speed and was forced to get off and find some way of tying it. Take her advice: keep a pack of hairbands in your sports bag and always tie your hair back.

🏃 Warpaint

It may seem hard to wipe off the warpaint altogether, but it will help your skin no end, allowing it to sweat out the impurities and breathe properly for a time, and will avoid clogging it with make-up, which leads to spots. Make sure you drink plenty, exfoliate after the run and wash the face properly before reapplying.

Sports bras

Whatever your breast size you should always wear a sports bra. Obviously, as a male author I have no experience of wearing a sports bra, but I've been informed by my PT clients and female friends that attempting to run without adequate support can be both painful and cause long-term damage.

Where possible it's important that you get yourself correctly fitted for your sports bra. Some of the better sports shops cater for this, otherwise there are instructions on the packs from suppliers such as Shock Absorber, Triumph, Adidas or Nike. I've also provided an idea of how to do it yourself below.

It's estimated that 75–80% of women wear the wrong size sports bra, which (again) I have on good authority is painful and makes running both more uncomfortable and more difficult. Furthermore, the wrong size sports bra can lead to sagging and therefore long-term damage to the breast tissue, including stretch marks.

Bad posture and a painful back can also result from an ill-fitting sports bra, as the breast tissue isn't controlled and therefore puts more pressure on the core and lower back, which over time leads to injury in these areas. By making running seem uncomfortable and painful you'll soon be put off, or have a good excuse for not doing it regularly, all because of a simple sizing issue. So to ensure you don't suffer discomfort from your breasts moving unnecessarily or your posture changing (bending forward and rounding your shoulders), which in turn leads to referred pain in the back and shoulders, get fitted for and wear the correct sports bra.

A better figure

Not only will the correct sports bra support your breasts during running, it will also lift them, just as any regular bra will when fitted correctly. Properly fitted bras make you look better by raising your breasts to a more appealing level and revealing the waistline, which immediately gives you a better figure.

Bad running gait

An ill-fitting or unsupportive sports bra leads to incorrect running technique, as the breasts are either held in the hands while running or stabilised by swinging the arms across the chest or holding them firmly in front of the body. This leads to a tense, unnatural style, which not only rounds the shoulders but burns far more energy, meaning you'll tire quickly and therefore feel more unfit and in turn become demoralised.

Your breasts can bounce up to 9cm when unsupported during exercise; even A cup breasts can move up to 4cm. So every woman should wear a sports bra when running.

Use and replace

Believe it or not sports bras wear out like trainers, as the shock-absorbing elastic weakens over time, and like trainers they should be replaced early to avoid injury and discomfort. The more often they're used, the sooner they'll need replacing. Most women will own more than one sports bra, and they'll be worn alternately, meaning that unlike trainers they'll possibly get used only once or twice a week. However, check all your sports bras regularly for elasticity, fit and wear and tear, and replace where necessary.

Losing weight as you run

Whether you're running for weight loss or a fitter, healthier you, remember that you may lose a considerable amount of weight over the course of your training programme. This may also be true if you're training following injury or a prolonged absence from running. Either way it's unlikely that your breasts will remain the same size, and it may be necessary to get refitted and/or buy a new set of sports bras. If in doubt get advice from a reputable sports shop. Don't put up with the old bras – you'll only become injured.

In terms of brands there are a number on the market. Whatever your budget, find one that works for you. We're all different shapes and sizes so the most expensive bras or brand leaders won't necessarily suit you. Always try them on in the shop. Jump up and down and sprint on the spot in the changing room, looking in the mirror as you do so, to see and feel which absorb the most movement.

🏃 Good support

There are no muscles in the breasts. They consist of ligaments, which stretch beyond repair to irreversible breast sag when exercised unsupported. Any bra is better than no bra, but a sports bra is best. Research shows that breast movement from running is reduced by 38% with ordinary bras and 78% with sports bras.

🏃 Fitting a sports bra

1. Measure around the rib cage just under the breasts.
2. Add 5in/12.5cm to this figure. This gives your band size.
3. Measure around breasts at widest point.
4. Compare the two figures using the table below to get cup size

Inch difference	Cup size
Up to 1in (2.5cm)	A
1–2in (2.5–5cm)	B
2–3in (5–7.5cm)	C
3–4in (7.5–10cm)	D
4–6in (10–15cm)	DD or E
Over 6in (15cm)	F

Women's health

That time of the month

In the past women of all ages were advised to stop exercising for a few specific days a month. Although this may be good advice if pain is particularly high, it's just not practical in today's busy world. Added to which, do you think professional athletes can afford to sit out a race because it's their time of the month? Of course they can't. They have to perform. Nevertheless, I appreciate that the pain associated with the menstrual cycle can be completely debilitating – which brings me back to my favourite mantra: know yourself. If you know you suffer badly, then take a break.

Research suggests that women in their premenstrual phase are more likely to suffer from running injuries. It's thought that the imbalance of hormones can affect the motor neurones and leave you less reactive than usual; added to which blood sugar levels tend to be lower, meaning energy levels will be lower too. As part of a downward spiral, motivation can also be a huge problem, as just getting started can seem a daunting process.

From my research for this chapter, I've found that simply powering through seems to be the general consensus, and often leads to a real feeling of achievement. Conversely, there's no harm in having a rest – especially if you're just a social/fitness runner – since your running gait may change due to pain or motor imbalances and you may cause yourself injury.

Having said that, many women report that running through the premenstrual syndrome actually helps alleviate the pain; be it the physical act of running, or the endorphins released during exercise, pain apparently subsides to some degree. Furthermore, women have reported that the general wellbeing felt during and after a run helps with the depressive, physiological aspect, so if you're feeling low a run can help boost the spirits. Lastly, the bloating associated with premenstrual syndrome, caused by sodium retention, can be vastly reduced and alleviated by running, as sweating clears excess sodium from the body – just make sure you drink plenty of water.

→ Sanitary towels

As I've said time and time again in this book, everyone is different and it's important to 'know yourself'. Consequently women report different things in terms of the effects of running and cessation or increase of blood flow. Try out a few different tampons and pads and see which works for you. If you have friends who run or have joined a running club, ask for other opinions. Key advice, though, would be to put fresh in before you set out and change it on completion. Furthermore, it would be advisable to wear underwear, even if you usually don't because your running tights or shorts mean you don't have to. It can save embarrassment if your run does encourage more flow than usual. Lastly, as you doubtless already know, avoid light colours, just in case. Black running tights are probably a good idea during this time.

Hormones

As we all know, women's hormones fluctuate through the month and can have various consequences on the body, from increased temperature to lethargy. But what effect does running have on hormone production? Research suggests that if you run regularly you actually produce a less potent form of oestrogen than if you were sedentary. This form of oestrogen is not problematic in any way, and is said to cut the risk of developing breast and uterine cancer by 50% and the risk of contracting the form of diabetes that most commonly plagues women by 66%.

The downside to running a lot or too much is that you develop amenorrhoea (lack of a monthly period), which means that little or no oestrogen is circulating in your body. Oestrogen is essential for maintaining healthy bones, hence a lack of periods and oestrogen will lead to serious health risks to your bones. By taking oestrogen, amenorrhoeic women can stop – but not reverse – the damage to their bones; taking a calcium supplement is also advisable. If your periods do become infrequent or absent, especially if you're a competitive runner unable to rest or reduce exercising, then consult a doctor as soon as possible.

Female athlete triad syndrome

This term refers to the condition of athletic women who train extremely hard and suffer from one of three interlinked disorders: amenorrhoea, osteoporosis and anorexia.

→ Amenorrhoea

As stated above, intense training can cease the menstrual cycle. It's thought this occurs due to oestrogen and progesterone levels being unbalanced along with very low body weight. The over-production of running-released endorphins and catecholamines could be blamed for the former.

→ Osteoporosis

This almost seems a paradox, as running is known to help promote healthy bones and increase bone density (see page 177). However, amenorrhoea is caused by low levels of oestrogen, and oestrogen is necessary for strong bones. This means female runners suffering from a lack of menstrual cycle are at risk from stress fractures and osteoporosis. This is true not only for women suffering from amenorrhoea, but also post-menopausal women.

Again, the answer is to cut back and seek medical advice. However, the problem can also be treated by taking calcium and vitamin supplements (vitamin D – see Chapter 6) and the contraceptive pill, which raises oestrogen levels and re-orders menstruation cycles.

→ Anorexia

Runners unfortunately have a high incidence of anorexia, particularly long-distance runners. This results from an assumption that the lighter and smaller the body, the faster a runner becomes. However, this notion is sadly misguided. Obviously large body-builders' muscles aren't required, but muscles are still needed for running to take place efficiently and properly. Furthermore, without adequate fuel performance is greatly hindered, and if the body becomes stressed from lack of fuel yet is asked to work hard, it metabolises itself. This muscle breakdown and lack of energy results in a fatigued runner with less muscular support than necessary, and injuries inevitably occur. The other side effects of anorexia should also be watched out for, and medical attention should be sought if this becomes a problem.

Overheating

As you run and eat correctly you'll change your metabolism. It will speed up and thus you'll feel hotter, especially at night. This is not a bad thing. It means you'll burn more calories and be less inclined to hold on to fat stores. During your menopause you may feel even hotter. This again is nothing to worry about. If you've done a long, hard run or an interval session and it's 'that' time, you may find you sweat a little in the night. This is quite normal.

Women's diet

Chapter 6 outlines diets in general, what to eat, when to eat and what to avoid, and applies to women as well as men, except for two specific minerals: calcium and iron. Calcium is needed for bone health, particularly if oestrogen levels are low. Iron is needed (especially for menstruating women) to enable the blood to carry oxygen more readily. Women require more iron than men each day, as much as 18mg when menstruating. A high proportion of women are in fact iron deficient. This is especially true for vegetarians, who can develop anaemia relatively easily if running quite long distances each week. This is due to iron being used more excessively by distance runners. Sources of calcium include dairy products, dark leafy vegetables, broccoli, and canned oily fish, like sardines and salmon. Foods rich in iron include liver, fortified dry cereals, beef and spinach.

If you find you suffer from amenorrhoea for a few months, cut back on your training or rest completely for a week or so and then restart slowly.

Differences to men

Added to the biomechanical differences in the legs, hips, knees and feet mentioned above, there are physiological differences that are important to factor in, especially when starting running or running with a male training partner. In general women's cardiovascular systems are proportionally smaller than men's. This means they have to work harder for similar gains. In addition women have less oxygen-carrying haemoglobin than men, which again means the heart (which is already smaller) must beat more times to get the haemoglobin to deliver oxygen around the body. However, don't be disheartened. Despite these differences women generally show greater improvements than men during training. The key, then? Stick with your training, work hard, but compete with yourself, never (unless your name's Paula) with the man next to you. Lastly, women's heart rates take longer to return to resting levels than men's.

The tip, then, is to remember the differences and try not to get too competitive when training alongside men. Know yourself, compete with your times, your heart rate and your personal best; use the men (and women) in your training group to push you, but accept that there are physiological differences.

Having said that, there's an old theory that women are better marathon runners than men because they have more body fat to burn. Over shorter distances men tend to use their strength to push ahead, whereas women are in general content to find a comfort zone and stay there, which is ideally suited to marathons. So if competition is your aim, why not sign up for a marathon and convince him to do the same?

Conclusion

Men and women are different. We need slightly different kit, we can suffer slightly different injuries, and we're capable of slightly different achievements as runners. So know yourself – take a look at your running schedule, ensure you're fit and healthy and doing everything you can to be the best you can, be that by wearing a good sports bra, resting at 'that' time of the month, changing your training while pregnant or seeking medical advice if your periods have stopped. Safety and a happy lifestyle must be paramount.

Pregnancy

Simply put, the best advice is that if you already run, then you can continue to run at the start of your pregnancy. If you don't, then taking up running while pregnant probably isn't the best idea – your body won't be used to it so will start to make the adaptations that any human does when they start running. However, unlike most people your body is also adapting to the foetus inside. Both adaptations occurring at the same time isn't advisable. However, consult a doctor and do what you feel comfortable doing.

→ Major drawbacks of running during pregnancy

1 **Overheating** – Exercise makes us hotter when we train, it also raises our metabolism after we train. Both of these raise our temperature. If your body temperature gets too high it can harm the foetus.

2 **Dehydration** – This can reduce blood flow around the body and specifically to the uterus, which can cause contractions to start. If you do choose to run make sure you drink a lot of water, perhaps more than you did before you became pregnant.

3 **Injury** – Hormones released during pregnancy make the joints loose. This can lead to injuries occurring far more readily, so whether running or not take extra care when active.

→ Major advantages to running during pregnancy

1 **Healthier mother and baby** – Women who were regular runners before becoming pregnant are more likely to have a larger baby. This isn't something to wince at, as larger babies tend to be stronger and cope better with physical adversity.

2 **Blood pressure** – As long as its comfortable and not painful in any way, running during pregnancy can keep your blood pressure down, which is more healthy for you and the baby.

3 **Weight loss** – Weight loss after pregnancy will be easier if you continue to run through the early stages, as you'll have kept your metabolism high. However, this is again only good if comfortable, otherwise rest-up, for both your health and the baby's.

Morning sickness is quite common, it is not something to be scared of, but must be dealt with. Apparently ginger helps.

→ A few guidelines

Pregnant women are far more robust than people give them credit for. African and Amazonian tribeswomen, for example, are known to walk for around ten miles to pick up huge bowls of water while in their third trimester. This is something that occurs naturally and isn't going to change any time soon. We in the Western world, however, have developed a culture of protection and segregation towards pregnancy. I'm not knocking this at all – we should still give up our seats on the bus to pregnant women and be aware that pregnant women lose their breath or feel sick doing mundane tasks. However, we should also remember that as long as a pregnant woman is healthy and not ill in any way she's robust and strong enough to carry on exercising, so long as a few guidelines are kept to. Having said that, it's important to use common sense and if something doesn't feel right, stop, and perhaps check with your doctor.

If you were active before becoming pregnant, then stay active, perhaps just cut back. Always err on the sensible side. If you weren't active before pregnancy, you must ease in very gently and ensure careful progression.

Strange cravings during pregnancy are said to be the body's way of telling you it requires a vitamin or mineral that it's lacking, so take a multi-vitamin and multi-mineral supplement and ensure you're getting enough red meat and calcium.

Choose a softer surface to run on to avoid too much impact to the foetus. This may also help avoid too many stretch marks. The local park or a running track are ideal.

Despite the extra cost, don't scrimp if you need a larger sports bra (many companies produce maternity sports bras) or leggings. Just get the one set and wash them to death for six months. It'll be worth it. The same is true for shoes – wear a more cushioned pair during your pregnancy just to save your joints.

Pregnancy itself

There are three trimesters that last three months each. They're all very different, and each has things that you can and can't do. Again, the key is to listen to your body – whether you're tired, hungry or have aches and pains, just make sure you act accordingly.

→ First trimester

It's fine to run, but ensure you keep it aerobic and not anaerobic, ie long, slow, steady runs are fine, but don't make them too intense. Intervals and Fartlek training will quickly take you into anaerobic glycolysis (see Chapter 5), which is too intense and can be harmful to the foetus.

→ Second trimester

At this point all your life's needs are being split between you and another little person. For this reason you'll start to feel breathless when active. This isn't for fitness reasons, it's due to your diaphragm being unable to move as freely due to the little person sitting on it. You therefore breathe far more shallowly than usual and hence have a real lack of breath.

At the end of the second and beginning of the third trimester a woman's body starts producing a hormone called relaxin. Its main role is to relax the pelvis to allow it to enlarge during birth; the problem is it acts on the other joints too, and leads to them becoming hypermobile. Advice at this stage would be not to do any high-impact training and to stick to 'closed chain' exercises. These are exercises where the feet stay on the floor (eg static squats), whereas 'open chain' exercises involve the feet leaving and hitting the ground repeatedly (eg running), which isn't recommended for ankles, knees and hips weakened by relaxin. Weighted exercises shouldn't be done for the same reason. Body weight exercises are fine, if they're closed chain, but avoid exercises that open the joints and pelvis, like sumo squats. However, always listen to your body and err on the side of caution.

→ Third trimester

By this stage the breathlessness of the second trimester has eased off, as the 'bump' has dropped, but due to the size of the bump you can't run anyway, even though your energy levels actually increase. However, staying active remains important, though only lower-impact exercises must be done, again due to relaxin's effects on some ligaments and tendons, which will make you more vulnerable to injury. Walking, swimming, stationary cycling and aquarunning (you'll be even more buoyant than usual) are all excellent exercise sessions. Never exercise to the point of breathlessness, as this would divert oxygen away from the baby. For many mothers to be, brisk walking is enough at this late stage.

→ Post-pregnancy

Relaxin can stay in the body for up to six months after birth for some women and up to six months after breastfeeding ends for others. This unfortunately means that hypermobility continues

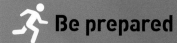

Be prepared

Research has suggested that babies dislike the taste of post-exercise breast milk as it's high in lactic acid, which gives it a more sour flavour. Therefore either collect milk before a run for feeding afterwards, or do the breastfeeding before running and drink a little more than you normally would.

and exercise must be progressive, done with low weight, and care must be taken when doing exercises that involve opening the legs, which can be detrimental to the pelvis. It's a good idea to do core strengthening exercises to reverse the action of relaxin and pregnancy; a strong core will prevent most injuries.

Don't rush back to exercising too soon, especially if your ambition is to lose weight. The weight will come off, just be patient. The walk/run beginners' programme in Chapter 9 is a good start.

Another thing to bear in mind when getting back into training is the effect the new addition is having. It's likely that baby feeding through the night, added worry and the realisation that life will never be the same again will be taking its toll. Therefore bear in mind the effects of a child on your training programme. Above all, eat well, ensure you remain well hydrated and use your common sense: listen to your body, know yourself and act accordingly.

Children

Although starting young in any sport is encouraged, as what's learned in our formative years is often carried on through life, real running training is difficult to organise for a young child. Historically, running training for children hasn't usually taken place until secondary school age, as this is when the point and advantages of training become understandable. Furthermore, it's not until reaching its teens that the body is ready to be trained like an adult.

→ Conditioning
Children should steer clear of weight training and conditioning until the age of around 14. Prior to this the bones and muscles are still growing, therefore any serious weight training is likely to lead to stunted growth. The same is true for conditioning for running, be it sprinting or long-distance; body weight is OK for children and can be novel and fun for them. However, weighted exercises should be avoided until their teens.

→ Sprinting
Children can begin sprinting as soon as they're confident enough to run, but real training shouldn't take place. The school sports day sprint across the playground is fine, but training for it is neither worthwhile nor likely to grab a child's attention. However, it's fine to encourage a child to do it. Where possible get them to warm up with a few laps of the playground, but even if this is impossible children are so limber that the chances of pulling a muscle are slim. The way to train a child for sprinting is to make it a game – chase a ball, chase a Frisbee, etc.

→ Kids on the run
The biggest problem with children is keeping them entertained. Asking them to run round the football pitch three times usually starts way too quickly as a race and fun and games, then leads to cutting corners and trying to cheat, before breaking into a walk and chants of 'Do we have to?' Without an understanding that this helps them keep fit and lose weight (not something most pre-teens worry about) they need other incentives. Yes, you can offer incentives in the form of treats, but this seems counter-productive. The best way to get kids running is to play games. This can be normal sports games such as football, tennis or touch rugby, but kids games like 'stuck in the mud', 'bulldog' or 'one, two, three and in' are better. These keep the children's attention, have a competitive and adventurous edge, which they love, and usually get them running for the entirety, either continuously or in short sprint-type intervals. My advice is don't worry too much about times, distance, pace, conditioning and prehab – just keep children active to avoid childhood obesity and keep their CV system developing, and when they reach secondary school and real competitive sports introduce them to athletics and running. If they have a talent it will shine through and the real running can begin.

→ Relay races
Kids love to sprint. As fast as they can. They don't understand pacing themselves. Furthermore, they love being part of a group, part of a team, with a shared common goal. And lastly they love competition, so combining all three over relatively short distances will keep them occupied for some time. Simply split them into two teams and race to and from selected points. Simple, fun and CV-wise a good workout for them.

→ Children and running shoes
Medical advice is that once a child reaches the age of around five or six and is starting to do PE and play games that involve running, fitting them for running shoes can't do any harm. The problem with kids is that their feet grow individually, and fitting them for shoes can highlight this. As a teen I had a slight leg length difference – not an issue for most people, but I was running cross-country races twice a week and training five or six times a week, and the mileage led to a damaged medial collateral ligament. In short, the lack of proper shoe support can lead to injuries, and as shoe manufacturers make running shoes in youth sizes, why not get the kids kitted out?

⏱ Conclusion

Keep running fun. Kids will enjoy it more, and so will you. If they want to join you on your daily run at some point, fine, but it's their choice – don't push them, and be aware they may get bored after 200m! For childhood obesity problems, diet is far more important than encouraging a child to do a 5km race; just give them the nudge to play outside and enjoy games with other children instead of sitting in front of a PlayStation.

The elderly

Short of disability or health issues, there's no reason why anyone of any age can't start running. So whether you're 40 or 80, if you fancy running get checked out by your doctor and, if given the all-clear, give it a go.

→ Start slow and aim low

Although I'm not one to dampen anyone's spirits or ambition, it's worth being realistic regarding what can be achieved. Having said that, runners in their 70s have clocked up marathon times of under three hours. However, attempting to outpace good runners in their 20s and 30s is unrealistic, so it's better to aim low and surprise yourself rather than aiming too high.

→ Walk before you can run

It's important not to rush into things too quickly, especially 'what you used to be able to do'. Start with a period of walking and conditioning to build up the muscles so that they won't become injured and can protect the ligaments and tendons. Walking will also give the heart time to get stronger, so that running will be easier and safer.

Be aware that you may have forgotten (in a muscle/motor neurone sense) how to run. Be patient, you'll soon get back to it. To help, try the six-week beginners' programme in Chapter 9. Alternatively (or in addition, ideally), purchase a heart-rate monitor as discussed earlier, and use it from the start.

→ Cutting back

Unfortunately, even if you've been running your entire life, there will come a point when you must reduce your weekly mileage or stop running altogether. As long as you're still running correctly there's no reason (unless medically advised otherwise) to stop. However, stop your session as soon as your running gait becomes unnatural and 'sloppy'. This may be after 50 minutes now, but in five years it may be within 30 minutes. Softer running surfaces are better for ageing joints and may prolong good form a little longer, but avoid real off-road cross-country routes, as uneven, obstacle-strewn terrain will encourage falls. Listen to your body and act accordingly. If you get to the point where you can't run any more, then try non-impact exercises like swimming or cycling.

→ Diet

If you're starting to exercise you'll need to eat more to provide the necessary energy. Protein intake must be increased, as should carbohydrate. Try and lower your fat intake, just to be healthier. Running doesn't give you an excuse to indulge more, since another symptom of ageing is a slower metabolism.

→ Hydration

As we age our body temperature rises, therefore older runners tend to have more dehydration issues. This can also be attributed to the body's homeostasis receptors being less functional than they used to be: you just don't realise you're thirsty soon enough. The best piece of advice is to carry a water bottle and drink every two to five minutes as you run.

→ Conditioning

Conditioning exercises and prehab are still just as important, and in some ways more so. Strengthening the muscles will help avoid new injuries, stop old injuries redeveloping, and ensure a correct running gait. Men tend to experience about twice as much muscle wastage as women, so exercising to avoid this is paramount if you're going to run safely and strongly. Try not to do anything too dynamic, stick to 'closed chain' compound exercises, ie exercises involving multiple muscles that keep the feet fixed on the floor. Great examples are squats, feet-fixed lunges and hamstring bridges. Don't try to lift large weights – keep them light and repetitions high (15 or above), as this will increase muscular endurance.

→ Osteoporosis and arthritis

If you or your family have a history of either osteoporosis or arthritis you should consult your doctor before starting any exercise plan.

It was originally thought that exercise for the over 50s would encourage the bone and joint damage seen in osteoporosis and arthritis. I would advise avoiding exercises with dynamic movements (sprints, twisting and turning), like football and rugby, or jumping and landing, like volleyball and basketball. However, running – like cycling and swimming – helps reduce the onset of these problems.

Going for runs, stretching after runs and some light conditioning exercises for running all strengthen the muscles, tendons, ligaments and bones and can increase movement to stiff joints.

Your bones become denser from the impact of running, helping to offset or ward off osteoporosis. Furthermore, the movement of running encourages joints to release their natural oil (synovial fluid), and also strengthens cartilage, warding of osteoarthritis. The only downside is that cartilage wears away with years of running, and this will eventually catch up with us. Wear good cushioned shoes, run off-road where possible, and perhaps cross-train with non-impact cardiovascular sessions like swimming or cycling.

⏱ Conclusion

If medical advice allows, it's never too late to start running. Make sure your kit and equipment are going to protect you properly, drink lots of water and take supplements like calcium and glucosamine to help with bone strengthening and joint lubrication. Also, eat a little more (healthy!) food than you did. However, know yourself – when the body hurts and doesn't recover, ditch the running shoes and hit the swimming pool.

CHAPTER 15
INJURIES & REHAB

Injuries are the nightmare of all sportspeople. If your life revolves around your sport, or your daily or weekly run is your de-stresser, then being injured will be very demoralising. The purpose of this chapter is to describe the most common running injuries and provide ideas on how to avoid and treat them. Above all, remember things will get better. You will recover, but you have to give yourself time to heal. Don t train on an injury, it will get worse!

Losing all you've worked for

If you become injured or simply have no time to train, the effects of 'detraining' can seem devastating. However, believe it or not detraining isn't all bad. First of all, think of it as another motivation to continue training wherever and whenever possible. Put a positive, not a negative, spin on it.

→ A few days off

Research suggests that losses in performance and efficiency occur when training stops for around two weeks, so taking a few days off for a cold or a niggly hamstring isn't going to do you any harm. For most of us the contrary is true – it'll do us some real good to have a rest. However, if a few months pass due to serious injury, illness or any other reason, then the majority of real fitness gains and physical improvements made will be lost – in fact studies show that VO_2max levels can decrease by as much as 25% over 20 days if injury or illness means you're almost sedentary.

→ Regaining past glories

If illness or injury does prevail, and fitness levels are lost, it's not the end of the world. For example, a nasty injury to my right hand meant I couldn't use my arm for the best part of six months or run for the best part of three (the scars had to heal without getting sweaty). Obviously I was distraught, as prior to the injury my fitness levels were pretty respectable. However, studies suggest that once a certain level of fitness is gained, even if it's lost again, it's easier to regain than it was to gain first time round. I've now surpassed my previous fitness and found more ways to train and improve, as I had to adapt and 'think outside the box'. Furthermore I enjoyed striving to regain my old fitness level as it gave me another motivational goal. So the answer is to know when you're beaten, find a new way round the obstacle and never, ever give up.

Common runners' injuries

Overtraining, fatigue or plain bad luck can all lead to injuries, but being aware of them and their causes can help you avoid becoming another victim. The following are the top eight injuries that runners tend to suffer from.

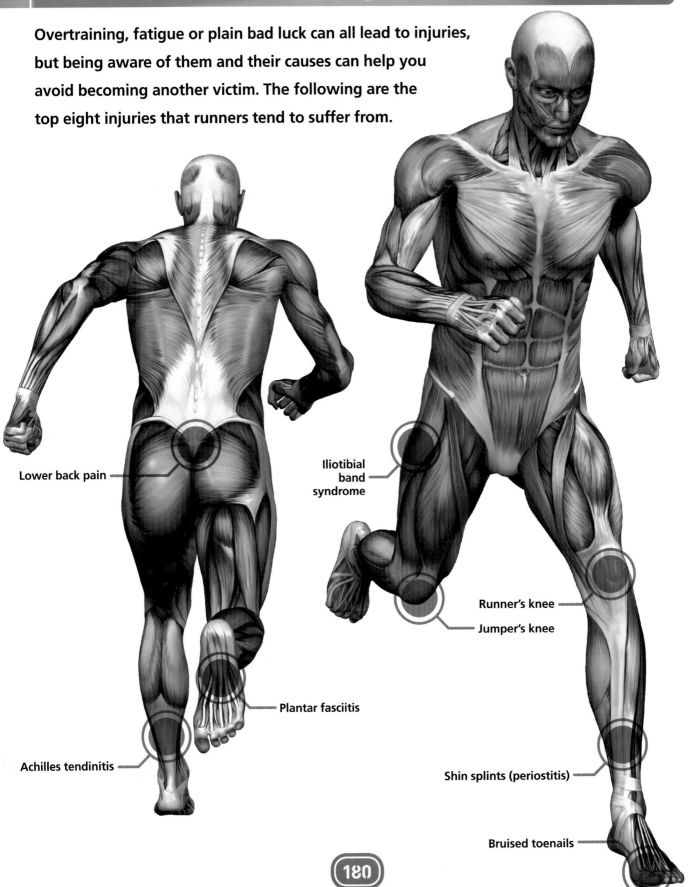

Lower back pain

Iliotibial band syndrome

Runner's knee

Jumper's knee

Plantar fasciitis

Achilles tendinitis

Shin splints (periostitis)

Bruised toenails

Achilles tendinitis

→ What is it?
Inflammation of the Achilles tendon, the strongest tendon in your body, which connects the large calf muscles to the heel bone and provides the power in the push-off phase of the running gait cycle. It presents as an ache just above your heel that increases as you run or walk. Studies suggest that it makes up 11% of all running injuries.

→ Causes
In general it's due to your calf muscles being too tight or your ankles being slightly inflexible. Increasing the miles per week too quickly (ie overtraining) and the back of your trainer rubbing on the Achilles tendon area can also be factors.

→ Treatment
Replace old inflexible trainers with new more cushioned ones. Increase the flexibility of your calf muscles by stretching and reduce or stop training until doing it is pain-free. Reducing hill training and sprints is also a good idea. Lastly, ice the area after any training to help reduce the pain.

→ Prevention
Stretch, stretch and stretch. Also, don't run too many miles per week too quickly.

Shin splints (periostitis)

→ What is it?
Shin splints refers to any shin pain picked up by an athlete, but originally and still most commonly to medial tibial stress syndrome. This is basically inflammation and the resulting pain of the inner part of the shin, which feels almost like a bruise.

→ Causes
Usually too much running, particularly on hard surfaces. If biomechanical weaknesses such as overpronating or weak muscles below the knee are also present these can be the major cause.

→ Treatment
Ice and possibly massage of the area to reduce inflammation and relieve pain. Cut down on running – stretch and train the muscles of the lower leg before building mileage back up. It's a good idea to run on softer surfaces where possible. Don't be tempted to run through the pain. Warming up the area passively and actively prior to running can help alleviate the problem.

→ Prevention
Don't run too many miles per week too quickly. Condition and prehab, ie keep up strength-training of the lower legs, including flexibility. Vary training so that not all runs are on concrete: include some on fields and treadmills and attempt the odd trail/cross-country run.

Runner's knee

→ What is it?
Runner's knee – chrondromalacia or patellofemoral pain syndrome (PFPS) – is characterised by pain at the front of the kneecap. The pain usually increases going downstairs after long periods of sitting.

→ Causes
There are multiple causes including overpronation, too much downhill running, overly tight hamstrings, weak quad muscles and overtraining.

→ Treatment
Reduce and remove inflammation through 'PRICEA' (protect, rest, ice, compress, elevate and anti-inflammatory medication, ie ibuprofen). To protect or rest, cut down or stop running and avoid activities that cause pain. Build up imbalances of the quads and gluteus medius – stabilising exercises do this very well.

→ Prevention
Get your running gait analysed, as overpronators are more prone. Replace your running shoes regularly. Avoid running on hard surfaces all the time and avoid steep downhills, especially on hard surfaces. Ensure you maintain your flexibility by stretching and keep on top of prehab/conditioning so leg muscles are strong.

Jumper's knee

→ What is it?
Jumper's knee or patella tendinitis is characterised by pain at the front of the knee underneath the kneecap. The pain is usually increased with prolonged use, such as standing, walking or driving holding the clutch pedal!

→ Causes
Like runner's knee there are multiple causes, such as direct impact and trauma leading to the chronic problem, or jumping sports such as basketball, gymnastics and Parkour. Tight and overworked quadriceps can also be a major cause.

→ Treatment
Reduce activity and remove inflammation with PRIA (protection, rest, ice, anti-inflammatories). Cut down or stop running in favour of seated cycling or swimming, to allow the tendon to heal and calm down. Build up imbalances of the quads and gluteus medius – stabilising exercises are perfect for this.

→ Prevention
Replace your running shoes with cushioned versions and avoid running on hard surfaces all the time. Avoid steep downhills, especially on hard surfaces, and where possible avoid the sports that have led to the problem.

Iliotibial band syndrome

→ What is it?

ITBS is a dull ache felt on the outside of the knee. The iliotibial band is a thick, fibrous band of fascia that runs down the outside of the thigh and inserts just below the knee. The pain can be severe enough to make running too difficult to continue, especially as tenderness may also be felt in gluteal area in more severe (very tight ITB) cases.

→ Causes

Overtraining or running without sufficient rest periods. If the IT band becomes tight it can rub against the outside of the knee, causing pain and inflammation. This pain is aggravated by running, particularly downhill. In severe cases pain is felt even when bending the knee.

→ Treatment

PRICE (see page 184) and stretching your ITB using a roller is by far the most successful way of alleviating this injury. However, running on even ground, general stretching and increased flexibility and strengthening of the leg, hip and muscles in the backside can help.

→ Prevention

Stretch at the end of every session. Try not to run downhill on hard surfaces too often and ensure cushioned and correct-fitting shoes. A good conditioning routine to ensure leg muscles are strong is imperative.

Plantar fasciitis

→ What is it?

The plantar fascia is a broad, thick band of tissue that runs from under the heel to the front of the foot. Plantar fasciitis is a pain felt under the heel and usually on the inside at the origin of the attachment. Pain is usually worse first thing in the morning, as the fascia tightens up overnight. After a few minutes it eases as the foot gets warmed up.

→ Causes

The most common cause is thought to be very tight calf muscles, which leads to overpronation of the foot. This causes overstretching of the plantar fascia, leading to inflammation and thickening of the tendon, which in turn leads to a loss of flexibility and strength.

→ Treatment

Correct footwear at all times is imperative, especially when running. A decent pair of flat, lace-up shoes with good arch support and cushioning are a must. Beyond that, rest as much as possible. Ice and anti-inflammatories can also help.

→ Prevention

Overweight individuals are more at risk of developing the condition due to the excess weight impacting on the foot, so a weight loss programme may be of benefit. Stretching techniques such as rolling the bottom of the foot on a golf ball work as treatment and prevention.

Bruised toenails

→ What is it?

Repeated bashing of the toenail causes it to bruise underneath (blood pools under the toenail) and turn black.

→ Causes

I lost five toenails from this on one military course. I think on that occasion it was down to my boots being half a size too tight. Usually it's due to the impact of the toe against the end of the shoe or by blood being pressed into the toe from the shoe being too tight. Too much running, especially downhill, can also be a cause.

→ Treatment

The toenail will eventually fall off of its own accord and a new one will have part grown up underneath. Don't pull the old toenail off prematurely – it's protecting the soft skin underneath and removing it will cause pain and long-term damage. If the nail is catching on socks or in bed, visit your local surgery and they can remove it. Removing it yourself often leads to an ingrown toenail.

→ Prevention

Try a new set of running shoes, perhaps a different brand, or at least a half-size bigger. Less running downhill, especially on hard surfaces.

Lower back pain

→ What is it?

A dull aching in the lower back, centrally or to one side. Often leads to restricted movement, which in turn leads to cessation of running.

→ Causes

Most common cause is a previous pain in that area that's worsened by activity or running. However, poor technique and bad footwear can also be to blame, as well as bad posture from sitting at a desk all day. Tight hamstrings or weak abdominals can also play a huge part.

→ Treatment

Anti-inflammatories will drastically reduce the pain and inflammation but won't cure the problem. Improving posture and addressing core weakness is of utmost importance. In particular, strengthening the transverse abdominals, glutes and erector spinae can help. Flexibility can also be an issue, so if you tend to neglect stretching after a run start performing a good stretch routine. Ice and heat on the area can help relieve pain and tightness, as can a good sports massage to relieve tightness and knots from any previous injuries.

→ Prevention

Only run pain free, whether on grass or a treadmill, or not at all. Ensure you have your running gait assessed by a professional and then wear the appropriate cushioned trainers to run. Improving your core strength and abdominals is an absolute must.

Overtraining

Overtraining is a problem that I see daily, be it in myself, Marines I used to work with, fellow fitness industry professionals or members of the gyms I use. I honestly admit that I'm an exercise addict and have been guilty of overtraining, but more importantly I've suffered the consequences. So I cannot stress strongly enough the importance of being aware of overtraining.

What is overtraining?

Overtraining is an emotional, behavioural and physical condition that occurs when the volume and intensity of exercise exceeds the recovery capacity of the body. Simply put, overtraining is attempting to complete more exercise than the body can tolerate. The downside to overtraining is that is doesn't just halt progress, it causes a loss of strength and fitness.

Rest

The most effective weapon against overtraining is rest, and the following acronym will help you remember why:

- Recovery
- Ensures
- Successful
- Training

Basically, to stop overtraining be sensible and listen to your body: if you feel overtired and fatigued you probably are, so combat this with a few days' rest and appropriate nutritional intake. If you think of rest as a tool to aid your training and help you improve your running then you'll use it effectively and appropriately.

Allowing your body to recover from exercise fatigue is so important. To push on not only degrades the body, but doesn't allow the little aches and pains – or DOMS (delayed onset muscle soreness) as they're known – to recover, and can therefore lead to injury. For runners, not allowing the body to recover adequately will lead to slower times, which leads to frustration and a feeling of needing to train harder; a vicious circle will ensue and possibly a downward spiral of continued fatigue and overtraining, leading to short-term or possibly long-term injuries.

Pushing the boundaries

The fitter you get, the more intensely you'll be able to train. Furthermore, your rate of recovery may be greatly increased, and therefore training can be done for longer or more frequently without as much rest. This isn't an excuse to start overtraining, but you must be aware that your individual rate of adaptation to exercise is different from the next person's, so whereas they need a rest today you may not need one until tomorrow, or vice versa. Just remember, we all have a limit at some point.

No one can force their body to adapt and improve when there's no capacity left, and this is where training with a group or partner can backfire. If your partner is a little fitter, or their body is adapting and improving faster, they may be able to cope with the excessive intensity and frequent sessions while you can't. Although it goes against your competitive nature and may hurt your pride, it's important to take the rest your body craves, even if your running group or training partner is raring to go. Remember that only you have to cope with the consequences of overtraining.

Symptoms of overtraining

The following are all indications of overtraining:

- Loss of performance
- Inability to progress
- Increased difficultly of easy sessions
- Lack of enthusiasm
- Increased recovery time
- Muscular atrophy and associated weight loss
- Heart rates (working and resting) higher
- Blood pressure higher
- Lowered immune system (leads to cold, infections and allergic reactions)
- Nausea
- Loss of appetite
- Emotional and psychological effects (lethargy, listlessness, procrastination, fear of failure, unrealistic high goals)
- Disturbed sleep patterns
- Loss of libido

Acute or chronic

Injuries are either acute or chronic. An acute injury is one that's happened recently and from a known cause; a twisted ankle is a perfect example. A chronic injury is one that's been around for some time and persists; patella tendinitis is a good example. An untreated or unrested acute injury can become a chronic injury.

Medical advice

With any injury, whether acute or chronic, it's worth seeking medical advice to ensure serious damage hasn't been caused. If your injury is to the head, neck or back seek medical attention immediately. In general running injuries are lower limb or core/lower back related, but it's not uncommon to hear of injuries to the shoulders and – if we consider asthma or allergies as injuries – to the cardiovascular system. Whatever the injury, seek professional advice, since if it's nothing to worry about you've at worst wasted your time, but if it is something you'll have stopped yourself running on the injury, which nine times out of ten would make it worse.

Always seek medical advice if you're ever in any doubt. If you're positive medical advice isn't needed, or have sought advice and the injury is minor rather than major, the following information may be of use.

Injury treatment

The acute phase of an injury is said to be the first 48 hours, and this is the period in which to use ice. The types of injury you can treat yourself are sprains to ligaments (eg going over on your ankle), strains to muscles (eg a pulled hamstring) or impacts causing bruising (usually from a fall or contact sport). If left unattended all of these will be dealt with by the body's natural biological pathways, but icing can drastically speed up the process. Such injuries lead to classic inflammatory responses, ie heat, pain, redness and swelling, all of which are to protect them from further injury and are characteristic of this acute phase, along with discolouration and loss of function.

PRICE

'PRICE' is a simple mnemonic to help you remember how to treat an injury, standing for protect, rest, ice, compress and elevate:

→ Protection

It's important to protect the injury to aid recovery and prevent further injury. No painful activities should be undertaken where possible, but obviously your everyday lifestyle and

If you have an injury to the chest or left shoulder it's worth asking for medical advice prior to icing due to their proximity to the heart.

 Medical attention

Following a fall I thought I'd sprained my wrist, but I left it for a month before seeking medical advice. Following X-rays, an MRI and finally an arthroscopy I was diagnosed with a complete rupture to some major ligaments of the wrist, which if left much longer could have seen me lose the use of my thumb. I required surgery to repair the damage and was left with a reduced range of movement for some time.

work commitments have to take priority. Where possible, immobilise the injury entirely and never be tempted to just press on, as there's huge risk of making the injury worse.

→ Rest

Rest is arguably the most important part of injury management in the first 48 hours, and makes a direct contribution to the healing process. Again, where possible anything causing pain and/or discomfort must be avoided. Having said that, as soon as activities can be done pain-free it's important to begin active recovery.

→ Ice

Ice is THE tool for injury treatment. It reduces swelling and heat by narrowing the diameter of the blood vessels; the cold also numbs the area, which reduces pain. Once ice is removed the injured area reheats and blood rushes in, bringing with it all the nutrients to aid healing.

Leave your ice pack in the freezer ready to go, as you never know when you'll be injured and you won't want to have to wait for it to freeze, as speed is vital to quick recovery.

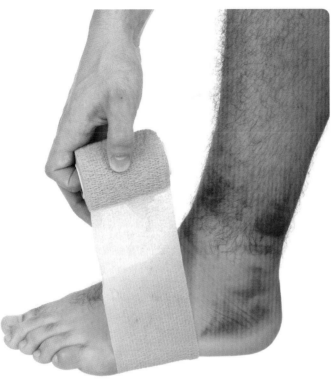

Icing

Although a simple bag of frozen vegetables can be used, it may be worth purchasing an ice pack system from a sports shop. Most are under £10 and consist of a gelatine ice pack for the freezer (which can also be microwaved to act as a heat pack), a cover to put it in (to protect the skin from hot or cold burns) and an elastic Velcro strap for attaching it to the injured site.

→ How to ice

Ice should be applied until the injured site is numb, which usually takes around 10–20 minutes. Where possible this should be done every two hours while awake. It's important to protect the skin from ice burns by wrapping the ice or icing implement in a damp towel or cloth (or the cover an ice pack is provided with). Additionally it's important, when icing a joint (knee, elbow, ankle, wrist etc), that the ice is removed briefly every five minutes or so to allow movement of the joint in the pain-free range. Due to the cold's numbing effects this pain-free range may be greater once iced.

→ Compression

Compression helps to control swelling by providing counter-pressure to the injured area. Pressure can be applied in a number of ways, from a 'tubigrip'-style bandage to a regular crepe bandage or a 'compression bandage'. However, it's imperative to check the circulation of the compressed area by pinching the body below the injury (for most running injuries this will be the toes) to ensure that blood is seen to return. If pain is felt above or below the injury the compression is probably too tight and should be removed or at least loosened.

→ Elevation

The injured area (a leg, most likely) should be elevated above heart level, eg by putting the feet up. This allows the return of blood and inflammatory fluids from the injury site, thereby reducing swelling. While elevated it's important to perform active recovery exercises within the pain-free range, ie static exercises and joint mobility (like rotating the ankle left and right after an ankle inversion). This encourages the muscles to aid drainage of the swollen area as they 'pump' while they contract.

Other runners' injuries

Athlete's foot
→ What is it?
This is a fungal infection that infects the skin of the foot. True athlete's foot is where the skin splits and cracks between and underneath the toes. Serious and untreated cases are extremely painful as the wounds can be deep, with raw skin exposed.

→ Causes
Athlete's foot is generally transferred from others already infected, in particular from the floor in damp changing rooms.

→ Treatment
Keep the feet aired and dry and use anti-fungal creams, athlete's foot powder and sprays to remove the fungal infection.

→ Prevention
Don't share towels or kit. Wear flip-flops in changing rooms and around swimming pools. Keep your feet as dry as possible and always dry thoroughly after cleaning. Use of talcum powder, particularly anti-fungal types, can help. Also, ensure trainers have completely dried out before using them again.

Blisters
→ What are they?
Blisters can occur anywhere on the body, but for runners they're generally found on the feet. The human body protects itself from friction by forming a bubble of fluid over the affected area.

→ Causes
Many things can cause blisters, from ill-fitting trainers to ruffled socks and dampness.

→ Treatment
There are two schools of thought. Either leave the blisters to disappear or burst by themselves, by wearing shoes that don't rub the same area or by protecting them with plasters or a blister-specific medical kit; or, if wearing other shoes isn't realistic (as was

the case during my time in the Marines), burst the blister with a sterile needle by making two holes – one to let the fluid out, the other to let the air in. Clean the area immediately by soaking up the fluid and dressing the wound. However, don't remove the dead skin, as this protects the tender new layer underneath; it will die and fall off when the new skin has grown. Removing it before this will cause far more discomfort than the blister itself and delay the healing process.

→ Prevention
Ensure footwear fits correctly and try to keep your feet dry and clean. The use of talcum powder will help. If 'hot spots' are felt where friction is beginning, use Vaseline on those areas.

Hyperkeratosis
→ What is it?
Hyperkeratosis is the thickening of the skin on the feet, particularly the heels and balls. Calluses (layers of skin) build up on top of each other to protect the area that's constantly under stress to avoid blistering. Problems arise when these hard areas become painful.

→ Causes
There are multiple reasons for the skin to form calluses, from simply running for long periods to ill-fitting shoes that cause rubbing. Overly large trainers and trainers done up too loosely are major causes.

→ Treatment
Removal of some of the callused skin with a pumice stone can help, as can moisturising the area.

→ Prevention
Ensure shoes fit well and are replaced often. Treat and repair your feet – if you ignore them they'll get infected and cause you pain. A god foot admin routine of exfoliating and moisturising and removing hard skin can be the answer.

Mid-foot pain
→ What is it?
Simply pain felt in the middle of the sole, similar to that of plantar fasciitis. For the most part the pain isn't felt when resting or not using the foot.

→ Causes
Can be due to any of the following:

● Supination, which causes the foot to be inefficient at cushioning because it doesn't bend inwards correctly.
● A stress fracture of the mid-tarsal (the joint that connects metatarsals to the top of the ankle).
● A strain to the tendons that pull toes upwards.
● Arch strain/collapse, especially if high foot arch isn't being supported properly and impact causes it to start collapsing.

→ Prevention
Buy new, well-cushioned trainers to lessen impact and support the arch; get your gait analysed and see if supination is the cause – if so, purchase orthotics (www.simplyfeet.co.uk) (an insert or brace for high arches may also be necessary); and if pain still persists check for tendon inflammation and PRICE the area, ensuring you don't tie shoes too tight when running.

Stress fractures
→ What are they?
Stress fractures are small cracks in or fragmentations of the bones. For runners (and other sportspeople who spend most of their time on their feet) they most commonly occur in the metatarsal bones and shins. Symptoms are chronic pain that gets worse when running, tenderness to the touch and swelling.

→ Causes
When muscles, tendons and ligaments become too fatigued by training and stop providing adequate shock

absorption the bones of the feet end up taking the brunt instead. Worn-out trainers that lack cushioning can also be a major contributor – as can running in shoes not designed for running, or running barefoot with bad technique. However, sometime stress fractures occur due to overuse, especially if run distances or times are increased too quickly.

➜ Treatment
PRICE must be rigidly followed for anywhere between four weeks and four months depending on the severity of the fracture. All running must cease until completely healed or the injury will be back to square one.

➜ Prevention
Wear shoes with cushioning and replace them often. If attempting barefoot running, ensure you understand the technique and increase very gradually. The same goes for progressing any running – increases distances gradually and carefully, and where possible have a day's rest between each session.

Sprained ankle
➜ What is it?
The over-stretching or, worse, tearing of the ligaments that connect the three bones of the ankle. The initial injury is general an inversion or eversion that feels like a sharp pain and then like an ache. The ankle generally swells considerably quickly following injury.

➜ Causes
Any twist, eversion or inversion that damages the connective tissue of the ankle, often caused by uneven ground or weary muscles, tendons, joints and proprioceptive sensors.

➜ Treatment
PRICE as soon as possible. It's often necessary to keep activity to a minimum and where possible stay off the ankle completely for two weeks, at which point the majority of swelling should have gone down.

➜ Prevention
If you have a tendency to sprain your ankles, perform proprioceptive exercises during prehab/conditioning session to strengthen them (see Chapter 11). Avoid runs over uneven ground and ensure your running shoes have good support and stability. A thorough warm-up is a good avoidance measure. However, most ankle sprains are just unfortunate accidents.

Muscle strain
➜ What is it?
Any tear within a muscle, for runners most likely the calf, hamstring, quad, adductors or perhaps glutes. They range from minor micro tears (or pulls) to full-on ruptures. Micro tears are characterised by a dull ache that gets continually worse as it's run on and gets steadily bigger. A full rupture is felt as a sharp stabbing pain and sometimes an audible noise.

➜ Causes
The most common cause is overexertion of a tight, cold, unwarmed muscle. For runners, the most common causes are sudden acceleration or anything that puts undue and unnatural stress on a muscle.

➜ Treatment
Yet again PRICE is the only real remedy, along with resting until pain subsides. Length of rest can be anywhere between two and eight weeks dependent on severity. On return to activity, be very careful. Do thorough warm-ups, including dynamic stretching, and a shorter/easier session than normal to start with.

➜ Prevention
Correct technique and correct kit and equipment, especially cushioned or stability-controlled trainers, and most importantly a thorough warm-up and post-workout stretch routine.

Bursitis
➜ What is it?
Bursitis is the swelling of a bursa in any joint, which occurs most commonly in a runner's knees, ankles (Achilles area) or hips. The bursae are sacs of synovial fluid that lubricate the movement of tissue and bone against bone and cartilage. Pain and stiffness is felt in the joint itself and is usually worse in morning or after long periods in one position.

➜ Causes
Usually associated with impact injuries or overuse, ie long periods of repetitive movements or wearing running shoes without cushioning.

➜ Treatment
Yet again PRICE is the answer. Rest allows recovery and ice helps remove the problem over time. Don't run again too soon, as injury reoccurs if not fully healed.

➜ Prevention
As this injury is related to impact, well-cushioned shoes are imperative. Where possible run on softer surfaces, like grass or a treadmill. Lastly, good running technique can avoid the problem (see Chapter 4).

Collateral ligament injury
➜ What is it?
The ligaments (medial collateral and lateral collateral) that run laterally and medially (either side of the knee) are ruptured or stretched, causing immediate pain and swelling.

➜ Causes
Usually an impact or a long-term wear and tear injury if the knee isn't working correctly by even a minute amount. These ligaments stop the knee from moving too far left or right, so sudden or consistent repetitive movement in either direction can cause damage.

➜ Treatment
Yet again PRICE, and stop running as it will make matters far worse. For stretched ligaments two weeks should see them healed; for a tear/rupture a few months' rest may be needed.

➜ Prevention
Prehab and conditioning of the legs, particularly the quads and hamstrings that ensure the knee is strong.

Cruciate ligament injury

→ What is it?
A very common injury to footballers or skiers is a full 'ACL rupture'. The ACL and PCL or anterior and posterior cruciate ligaments are those found in the knee joint between shin and thigh bones. The anterior is more likely to suffer damage than the posterior. A rupture or stretch of either leads to severe pain inside the knee and a large amount of swelling and even discolouration. Most worryingly, though, you'll also be unable to support yourself on the injured leg.

→ Causes
The ACL and PCL are there to ensure the integrity of the knee joint, to hold it together for want of a better phrase. Any violent twisting or backwards movement can damage them.

→ Treatment
Use crutches. PRICE is key. If an ACL or PCL rupture is suspected seek medical advice ASAP, as surgery is the only real option. If advised it's only a stretch, rest and ice for two weeks then test carefully.

→ Prevention
Again, prehab and conditioned legs, especially the hamstring, as like these ligaments it supports the knee, so can go some way towards protecting them.

Lateral meniscus tear

→ What is it?
A surprisingly common injury in which a crescent-shaped piece of cartilage in the knee joint is torn. The injury causes severe pain in the knee and swelling within hours. Often clicking in the knee can be heard and straightening the leg becomes impossible due to a detached piece of cartilage obstructing the joint.

→ Causes
The cartilage's job is to act as a shock absorber for the knee. Much like ACL or PCL injuries, damage from twisting or violent impact causes damage to the menisci.

→ Treatment
PRICE once again, and seek medical advice. Surgery is often required, to remove the detached cartilage and sometimes to rebuild the joint itself.

→ Prevention
Prehab and conditioning will ensure the quads and hamstrings are strong and will make the knee more stable. Avoid sports more likely to cause impact to the knee (football, rugby, skiing etc).

Sciatica

→ What is it?
A numbness or electric-shock type pain in the glutes, lower back or in some case the back of the entire leg, caused by some form of compression or irritation of sciatic nerve.

→ Causes
There can be multiple causes, such as an uneven running posture which is in turn often caused by particularly tight glutes, hamstrings, calves or iliotibial bands. In more severe cases damaged vertebrae can be to blame.

→ Treatment
Sitting in one position for long periods, such as driving, can sometimes aggravate it, so ensure plenty of stops and rests. Stretching and mobility, particularly of the spine, is important. If the problem persists seek medical advice, and in the meantime combat pain with painkillers and anti-inflammatories.

→ Prevention
Compression wear, mobility and stretching.

Chaffing

→ What is it?
Chaffing occurs where areas of the skin become irritated (usually by friction) and can be rubbed raw.

→ Causes
Your skin rubbing against itself or your clothing. It's especially common when clothing becomes soaked in sweat.

→ Treatment
Chaffing was very common in the Marines, as we'd often get ridiculously sweaty running in boots, full combat dress and body armour and carrying loads of kit. I personally found two things helped: applying Vaseline to known problem areas and wearing cycling shorts and UnderArmour-style vest tops that are skin-tight but quick-drying. It's also important to use antiseptic cream on any raw patches to prevent infection.

→ Prevention
Use plentiful amounts of Vaseline on problem areas before starting. Purchase and wear running-specific, well-fitting clothing and replace where necessary. Furthermore, wash it after every use! Lastly, stay hydrated, as this can help reduce chaffing as well.

Cramp

→ What is it?
Cramps are spasms that cause muscles to contract but won't release. When severe the muscle or affected limb can't be used normally. Severe cramps can last for a considerable time.

→ Causes
Cramps result from an imbalance of the minerals/ions that generate the electric impulse that allows a muscle to contract. A number of factors can lead to this: fatigue, dehydration, salt deficiency, overtraining and performing a session too difficult for present fitness levels.

→ Treatment
In most cases it's a case of rehydrating and eating to rebalance mineral and electrolyte levels. However, gentle stretching and massage of the affected muscle can help.

→ Prevention
Ensure you eat and drink prior to sessions and don't exercise too long without topping up, especially in extreme heat. A thorough warm-up and stretch can help prevent cramp.

DOMS (delayed onset muscle soreness)

→ What is it?
Soreness that occurs in muscles between 12 and 72 hours after an exercise session.

→ Causes
The aches result from microscopic tears in the muscles. They're usually worse the day after, as this seems to be when the proteins of the muscle are broken down and repair occurs. DOMS are always worse if you're returning to exercise after a sedentary period, trying something new or extending a distance or time considerably.

→ Treatment
If symptoms are bad PRICE can help. Other than that, rest the painful muscles and massage gently if necessary. Anti-inflammatories can be taken but shouldn't need to be.

→ Prevention
Warming up, cooling down and stretching can help reduce the onset. Compression gear (see Chapter 3) and building up slowly after sedentary periods can help.

Heat exhaustion

→ What is it?
The body overheats and symptoms such as nausea, dizziness, disorientation and headaches take hold. If left untreated it can lead to potentially severe, even life-threatening heatstroke.

→ Causes
Generally results from lack of fluid and increased sweating, which leads to severe dehydration and causes the body temperature to climb rapidly.

→ Treatment
Immediately you feel you're suffering stop exercising, and if you're in a hot place or the sun get out of it as quickly as possible. Sit down and drink water slowly without gulping. If you gulp you're more likely to be sick. Energy drinks can also be used at this point to replace electrolytes, but make sure water is taken as well.

Personal experience...

Some people swear by wearing plasters over their nipples or taping problem areas. I did this for a couple of weeks on one military course to prevent 'webbing burns' (where the belt supporting your kit and equipment causes friction and therefore severe chaffing on the hips). However, I left the tape on the area for the best part of two weeks and am now allergic to zinc oxide tape and most plasters! My advice is steer clear if you can to prevent becoming allergic. Vaseline is the answer.

→ Prevention
Eat and drink sensibly before your session, and if you're susceptible to the heat run early or late in the day when it's cooler. If you have to run in the heat take it slowly at first and acclimatise. The correct kit and equipment is imperative, so make sure you're dressed appropriately for the conditions and have some way to hydrate throughout your run and afterwards, such as a water bottle or hydration pack (see Chapter 3).

A stitch

→ What is it?
A sharp stabbing pain just under the rib cage, usually on the right-hand side. It's said to be straining of the ligaments that connect the diaphragm to the other internal organs.

→ Causes
Results from the diaphragm and organs receiving impacts as running occurs. Simply put, if you breathe out as the left foot strikes the ground you shouldn't suffer, but if your routine gets interrupted and you breathe out as the right foot lands, then the ligaments connected to the liver get stretched by the movement of the diaphragm (allowing you to exhale) and a stitch occurs. Eating too soon before a run can also cause the problem, as a full stomach affects the whole process.

→ Treatment
Try to run through the pain and regulate breathing by slowing down. If this fails to cure it, stop and walk and control breathing that way. Breathe in deeply and stretch the side of the body (usually the right-hand side) by leaning away from it. Stretching usually alleviates the pain.

→ Prevention
Ensure you exhale as the left foot strikes. Breathe deeply and evenly when running. If you get breathless and get stitches regularly then run slower until fitness improves. Don't eat within two hours of your session and drink plenty, as dehydration can cause the cramping pains associated with a stitch.

Conclusion

As careful as you are, as much conditioning and prehab as you might perform, as good as you are at avoiding overtraining, you'll eventually pick up an injury. It's inevitable and almost unavoidable. However, by being aware of the common injuries, what causes them and how to avoid them you can lessen your chances and limit the onset of common or recurring injuries. Just ensure that when you do become injured you rest up, use PRICE and take your time coming back – see it as another challenge, not a setback.

Glossary

Aerobic
Used to refer to running or other exercise at an intensity that's sufficiently easy for your respiratory and cardiovascular systems to deliver all or most of the oxygen required by your muscles, and slow enough that lactic acid doesn't appreciably build up in your muscles. Generally, you can sustain a slow aerobic pace for long periods of time, provided you have the endurance to go long distances.

anaerobic
Used to refer to running or other exercise at an intensity that makes it impossible for your respiratory and cardiovascular systems to deliver all or most of the oxygen required by your muscles, and fast enough that lactic acid begins to build up in your muscles, thus producing a tired, heavy feeling. The pace associated with anaerobic running cannot be sustained for very long.

anaerobic threshold (AT)
The transition phase between aerobic and anaerobic running. Good training will increase AT by teaching the muscles to use oxygen more efficiently, so that less lactic acid is produced. Also known as 'lactate threshold'.

cool-down
Slow running or jogging done after a workout or competition to loosen muscles and rid the body of lactic acid.

cushioning (or shock absorption)
The ability of a shoe to absorb the impact of footstrike.

DOMS
Delayed onset muscle soreness. This type of muscle soreness normally peaks about 48 hours after a particularly intense or long run.

elite runner
An athlete who has reached the highest level in his/her sport.

endurance
The bodies ability to resist fatigue while performing medium to long periods of low to moderate intensity work

fartlek
Swedish for 'speed play', variable pace running; a mixture of slow running, running at a moderate pace and short, fast bursts. Fartlek training is a 'creative way' to increase speed and endurance.

'hitting the wall'
The dreaded point (and awful feeling similar to what your body would feel like if you ran into a wall) during a race when your muscle glycogen stores become depleted and a feeling of fatigue engulfs you.

intervals
Training in which short, fast 'repeats' or 'repetitions' often 200 to 800 meters, are alternated with slow 'intervals' of jogging for recovery; usually based on a rigid format such as six times 400 meters fast (these are the repeats) with 400 meter recovery jogs (the intervals). Interval training builds speed and endurance.

lactic acid
A substance which forms in the muscles as a result of the incomplete breakdown of glucose. Lactic acid is associated with muscle fatigue and sore muscles.

lactate threshold
See 'anaerobic threshold'

lateral
Refers to the outer edge of a shoe/body or muscle.

Marathon
26.2 miles; According to legend, in 490 BC, a Greek soldier name Philippides ran the distance from the site of the battle of Marathon to Athens, where he died after the Greek victory over the Persians.

maximum heart rate
The highest heart-rate reached during a specified period of time.

medial
Referring to the inner side (or arch side) of a shoe/body or muslce.

'metric mile'
1500m, the international racing distance closest to the imperial mile.

midsole
The area of the shoe between the upper and outsole that's primarily responsible for the shoe's cushioning. Most midsoles are made of foams: either EVA (ethylene vinyl acetate) or polyurethane. EVA is lighter and more flexible than polyurethane, but it also breaks down more quickly. Many midsoles also have additional cushioning elements such as air, gel and various embedded plastic units.

mile
1609 meters, 5280 feet, or 1760 yards. Note: 1600m is not a mile.

motion control
The ability of a shoe to limit overpronation.

outsole
The material, usually made of hard carbon rubber, on the bottom of most running shoes; the layer of the shoe that contacts the ground.

overpronation
The excessive inward roll of the foot before toe-off. Overpronation is believed to be the cause of many running injuries.

plyometrics
Bounding exercises; any jumping exercise in which landing followed by a jump occurs.

post (or medial post)
Firmer density of midsole material added to the inner side of the shoe. A post is designed to reduce overpronation.

pronation
Pronation begins immediately after the heel contacts the ground. It is a normal and necessary motion for walking or running. Pronation is the distinctive, inward roll of the foot as the arch collapses.

PB
personal best.

runner's high
A feeling, usually unexpected, of exhilaration and well-being directly associated with vigorous running; apparently related to the secretion of endorphins.

running economy
Refers to how much oxygen you use when you run. When you improve your economy, you are able to run at a smaller percentage of max VO2 (your maximum rate of oxygen utilization).

stability
The ability of a shoe to resist excessive foot motion

stamina
The bodies ability to resist fatigue while performing short to medium periods of high intensity work

supination
The opposite of pronation. It's an outward rolling of the forefoot that naturally occurs during the stride cycle at toe-off. Oversupination occurs when the foot remains on its outside edge after heel strike instead of pronating. A true oversupinating foot underpronates or does not pronate at all, so it doesn't absorb shock well. It is a rare condition occurring in less than 1% of the running population.

taper
Runners usually cut back mileage (or taper) one day to three weeks (depending on race distance) before a big race. Tapering helps muscles rest so that they are ready for peak performance on race day.

target heart rate
A range of heart rate reached during aerobic training, which enables an athlete to gain maximum benefit.

tempo runs
Sustained effort training runs, usually 20 to 30 minutes in length, at 10 to 15 seconds per mile slower than 10-K race pace. Another way to gauge the pace of tempo runs: a pace about midway between short-interval training speed and your easy running pace.

threshold runs
Runs of 5 to 20 minutes at a pace just a little slower than your 10-K racing pace; Threshold pace is roughly equivalent to what exercise physiologists call 'lactate threshold' or the point at which your muscles start fatiguing at a rapid rate. Running at or near lactate threshold is believed to raise your lactate threshold, which should allow you to run faster in the future.

underpronator
Underpronation is less common than overpronation. The shoes of underpronators show outsole wear on the lateral (outer) side not just at the heel but all the way up to the forefoot. Typically, underpronators tend to break down the heel counters of their shoes on the lateral side.

upper
The leather or mesh material that encloses the foot.

veteran
Older runner: men become 'veterans' on their 40th birthday; women, on their 35th birthday.

VO₂Max (maximal oxygen consumption)
The maximal amount of oxygen that a person can extract from the atmosphere and then transport and use in the body's tissues.

wall
See 'hitting the wall'.

warm-up
Five to twenty minutes of easy jogging/walking before a race or a workout. The point of a warm-up is to raise one's heart rate so the body (and its muscles) are looser before a tough workout begins.

WR
World record.

Index